Sexuality, Gender and Schooling

The sexuality of young people arouses controversy and remains a source of concern for parents, teachers, policymakers and politicians. But what young people really think about sexuality and gender and how these issues impact upon their lives is often marginalised or overlooked.

Based upon extensive ethnographic research with young people and teachers, *Sexuality, Gender and Schooling* offers a telling and insightful account of how young people acquire sexual knowledge and how they enact an understanding of their own gender. It highlights the ways in which young people's constructions of gender and sexuality are formed outside the school curriculum, through engagements with various forms of popular culture – such as teen magazines and television programmes – and through same-sex friendship groups.

Offering a fresh perspective on a subject of perennial interest and concern, *Sexuality, Gender and Schooling* provides accounts from the inside – some of which may challenge and eclipse current approaches to sexuality education. It has significant implications for policy and practice in Personal, Social and Health Education and is also an excellent introduction to key debates and issues in the study of gender and sexuality.

Mary Jane Kehily is a lecturer in Childhood Studies at the Open University.

041528046X

Sexuality, Gender and Schooling

Shifting agendas in social learning

Mary Jane Kehily

London and New York

First published 2002 by RoutledgeFalmer
11 New Fetter Lane, London EC4P 4EE

Simultaneously published in the USA and Canada
by RoutledgeFalmer
29 West 35th Street, New York, NY 10001

RoutledgeFalmer is an imprint of the Taylor & Francis Group

© 2002 Mary Jane Kehily

Typeset in Times and Gill by BC Typesetting, Bristol
Printed and bound in Great Britain by
TJ International Ltd, Padstow, Cornwall

British Library Cataloguing in Publication Data
A catalogue record for this book is available from the British Library

Library of Congress Cataloging in Publication Data
A catalog record for this book has been requested

ISBN 0–415–28047–8 (pbk)
ISBN 0–415–28046–X (hbk)

To Anoop and Sean, with love and thanks

Contents

Acknowledgements   xi
Foreword   xiii

Introduction   1
Contextualising the research and the researcher 1
The context of the study 2
A note on methodology 5
*'Stop teaching sex education or reconsider your position
   in the school' 8*

1 **Fragments from a fading career: personal narratives
   and emotional investments**   10
Educational routes and biographical moments 10
Auto/biographical methods 11
Just call her 'rat-face' 14
Lose control/maintain control 19
Kehily is a bitch 25
The girl in the toilet 28
Concluding comments 31

2 **Ways of conceptualising sexuality, gender and schooling**   33
The impact of social constructionism 33
Socio-historical approaches 35
Psychoanalytic approaches 38
Contemporary approaches 41
Turning queer 43

The work of Valerie Walkerdine 45
Sexuality, gender and the domain of the school 49

**3   Producing heterosexualities: the school as a site of
    discursive practices**   52
Schooling and the domain of the sexual 53
Approaches to heterosexuality 54
Discursive practice: the official curriculum 57
Discursive practice: pedagogy 60
Discursive practice: student cultures 65
Concluding comments 71

**4   Agony aunts and absences: an analysis of a sex
    education class**   73
The lesson 74
Everything was perfect but . . . 75
Late period: girls and reputation 78
*A boy and his friend: the homosocial or the homoerotic
    heterosexual? 80*
The Flasher: the gaze and its object 82
'I feel so dirty . . .': discussing sexual abuse 87
Scared to be gay: homophobia and the power of girls 91
Concluding comments 96

**5   More Sugar? Teenage magazines, gender displays and
    sexual learning**   99
Magazines in context 103
School-based reading practices and gender difference 106
Sexual learning – problem pages 110
Sexual learning and cultures of femininity 114
More! *is too much 117*
The jigsaw puzzle of sexual learning 121
*Connections and disconnections: the burden of assumed
    knowledge 122*
Concluding comments 125

6   Understanding masculinities: young men, heterosexuality and embodiment   128

Theorising the body 129
Bodies in school: institutions and the embodiment of masculinities 132
Constituting heterosexuality: sex-talk, masturbation and pornography 133
Consolidating heterosexuality: relationships with women 140
Masculinities and homophobias 145
Young men and lesbianism 149
Fear of engulfment – fear of female sexuality 151
Heterosexual activity and reputation 154
Masculinities and ethnicity 156
Concluding comments 162

7   Sexing the subject: teachers, pedagogies and sex education   164

Teachers and the labour process 164
Life history approaches 167
Teaching and relations of desire 168
Teaching sex education 169
Five teachers and a school nurse 172
Sexual biographies, teaching and learning 176
Teachers and sexual diversity 185
Approaches to students 193
Concluding comments 198

8   Sexuality, gender and schooling reconsidered: notes towards a conclusion   200

Summary of the research findings 200
Research findings in brief 207
Implications for the practice of sex education 208
Implications for pedagogic practice in brief 211
Implications for further research 212

Notes   215
Appendix   217
Bibliography   218
Index   236

Acknowledgements

I am indebted to the many friends and colleagues who have contributed to this project in different ways. First of all I would like to thank the students and teachers who shared their experiences with me. I wish to express my gratitude to Debbie Epstein who supervised this study as a thesis and gave me generous support and guidance especially through the final stages. I wish to acknowledge the Institute of Education, University of London, for the financial support of a studentship. Thanks are also due to Janet Holland and Beverley Skeggs for their painstaking work in examining the thesis.

Many other friends have contributed to this work and sustained my interest in the project. I am indebted to Kate Corr for her support over the years, her comments on the work, especially on psychoanalytic themes and for her careful proofreading of the chapters. I wish to thank Joyce Canaan for her insightful comments, many valuable discussions and for her emotional support. I am grateful to Mairtin Mac an Ghaill for discussions on earlier drafts of chapters. I am grateful to Tuula Gordon for her friendship, her enthusiastic support of this work and for many stimulating discussions.

I wish to thank members of the Birmingham Narrative Group for interesting discussions on themes of narrative and subjectivity: Leone Burton, Joyce Canaan, Mariette Clare, Chris Griffin, Richard Johnson, Peter Redman and Deborah Steinberg. Additionally I would like to thank Peter Redman and Deborah Steinberg for their comments on Chapter 4 and Richard Johnson for his comments on Chapters 5 and 6. Thanks are also due to Tarja Tolonen, Val Hey, Frinde Maher, Rob Pattman, Sean Escritt, Susan Johnson and David Spencer for help along the way.

I am indebted to friends and colleagues at the Open University for support during periods of study leave and beyond. I am particularly grateful to Peter Barnes, Rachel Burr, Mary Jane Curry, Liz Freeman, Chris Golding, Wendy Stainton Rogers, Joan Swann and Lynda White.

Finally, I would especially like to thank Anoop Nayak for always being there. His love and support are invaluable.

Foreword

Like all research and writing, *Sexuality, Gender and Schooling* comes
out of particular dialogues, traditions and networks. It belongs to a
distinctive body of work that has focused on the sexual cultures and
sexual and other identities of young people in Britain, especially in
the context of the schools. As Mary Jane Kehily herself suggests,
there are affinities and continuities between her own work and
Paul Willis' *Learning to Labour* (1977), Angela McRobbie's work
on popular culture and femininity (1978a, 1978b, 1991, 1996) and
much of Christine Griffin's work from *Typical Girls?* onwards
(1985). If these are older brothers and sisters, so to speak, there is a
peer group too which can be seen in the published work of Debbie
Epstein, Mairtin Mac an Ghaill, Anoop Nayak, Rob Pattman and
Peter Redman (see the bibliography to this volume), all of whom
studied in and around the Department of Cultural Studies at the
University of Birmingham in the late 1980s and early 1990s – and
who have often continued to work together in different ways.

In this Foreword I want to draw out some threads in this skein of
work, then suggest some ways in which Mary Jane Kehily's study
extends it in particular ways.

First, the focus on young people's cultures has stemmed from a
number of commitments which are as much personal, political and
ethical as academic. As Kehily herself puts it in her Introduction:

> The emphasis on student cultures can be seen as a way of 'giving
> voice' to school students who *receive* the curriculum but play no
> part in the structuring of the school as an organisation or the
> planning of the curriculum and the teaching of lessons.

In this work, young people's standpoints are valued in a number of
different ways. They are seen as active agents in their own and
others' lives. They are active sense-makers of their worlds. Mairtin
Mac an Ghaill strikes the same keynotes as Kehily: 'Young people
are active makers of sex/gender identities' (1994: 179). There is a
consistent thread here, through the whole skein, that questions the
dominant assumption of childhood 'innocence', even for the primary and infant school child. In her early work on anti-racist teaching among white primary school students, for instance, Debbie
Epstein questions the absence of the capacity to understand oppression and injustice among the children, arguing for 'starting with
areas of oppression that are meaningful to children' (Epstein 1993:
118). More generally, the cultural work of students is seen as a
key starting point for learning and for teaching. School students
are never 'empty vessels', nor letter-boxes through which a curriculum is to be 'delivered'. They have their own aspirations and projects
in life, group commitments and concrete knowledges already. This is
the awkward complex truth that cuts across and in practice will
always disrupt the (at best) teacher-centred, at worst state-and-
business-centred, curricular orthodoxies of today.

A second key finding is that these knowledges and forms of
'identity work' are diverse and contradictory, just as pupils' lives
most often are. Young people sometimes develop what seem to
the researcher stunning and productive insights. For Mac an Ghaill,
for example, the experiences of the gay male students in his study
of school-based masculinities were capable of providing 'a broad
agenda for sex/sexuality education that would be of value to all
young people and their development of their sexual and gender
identities' (1994: 180). In other contexts school students share the
dominant definitions and some very familiar closures, the aggressive
rejection of homo-erotic desire and gay and lesbian identity for
instance and the single-minded affirmation of heterosexuality. The
importance of methods (of both research and teaching) and the
significance of larger contexts can be seen in Rob Pattman's research
in *Young Masculinities* (Frosh, Phoenix and Pattman 2002) which
used individual interviews as well as the method favoured by
Kehily – the group discussion:

> The rich fluid and emotionally engaged accounts provided by
> the boys we interviewed refute popular notions of boys as

being emotionally illiterate. The absolute privileging of heterosexual identity for example (47).

This might be compared with the difficulties faced by the boys in this
study when asked to 'perform' against the girls' greater competence
and insight (and glee at their embarrassment) on sexual matters in
the public arena of the class room (see Chapters 4 and 6).

This double-take on youthful cultures runs right through the
(short) history of these 'cultural ethnographies'. For Paul Willis,
writing about working-class boys in the 1970s, the 'cultural processes of reproduction', especially of the identity of working-class
man/boy, 'pass through a moment of real penetration and potential
radical solidarity'. This much-debated formulation can be compared, thirty years later and in a very different economic and educational world, with Kehily's lucid appraisals of the questionings and
refusals of girls and boys in sex education lessons.

The commitment to listening to the meanings of young people has
immediate implications for methods. A shared methodology,
indeed, which has been increasingly made explicit, is a third
common strand. The project implies an attachment to what are
usually termed 'qualitative' research methods, especially to forms
of face-to-face meeting like group discussions, one-to-one interviews, and various kinds of observation and participation. These
methods in cultural studies have often been clumped together as
'ethnography' – with some justifiable resistance from anthropolo-
gists. Cultural studies has been distinctive, however, in *combining*
'ethnographic' research *with other methods*. The methods themselves
are not simply laid side by side in a pluralistic mode, but employed
together, in combination, in ways that mean that each is now applied
with a somewhat new inflection.

Auto/biography, by which is meant both autobiographical
'memory-work' and self-reflection and close address to the lives of
others, is a striking instance of this combination. Auto/biographical
self-reflection is central to Kehily's work and method, reviving, in
effect, a long tradition in cultural studies (see also Redman 1998
and Mac an Ghaill and Redman 1997 for sustained uses of a similar
method). Equally important is the literary input into method in this
and similar texts. In describing her approach to the 'moments' or
episodes represented in her transcripts, Kehily notes how she
treats them first as 'discursive clusters', then as 'literary text,
paying close attention to linguistic features and devices, particular

words and phrases and, occasionally, their absences too'. As she notes, this continues the crossing over of literary and ethnographic method developed by Paul Willis particularly, from the methods of 'reading' exemplified in Richard Hoggart's *The Uses of Literacy*. In ethnographic work perhaps 'close reading' is a way of *listening very closely*.

A fourth feature is to address the larger cultural and institutional context in which young people make their meanings. Their meaning-making is seen as part of a larger cultural formation. This marks an important difference with those ethnographic traditions that focus only on the life experiences of particular groups. In the school-based studies this means addressing the character of the school as a specific social and cultural site, the policies and forms of public representation that regulate schools, and, most importantly in this study, the whole sphere of popular culture on which young people draw for sexual models and knowledges. In each of these aspects, and also in relations between peer cultures in the school, questions of power and difference are taken as critical. The cultures of school students always take the pressure of the authority relations of the school, just as teachers, whatever else they do, have to find their own solutions to issues of order and control in the classroom and surveillance and regulation from 'above'. A key theme in Kehily's own work, and in her joint work with Anoop Nayak, has been how the sexual cultures of school students are developed as a kind of 'playground' or story-telling forum in tension with the official regimes of the school, especially the pressure towards de-sexualisation. All the studies are informed too by a recognition that schools exist within a social context of major inequalities on lines of class, gender and sexuality and race and ethnicity. In the Kehily study, though other differences are not ignored, the intersections of gender and sexual identities, of masculinities and femininities are particularly emphasised. Studies differ too in the relative stress on official policies, popular culture and everyday school experiences. Kehily's stress on popular cultural resources in the school might be compared with the strong concern with the formal politics of school-ing, state policies and new media in my own and Debbie Epstein's study, *Schooling Sexualities* (1996). In many ways the two studies are complementary.

A fifth feature concerns the disciplinary identities of the studies themselves. It is often hard to pin a disciplinary label; and in many ways (though not all) academic disciplines cease to matter.

I want to argue that work on young people's school-based cultures – and perhaps youth cultural studies more generally – is a good example of 'transdisciplinarity' in cultural research today, a situation which represents a new moment in intellectual development. As a new interdisciplinary area, cultural studies both drew on and influenced disciplines across the social sciences and the humanities. It was an element – though only one – in a larger 'cultural turn'. But now that the 'cultural agenda' has been taken up more generally, there are real convergences of research questions and of method, especially where cultural studies retains the openness to borrow back once more the elements of its own approach, inflected again by critical psychologists, cultural geographers, literary historians and sociologists of education, race, class and gender. Kehily's study is fully of this moment I think, drawing in new ways on a literary inheritance, dialoguing with psychoanalysis and with cultural psychology (Valerie Walkerdine especially), and, centrally, a study in 'education' in the most expanded sense.

A final feature is engagement with issues of strategy and practice. It is important to stress this aspect since it has become an issue in recent debates about cultural studies. There have been two related criticisms. The first, pursued especially by Jim McGuigan, has been a criticism of 'cultural populism' or the tendency to substitute a kind of celebration of popular agency for analysis of institutional and, especially, capitalist power and dynamics. The second criticism has concerned the neglect of 'policy', where policy is seen primarily to belong to governments and public institutions. There is an implication in much of this criticism that cultural studies has somehow lost the ability to make evaluations and criticisms. This is a description that sits rather oddly with this book and the larger body of work to which it contributes. There has always been a strand of work in cultural studies which has taken educational practices and policies as its object. In addition to the schooling ethnographies (to which we will return) this has included more 'historical' work on oppositional educational movements, on educational practice in higher education and on trends in state policy – the post-war 'social-democratic' consensus, for instance, and the emergence and hegemony of neo-liberal 'reform'. The criticism seems to assume, moreover, that only elites have policies and only elites can change things. By contrast much work in cultural studies does hold to a belief in popular agency and in the possibilities of a critical professional practice that can make a difference. As we have seen, this is not at all the same thing as celebrating popular resistance wherever it appears – or can be imagined.

This takes us straightaway to a key distinguishing feature of this book, which is the very close engagement not only with student cultures but with the experiences of being a teacher, especially in the tricky domain of the sexual. This is where the text begins – in the author's own teacher experiences; and this is where it ends – in the life histories and educational strategies of some of the teachers she talked closely with and whose practice she has observed. In so far as the charge of 'cultural populism' has some substance in school-based studies, it could refer to an exclusive identification with students' points of view. Cultural ethnographies of schooling have sometimes left the thoughtful teacher standing on the wrong side in a partly imaginary 'battleground' which the researcher has produced. Kehily, however, consistently addresses the dilemmas and strategies of the teacher. And although this book is not 'advice literature' or a 'handbook' in any sense, there is an open, accessible, thoughtful and suggestive treatment of key themes and dilemmas here, always posed in concrete terms, and inviting discussion and personal comparison. Perhaps, after all, teachers have had enough of benchmarks and standards, and all kinds of advice, prescription and surveillance. Perhaps it's time that teachers too were treated as 'grown-ups'! So perhaps they will welcome the calm, careful but often quite adventurous exchange of insights which this fascinating volume offers.

The educational reflections invite different readings and appropriations by teachers themselves. As myself an inveterate pedagogue, albeit not in a school, there are three things I have learned or re-learned from this text. The first is never to forget the differences of positionings and 'fore-knowledges' (prejudices if you like) within the class or group that I am teaching. What I teach and how will really have a different significance across the range of student experiences. What may work in one place may be very negatively received or blocked in another, just like the lessons based on readers' letters in girls' magazines in this text. Yet fore-knowledges and differences are not difficulties only but also resources, with which a teacher can work.

I take a third lesson from Kehily's use of psychoanalytic ideas, another innovative aspect of her text, and another learning also from Valerie Walkerdine. I learn, especially, the importance of understanding *ambivalence* both in myself as a teacher and in those

I teach. Thus the student who rejects most fiercely the knowledges I believe I teach may end up as the one who develops them the most productively.

Richard Johnson
May 2002

Introduction

Contextualising the research and the researcher

This study aims to explore issues of sexuality, gender and schooling. I am interested in the ways in which school students interpret, negotiate and relate to issues of sexuality within the context of the secondary school. In order to explore these themes I use the concept of *student sexual cultures*. I understand student cultures to constitute informal groups of school students who actively ascribe meanings to events within specific social contexts. Student sexual cultures refers specifically to the meanings ascribed to issues of sexuality by students themselves within peer groups and in social interaction more generally. My argument throughout is that this process of making meaning within the immediate realm of the local produces individual and collective identities, that is to say, ways of developing a sense of self in relation to others. This process of making sense of the world within the locale of the school can be seen as an active process that carries social and psychic investments for individuals and groups. These themes are elaborated upon and explored in subsequent chapters. The study documents the ways in which issues of sexuality feature in the context of student cultures and the implications of this for sexual learning and the construction of sexual identities. I am particularly interested in the inter-relationship between gender and sexuality and how school students negotiate complex social relations in ways that can be both creative and constraining.

The study focuses upon two key areas in the field of sexuality and schooling: firstly, the shaping of pupil cultures and the construction of sexual identities; secondly, teaching and learning in the field of Personal and Social Education (PSE), particularly sex

education. I am interested in exploring the frameworks informing
the teaching of PSE and the ways in which policy is *translated* into
practice in schools. Work in this area in the past (e.g. Lees 1993;
Wolpe 1988) has tended to focus on the *delivery* of sex education
programmes, rather than on the ways they are *received* by
students. I am concerned to explore the 'reading effect' – the ways
in which the meanings and messages of the official curriculum are
mediated by student sexual cultures.

The emphasis on student cultures can be seen as a way of
'giving voice' to school students who *receive* the curriculum but
play no part in the structuring of the school as an organisation or
the planning of the curriculum and the teaching of lessons. This
approach, however, can have a tendency to see teachers as an
oppressive, monolithic force, defined in opposition to students. I
am, therefore, also concerned to draw upon the experiences of
individual teachers, including my own experiences as a teacher, to
explore and analyse these personal accounts of teaching and learning in the field of sex education. I see this as an important element
in developing an understanding of current practice in contexts
where both teachers and students may have investments in the
construction and maintenance of symbolic boundaries in this area.
These themes are explored further in Chapters 1, 3 and 7.

The context of the study

The fieldwork for this study was carried out over a total of two
years, beginning in 1991 and continuing in 1995 and 1996. Ethnographic research was conducted in two secondary schools in the
Midlands area of the UK. My interest in issues of sexuality,
gender and schooling span many years, firstly as a teacher and
secondly as a postgraduate student at the Department of Cultural
Studies, University of Birmingham, UK. Sexuality and schooling
became the focus for my Master's dissertation, 'Tales we heard in
school: sexuality and symbolic boundaries' (Kehily 1993) and I
was keen to explore these issues further in a thesis. For many of
the reasons discussed in subsequent chapters, gaining access to
carry out research in schools was not easy. Several schools I con-
tacted during the early stages of the project did not want to participate in research in this field. In negotiations with these schools I
felt that staff were preoccupied with the legislative changes that
affected the organisation and management of schools in England

and Wales. Issues relating to marketisation, budgetary constraint and loss of control were powerfully felt in the implementation of policies such as local management of schools (LMS) and the National Curriculum. Teachers I spoke with appeared anxious about issues of sexuality and sex education generally. Senior staff in particular were fearful of 'bad publicity' and were motivated by a concern to keep their school out of the headlines in areas that they considered to be 'controversial'. In order to gain access to schools I drew upon contacts I had made as a teacher and, more recently, as a contract researcher at the Centre for Educational Development and Research (CEDAR), University of Warwick. Through personal contact with teachers who were known to me I was able to carry out ethnographic fieldwork in two schools, one in the West Midlands area (Oakwood School) and one in a large town in the East Midlands area (Clarke School). Negotiations with both schools were based on the understanding that my research would not bring the school into disrepute and that pseudonyms would be used in written papers and reports to protect the identity of teachers, pupils and the school. In one school I was able to offer support for staff who taught Personal and Social Education; additionally, I provided feedback on the research and discussed the implications for sex education practice in the school.

Both schools were open access secondary schools for boys and girls aged 11–16 and both schools served a largely working-class local community. Oakwood School was non-denominational and ethnically mixed with many students from south Asian and African-Caribbean backgrounds. Clarke School, however, was a Church of England school and the school population was mainly white. In both schools I formed closely binding relationships with students, especially girls between the ages of 14 and 15. At Clarke School in particular, I felt that students in the school associated me with certain groups of girls with whom I had developed a relationship during the research period. In order to speak with more boys in school I supplemented the ethnographic fieldwork with focus group discussions at an all-boys secondary school in a large city in the south east of England. This school was also accessed through personal contact with a senior teacher in the school who described the student population to me as 'very mixed' with a high percentage of students from African-Caribbean, mixed heritage and South Asian backgrounds.

In addition to the political changes referred to above that directly affected schools, both schools where I carried out research were located in an area that had undergone far-reaching economic change. The Midlands region of the UK has a history of factory employment as well as a former industrial heritage related to the manufacture of cars and skilled craftwork such as jewellery making. More recently the region has witnessed widespread de-industrialisation, the dismantling of former industries and the emergence of a competitive global economy. Furthermore, in the post-war period, the region has become synonymous with the settlement of diasporic communities from the New Commonwealth countries as well as large numbers of people who have arrived from Pakistan and Ireland. In these 'new times' of global change and development it is the convergence of time and space that has radically transformed English working-class culture. This study recognises the cultural specificity of the school as a local space that exists in complex interaction with wider global processes relating to migration, the economy and culture. At the local level the very fabric of the Midlands region seems to speak of an industrial heritage that can no longer be realised, functioning as a symbol of post-industrial alienation.

Willis's (1977) classic study of working-class male counter-culture (conducted in the same region) demonstrated the direct and functional relationship between school and work. For the 'lads', having a 'laff' at school was regarded as preparation for the workplace; the styles of trickery and subversion they engaged in became the means whereby young men 'learned to labour'. McRobbie's (1978b) study of working-class girls argues that popular cultural forms and the practice of female friendship help to prepare young women for their future roles as wives and mothers in the domestic sphere. In the post-Fordist era it appeared that the young people in my study were hardly 'learning to labour' or preparing for marriage and motherhood. Their futures in the workplace and the home were less certain and not so clearly defined. The materiality of young people's lives pose many big questions for schools concerning the nature and purpose of education in the present period and the relationship between school and society in the face of global change. The role of the school and its relationship to the local economy is seemingly less obvious as local industries and long-term manual work decline. At the same time multinational chains in the retail and service sector, together with new forms of 'flexible' employment have expanded. Observing the scope of economic change prompts more questions than answers. How has economic change impacted upon the lives of young women and men in school? What are the implications for versions of masculinity and femininity? Is there a new, emergent sex-gender order? In many respects the sex-gender identities of young men and women in the area appear strongly traditional and deeply embedded in older forms of social and cultural practice. It is against the backdrop of these changes and points of continuity that this study has been carried out.

A note on methodology

Researching sexuality in schools is a complicated business. Linking 'sex' and 'school' together as a focus for study brings the researcher into direct contact with many of the symbolic boundaries that shape contemporary schooling. Constructions such as public/private, adult/child, teacher/pupil, male/female, proper/improper organise social relations within the school in ways that seek to demarcate and prescribe the domain of the sexual. Researchers in this field have commented on the ways in which informal school-based cultures are saturated with sex – through humour, innuendo, double-entendre and explicit commentary – yet the official culture of the school frequently seeks to deny the sexual and desexualise schooling relations (Epstein and Johnson 1998; Jackson 1982). Sex education remains a small and discrete part of the curriculum, while abundant and pervasive ways of talking about sex flourish in social spaces occupied by teachers and students. The symbolic boundaries containing issues of sexuality in school juxtaposed with the simultaneous desire to speak the sexual, point to some ways of understanding the sexual politics of schooling. Foucault (1988a: 10) expresses the view that, 'the association of prohibition and strong incitations to speak is a constant feature of our culture'. This observation leads Foucault to suggest, in his later work, that people are 'freer than they feel' (1988a: 10). This way of looking emphasises the productive potential of constraint: policing produces rebellion, boundaries create and define the unbounded in contexts where constraint and freedom exist in a dialectical relationship of support and mutual definition. Researching sexuality in schools calls for an approach which renders visible the social relations of schooling, which recognises the context in which sexuality is at once present and absent, the forms it takes and the responses it generates. This approach involves the researcher in observations and actions. Observing the symbolic boundaries shaping sexuality in school necessarily incurs an interpretive understanding of the context of school relations and the development of an analysis of the dynamics that are shaping and informing these boundaries.

This study is indebted to three different methodological approaches developed in the fields of ethnography, feminist theory and auto/biography. Each approach has provided me with insights and considerations that I have drawn upon during the course of the research process. While there is not space here to discuss methodological issues in any detail, these understandings can be summarised as an abiding concern with issues of reflexivity and experience that value research subjects as producers of knowledge. Specifically, my approach to ethnographic work in school is to see students as meaning-makers, informing and shaping the research agenda in direct ways. Key themes in the study such as magazine readership and embodiment were sign-posted by the frequently articulated responses of the students I spoke with. During the research period I came to regard student sexual cultures as a significant site for identity production. In peer group interactions students collectively negotiated an acceptable 'line', defining, for that moment, legitimate realms of thought, words and actions. Where possible I discussed accounts of particular incidents with teachers and other students in an attempt to understand events from different perspectives. This approach to qualitative research has been described as triangulation (Denzin 1970) and is often discussed in literature on research methods as a checking procedure for researchers, a way of validating the social world of the field (see Burgess 1991). My approach to triangulation, however, was a little messier. Sometimes it produced counter-narratives (as in the Naomi and Nathan romance discussed in Chapter 3) and sometimes a particular reading was conferred by various parties (as in the boys and bodily disgust episode of Chapter 6). Talking to teachers and other students about particular incidents often raised the possibility of multiple readings rather than a verifiable and conclusive account. This development is reminiscent of Liz Stanley's (1987) study of Henry Mayhew that unfolds to point out, in powerful ways, that things look different depending on where you are looking from.

Poststructuralist insights into the importance of context and contingency in shaping social reality (see Weedon 1987 for a clear and detailed treatment of these themes) have been instrumental in the writing of this project. Recognising that there are *moments* of truth and writing (Stanley 1990) has influenced my approach to data collection and analysis. My approach has not attempted to recreate the reality-effect of field relations produced in a just-like-being-there linear narrative. Neither have I attempted to develop an overview of sexuality, gender and schooling based on empirical observations. Rather, I have looked for *moments* in the transcripts that provide a commentary on the relationship between the domain of the sexual and the domain of the school. Having identified these moments, I began to think of them as *discursive clusters* – instances where ideas and relations are condensed in particular ways. These discursive clusters became, for me, the 'text', the object of analysis which was instructive in pointing me to ways of understanding and interpreting the social encounter. Specifically, my approach to such moments drawn from the transcripts is to treat them as literary text, paying close attention to linguistic features and devices, particular words and phrases and, occasionally, the absences too. I regard speech as a form of action that requires analysis of the act of speaking as well as analysis of what is said. Moreover, I would argue that text produced by ethnographic fieldwork can be viewed and interpreted as a form of social practice. This method of analysis has evolved, in part, from my background as a former student of literature and from my experience as a postgraduate student at the Department of Cultural Studies, University of Birmingham. Here I studied work on youth sub-cultures (e.g. Hall and Jefferson 1976), Paul Willis's ethnographic work (Willis 1974, 1978) and his school-based study *Learning to Labour* (Willis 1977). In this body of literature I recognised and enjoyed the 'craft' of literary inspired analysis at work. Willis (1996) has since discussed his ethnographic method as an elaboration of the close-reading technique employed by his teacher and mentor, Richard Hoggart. Willis describes using this technique to study a Shakespeare sonnet and, later, applying the same technique to culture in his study of a gang of motorbike boys. For Willis this method is a way of documenting the creativity of working-class culture that is respectful of lived relations and the experiential as a site for art and artistry (see Willis 2000 for a full account of these themes).

'Stop teaching sex education or reconsider your position in the school'

From January 1979 until July 1990 I had a teaching career. It wasn't much of a career, that is to say it wasn't particularly well planned, organised or developed; but it was what I did for over a decade. It took up most of my time and a great deal of my energy. In the next chapter I discuss my personal and political investments in teaching through the retelling of specific incidents that occurred during my first two years as a newly qualified teacher. Here, however, I want to note that my approach to teaching and my identity as 'teacher' was a politicised one. In common with other activists during this period, I saw the teaching of English, sex education and anti-racist education as sites for political activity and social change. In 1982 I was teaching English and Personal and Social Education at a secondary school in the West Midlands. The PSE curriculum included sex education for all Year 10 students and in these pre-National Curriculum days teachers were free to teach their subject in whatever way they chose. Or so I thought. After a few weeks of teaching sex education to a Year 10 class the head-teacher summoned me to her office and presented me with an ultimatum: 'Stop teaching this or reconsider your position in the school'. Apparently some students from another Year 10 class had complained that their sex education lessons (with the Head of PSE) were not 'as good' as my lessons and the students requested 'proper' sex education like the Year 10 class I taught. This incident makes me sound like a dangerous radical educator with an agenda of sexual liberation. However, I should stress that, despite the politicised identity, nothing terribly radical was going on. I had borrowed some resources for sex education from the Brook Pregnancy Advisory Service, a voluntary organisation that offered counselling and advice on contraception for young people. I had been following their guidelines and using their material through-out. I regarded this approach as 'safe' and non-controversial, even a little unadventurous. Besides, the subtext at the level of the experiential was simple and pragmatic; I was too busy and too tired to think up new and exciting ways of doing 'sex ed.' every week. The headteacher's response, however, suggests that the troubling and contentious status of sex education extends beyond the actual pedagogic practice involved and also pre-dates issues of public accountability and marketisation introduced in the UK context by the legislation of the late 1980s. Sexuality, it seemed to me, aroused anxieties in school and I found it challenging to think about why this might be so. In the following chapter I explore in more detail the development of my interest in teaching sex education and the contradictory subject positions involved in being a teacher and an activist.

Chapter 1

Fragments from a fading career: personal narratives and emotional investments[1]

In this chapter I aim to document the personal journey by which I became interested in researching issues of sexuality and schooling. Something that has now become an academic quest did not start out as such. Through the use of personal narratives drawn from my career as a teacher, this chapter will illustrate the ways in which my present research interest is inextricably linked to my biography as a teacher and my political and emotional investments in certain forms of pedagogic practice. The style and scope of this chapter is indebted to contemporary feminist analyses which embrace auto/biographical modes of social research and stress the importance of self-reflexivity to the process of fieldwork and analysis (see Reissman 1993; Stanley 1990; Walkerdine 1986b). The chapter is also shaped by a reading of Jane Miller's (1995) critical commentary on the autobiography of the question which discusses the complex relationship between personal investments and research agendas.

Educational routes and biographical moments

Like many people in their final year of an undergraduate degree, I 'drifted' into the idea of doing a Postgraduate Certificate in Education. It wasn't so much a conscious decision to become a teacher, more an unconscious and unspecified panic about what to do at a more general level. Contemporary 'lifestyle' lexicon refers to these moments as 'life choices' and 'career planning'. I don't recall thinking about it in such clearly defined ways but I do remember that education appeared an obvious 'choice'. I had been to school, I knew about it and in a strange way it felt safe and challenging at the same time. At this stage my musings on 'what makes a good teacher' and 'what is education' were inevitably related to my personal experiences of schooling.

My journey to school was a short one, only ten minutes walk away, but in my mind it was another country. It wasn't like home or anywhere else I'd ever been. I don't necessarily remember the content of any of the lessons but I do remember what my teachers looked like, what they wore and whether they smiled or frowned. The significant others in my school life were the teachers who didn't explode into a fury for seemingly no reason. They were the ones who didn't instil me with fear. My two sisters and I were in awe of teachers, keen to please and fearful of incurring their displeasure. As adults we still recall stories of life in primary school and remember with clarity and a great deal of hilarity whether particular teachers were *nice* or *nasty*. The marker for us as children was whether we felt able or afraid to ask to go to the toilet. The high point of our recollections is a proverbial tale of the incident where my sister did a wee over Miss Costello's shoe. The teachers we admired were the ones who were *nice*. They encouraged us to follow up ideas, explore details, ask the odd question. Based on this partial and personal retrospective, good teachers, I decided, were the ones who had a vision that went beyond the curriculum and beyond the boundaries of the school walls. As a young adult I thought that education was about making a difference, making a difference to people's lives. In the development of this home-spun philosophical position I was assisted by my involvement with student and socialist/feminist politics during the 1970s and a generally haphazard and incomplete reading of literature concerned with the politics and practice of radical pedagogy (e.g. Illich 1971; Freire 1972; Searle 1974; Bowles and Gintis 1976).

Auto/biographical methods

With my philosophical position 'sorted' and my commitment to 'making a difference' firmly intact, I began a teaching career in January 1979. My first appointment was as an English teacher in a comprehensive school in the West Midlands. To explore some of the feelings, themes and complexities of this period I have employed the concept of 'memory-work' (Haug *et al.* 1987; Kuhn 1995), a method of research whereby participants collectively remember aspects of their lives in order to analyse the relationship between the personal and broader social structures. This method was introduced to me while undertaking postgraduate study at the Department of Cultural Studies, University of Birmingham (1990–3). During this period I worked with a group of students, using personal narratives and photographs to explore issues of gender and sexuality in our past lives and current experiences, some of which formed the basis of an earlier study (Kehily 1995).[2] Michael Erben (1996: 159) suggests that the purpose of biographical method is 'to explore through the analysis of individual lives, the relationship between social forces and individual character'. For Erben, biographical method gives researchers access to the unfolding of people's lives that can be studied as 'an enacted drama of selfhood' (1996: 159). Erben suggests that a consideration of *how* consciousness is constitutive of self-formation lies at the heart of biographical method.

Auto/biographical methods have been utilised in productive ways by individuals and groups marginalised by dominant forms. Haug *et al.* (1987) developed the concept of 'memory-work' as a method for the generation of personal stories of gendered embodiment that could be told and analysed within the context of a feminist project. In this chapter I appropriate this method to critically examine my personal investments in teaching and my early interest in sexuality. In an early study, the Personal Narratives Group (1989) explored the reading of biographical accounts from a feminist perspective. In *Interpreting Women's Lives* they argue that the use of women's personal narratives offers a challenge to traditional bodies of knowledge, truth and reality that have been constructed as if men's experiences were normative. They suggest that women's personal narratives are capable of illustrating aspects of gender relations which explore the constructions of a gendered self-identity within specific social contexts. The Personal Narratives Group define individual accounts as 'verbal reconstructions of developmental processes' (1989: 5), indicating the interplay of agency and social dynamics in the shaping of gendered identities. Liz Stanley (1987, 1990) considers some of the methodological implications of feminist research and auto/biographical accounts. Stanley (1990) suggests that such work is reflexively concerned with its own production. Moreover, she sees the processes involved in this mode of analysis as problematising the notion of self; replacing unity and stability with 'an understanding of self as

fragile and continually renewed by acts of memory and writing'
(1990: 62).

Within the field of education, biographical methods have provided an insight into the lives and careers of teachers and their
relationship to structures of schooling (Sikes *et al.* 1985; Connell
1985; Goodson 1991, 1992). Cortazzi (1993) suggests that, as
teachers are often the motors of change in education, an understanding of teachers' experiences and perspectives can effect
improvement in educational systems, curriculum reform and classroom practice. In a similar vein Connelly and Clandinin (1988)
view teachers as holders of personal and practical knowledge
which can be utilised to understand and develop the processes
involved in teaching and learning. Further research in this field
indicates that teachers' pedagogic practice is shaped by their personal experiences of schooling as former pupils (Woods 1985;
Goodson 1992; Wood 1992). I have drawn upon this insight in my
analysis of teachers as sex education practitioners (Chapter 7). In
'Sexing the Subject' I consider teachers' approaches to sex education and relate their experiences as practitioners to aspects of their
biography that they discussed in interview. Hearing how teachers
learned about sex and *became* sexual subjects provided many
interesting reflections on the relationship of the past to the present.
As pointed out above, I have found auto/biographical methods
particularly useful for reflecting on my own investments in
researching issues of sexuality and schooling. In this chapter I aim
to offer a reflexive consideration of these themes which suggests
that doing research and being researched provide a further site for
the enactment of versions of the self. Viewed in this way, social
research can be seen as a modern technology producing research
subjects who can be 'known' through a dynamic where the
research encounter provides a performative space for the creation
of versions of the self (Foucault 1982a; Tagg 1980; Tolson 1990).

The stories that follow are my selected recollections of the years
1979–81, when, as a newly qualified teacher, I was attempting to
establish my career, develop ideas about pedagogic practice and
hold on to a personal vision. I use memory-work here to give my
stories a structure that will facilitate a reflexive approach to self-
generated memories of my past. Generally, however, the use of
memory-work to generate stories is a collective endeavour,
intended to produce different layers of meaning, understandings

and reconstructions of identity relevant to the research process. Past and current version(s) of self can be juxtaposed to develop a reflexive and critical relationship between individual concerns and broader social, political and cultural issues (Stanley 1990; Reissman 1993; Kehily 1995).

Just call her 'rat-face'

The fourth year class I inherited in my first year of teaching were 'out of control'. They were 'difficult' when I took them over and 'completely off the rails' by the time they left me. Teachers in the school had a whole vocabulary for describing such pupils and such classes. It was a language I felt uncomfortable with at first but found myself using, initially with a hint of irony and, in time, as a matter of course. It became a way of communicating frustrations to other teachers, allying with them and drawing a sharp distinction between what it means to be a teacher and what it means to be a pupil. 4Z, it was generally acknowledged, were an 'unholy bunch', 'a shower of shits', 'as high as kites' and 'off the planet'. Sometimes they were referred to as 'retards', 'cretins' and 'toe-rags'. Occasionally they were called 'seriously disruptive'.

I wanted to win them round, believed I could win them round if I persevered. Controlling them would be an achievement but teaching them that English could be fun was what I desired. After only a few weeks I settled for trying to control them. I tried every strategy I knew; being firm, being their friend, rewarding good behaviour, ignoring or punishing bad behaviour, shouting louder than them, isolating 'trouble-makers', rearranging the desks, group-work, whole class-work, individualised study programmes, detentions. Nothing worked. I was inexperienced and they knew it. The battle was lost.

There was a lot of pain and hurt for me that year. On one occasion in the war between them, me and my idealism, one of them, in a moment of open resistance, called me 'rat-face'. The whoops of laughter, banging of desk tops and unbridled excitement indicated to me that the rest of the class were very impressed by this and the name caught on in no time. Every lesson was a ritualistic humiliation, some worse than others. There was no way out.

This story of my relationship with 4Z coheres around the themes of control, teacher identity and pedagogic practice. The story begins with the details of my 'inheritance' as a newly qualified teacher: a 'difficult' class. My notion that this was a class I 'inherited' is suggestive of the level of responsibility and ownership teachers feel in relation to their classes, a notion which is not specifically taught in teacher training or through pedagogic literature, but is communicated informally through the culture of schools and teacher training colleges at the level of everyday talk and interaction. That teachers *own* their classes is an indisputable 'fact' of teacher existence, confirmed in numerous day-to-day exchanges ('Send one of *yours* to the office', 'One of *mine* will go', 'She's one of *Miss Green's*'). This feeling that your class 'belonged' to you and you were, therefore, responsible for them contributes to the associative link made between teaching and parenting (Steedman 1985; Walkerdine and Lucey 1989) where a discourse of control and protection operates to structure both roles. 4Z were *mine* whether I liked it or not and their decline could be directly attributed to my failure as a teacher. This is reflected in my deterministic view that 'there was no way out' – until, of course, the end of the academic year when they would be no longer mine.

4Z were a class with a 'reputation'. It was a generally acknowledged staff room 'truth', though one I resisted in the first instance. I had heard the stories teachers told about them, the catalogue of insubordination and deviance spanning four years that placed them utterly beyond redemption as 'no hopers' in the litany of the staff room. Ball (1981) comments on the assumptions teachers make of pupils based on their perceived ability, defined by the school in terms of the banding system.[3]

> As the band allocation of the pupils was a 'given', a label imposed from outside prior to any contact with the pupils, the teachers were 'taking' and deriving assumptions on the basis of that label, rather than making their own evaluations of the abilities of individual pupils.
>
> (Ball 1981: 36)

As a band 3 class, 4Z were regarded as 'non-academic' and in need of 'remedial attention' or as the official school discourse put it 'overcoming obstacles to learning'. It is, therefore, possible that 4Z 'acquired' a reputation in the minds of the teachers before the history of misdemeanours, where any negative event may serve to confirm teacher expectations of 'non-academic' pupils. My limited sociological understanding, combined with a politics which spoke of a sense of 'justice', produced an awareness of the power of the self-fulfilling prophesy. I did not want to be guilty of preconceived notions, labelling pupils and writing them off in the ways that I could see other teachers doing. I thought that if I adopted a different approach I would achieve a different outcome. Studies of teachers, teaching and the generation of school-based knowledge (e.g. Holt 1964; Esland 1971; Gorbutt 1972) led me to believe that this was the case – I had the power to change perceptions through practice. However, while this body of literature suggested the possibility of an alternative practice, the process by which this could be achieved was less well documented.

Geoff Whitty (1985) has commented on the ways in which the 'new' sociology of education of the 1970s tended to overstate and overestimate the potential for social change through schools. As a newly qualified teacher I had internalised this potential as a personal mission, *'teaching them that English could be fun was what I desired'*. It was part of a personal and political quest I had embarked on without reference to anyone else in the school or the community. What was to be done when it became clear that my open-minded optimism was not going to transform 4Z? Can the vision be dismantled and reconstructed in a different way? Is it my problem/fault or is it that of 4Z? Does the failure of the practice necessitate the abandonment of the dream? In the story I interpret the failure as *my* failure, a consequence of my inexperience as a teacher. As I was unpractised in the teacherly skills of organising and managing a class, 4Z were quick to spot my weaknesses and exploited them to the full. This analysis, plausible to me at the time, sees teacher/pupil relations as structured by and through the free-play of interactions within the classroom, where positions are negotiated and understandings reached. Within this conceptualisation it is possible for me to see teacher identity as open to reformulations of a positive and transformative kind, *'making a difference to people's lives'*. In retrospect I realise I overlooked, consciously and unconsciously, the ways in which teacher/pupil relations are *already constructed* through the social relations of the school where hierarchies of privilege and status provide a context for the construction and negotiation of pupil and teacher identities. At a conscious level this oversight can be rationalised in terms of my resistance to the 'how it is' set-up with its negative labelling and low teacher expectations which I saw, somewhat naively, as maintaining and perpetuating class relations and educational mediocrity. At the level of the unconscious there may have been other forms of resistance: the difficulty of recognising different and contradictory subjective investments and the need to forge a coherent identity invested in resolving contradictions through the 'unitary' identity of *teacher*.

Within the story, the shifting formations of my teacher identity can be located in my feelings regarding the language used by teachers to describe 4Z. I didn't know the word 'discourse' at the time, at least not in the poststructuralist sense, but I felt '*uncomfortable*' with the epithets used and was concerned to define myself *as against* the popularly held assumptions and beliefs relating to band 3 pupils. Such a position, however, was difficult to sustain within the context of the school, where discursive patterns extended beyond any individual attempt at disavowal. To communicate my experiences and frustrations to other teachers I found myself using the same language as they used, 'initially with a hint of irony and, in time, as a matter of course'. Here, I make a transition from defining myself *as against* other teachers, where I refuse to acknowledge and own my power as a teacher to define pupils in negative terms, to an acceptance of the teacher identified discourse which assimilates teacher concerns through the Othering of pupils. This process can be seen as central to the formation of my 'unitary' teacher identity expressed in the story through the language of warfare that permeates the rest of the narrative. The lessons become sites of 'battle', I use 'strategies' to 'control them' and loss of control can be detected in 'open resistance', 'humiliation' and defeat.

'Rat-face' is not the worst thing I've been called, though in the story it signifies a great deal of pain and hurt which may appear disproportionate to the verbal abuse itself. Here, it is the context of the classroom which gives the name-calling event its emotionally loaded significance. Carolyn Steedman (1985) comments on the claustrophobic world of the classroom as a place of anticipation, where events are observed and dramas staged. With 4Z I viewed this theatricality as their constant public appraisal of my performance as a teacher. The display of *teacher* involves a specific enactment: maintaining control, not losing 'face', not exposing weaknesses. Investing in and performing a 'unitary' identity such as *teacher* involves expelling doubts and vulnerabilities that may call your authority into question, for the duration of the lesson at least. Pupil perceptions, however, may be different. Bronwyn Davies (1983) notes how classroom order is reliant on pupil co-operation. In not responding to teacher 'authority', pupils may register an unwillingness to collude in practices that invest teachers with the power to 'control' them in the classroom. This complexity within the notion of control, where mutual recognition establishes classroom order, contrasts sharply with my early conceptualisation. As a newly qualified teacher I felt that establishing my teacher credentials within the school involved the demonstration of control over a class: '*controlling them would be an achievement*'. My failure to control 4Z in terms that I understood creates the conditions for the 'ritualistic humiliation', the public loss which exposes vulnerabilities and signifies a breakdown in the 'unitary' identity of teacher and classroom order.

This analysis, however, does not account for the ways in which teacher vulnerabilities are often seen in terms of physical, gendered embodiment. There are many vivid descriptions of this in academic research and in literary accounts of fiction and memoir. Mrs Baxter in Walkerdine's (1981) study, Ursula in Lawrence's *The Rainbow*, Frank McCourt in his memoir *'Tis* and many other teachers, real and fictional, have a tale to tell, a moment of hurt and exposure when they are symbolically undressed/violated by their pupils. Pupils' interest in the physicality of teachers can be seen, in part, as a deliberate and defiant inversion of school values which prioritise 'mental' capacities over the physical and corporeal (Willis 1977; Shilling 1991, 1993). While male and female students may challenge teachers in this way, the gendered dynamics of these exchanges often suggest that there may be specifically sexual ways of 'looking' for (male) pupils in their observation of female teachers. The sexualised nature of the 'look', where looking is structured through a lens of power and desire (Fanon 1967), presents a challenge to the dominant power relations of the school where male pupils are involved in the sexual appraisal of female teachers. Within the context of the classroom, the 'male gaze' may be discursively constructed *as against* other school-based discourses such as child-centred pedagogy (Walkerdine 1981) and teacher as *knower*, in control of, and *owner* of her class. Chris Shilling (1991) comments on the importance of the body to human agency and the attainment and maintenance of status:

The management of the body through time and space can be seen as the fundamental constituent in an individual's ability to intervene in social affairs and 'make a difference' in the flow of daily life.

(Shilling 1991: 4)

Within the context of the classroom, the assertion of 'body' over 'mind' by pupils can be seen variously as a transgressive act signifying the pleasure of resistance, the othering of teachers and bonding of pupils and attempts to reformulate classroom relations in ways unanticipated by teachers. The ability to 'make a difference' from the perspective of pupils may operate in opposition to teacher notions of 'making a difference'. In the event of being called 'ratface' by a male pupil, the opposing differences are symbolically located upon the body of the teacher in situations whereby pedagogic practices, however 'radical' or 'critical', can position teachers simultaneously as powerful and powerless in the lives of pupils.

Lose control/maintain control

Happily, not all classes were like 4Z. 3Y, by contrast, were 'lively', 'bright' and 'highly motivated'. For most teachers in the school there was a direct and self-evident correlation between intelligence and behaviour. Put in very crude terms, intelligent 'top band' pupils were well behaved or at least open to 'reason' and responsive to disciplinary routines. Poorly behaved 'band 3' pupils and persistent offenders were 'thick'. This dichotomy permeated all school relations and, while I wanted to challenge it, I didn't know how to. All my best efforts failed.

While 4Z came to represent the first serious blow to my idealism and expectations, I was busy cultivating 3Y as a personal success story. 'Ideas into practice – it is possible', I thought. Maintaining control seemed to be working with this class and I was beginning to feel confident enough to try to make English lessons 'fun', stimulating and enjoyable. I'd never whole-heartedly agreed with maintaining control anyway. It contradicted my ideas on radical pedagogy and particularly the central idea that education was also about liberation – making a difference. With this class I wanted to resolve the contradiction. Here, I was keen to risk radical pedagogic practices and student-centred approaches, discovery learning, small group discussion, less teacher-led material. I thought it could work with this class and I needed it to work. Then, at least, I could preserve some of my earlier values, albeit in a much modified form. Well, I was wrong. I made a terrible and irretrievable error of judgment. It was a complete disaster.

Moving to a less formal structure was a difficult adjustment for 3Y and the lack of teacher intervention in small group activities produced a myriad of disputes and conflict among members of the class. Of course, I hadn't anticipated this and the effort of developing different 'control' strategies when I wanted to be progressive, free and facilitative wore me out. What was an OK, if limited, pupil–teacher relationship degenerated into a series of minor skirmishes, battles and, on one occasion, open confrontation. At the end of the summer term, exhausted and emotionally drained, the nightmare pierced through day-light and I completely lost control of the class. They rampaged through the classroom, throwing books, paper and bags at each other with rapturous glee. Felt pens became missiles and when the excitement of that wore off they started writing on the desks, walls, display work and each other's shirts and blouses. Order was restored by the Deputy Head teacher, known to all the pupils as 'Granny Green-Teeth', an ex-grammar school mistress in her 50s who knew there was something suspiciously different about me and now had all the proof she needed.

Maintaining control became a central preoccupation in my first year of teaching. Well, in many ways it wasn't so much the desire to maintain control as the fear of losing control. Losing control of the class came to signify something more than the temporary shortcomings of a newly qualified teacher. Although I could not have articulated it at the time, I recognise the fear now as about a form of psychic damage, a personal loss, an abandonment of Self. So the investment in maintaining control was being played out on many levels, socially, emotionally and psychically. My self-styled formulations and expectations of what teaching and education was all about were leading me into dangerous and uncharted territory. Everyone was a visitor here and it didn't feel very welcoming.

This story of my relationship with 3Y elaborates on the theme of control introduced in the 'ratface' story. Here I am concerned with the tensions and contradictions between the ideology of radical pedagogy and my attempt to put some of the ideas into practice. 3Y were a band 1 class and, according to the discourses of the school, much more could be expected of them. Differences between classes and the teacher-centred discourses that sustained them were rarely acknowledged in the radical pedagogy literature (e.g. Anyon 1981; Shor and Freire 1988; Giroux 1988). Within this body of literature a binary of oppression/liberation operates to structure school relations in ways that suggest the school can be seen as a site for the oppression of pupils, and liberation is possible through teacher intervention. Here the teacher as radical educator recognises inequality and, through the adoption of radical pedagogic strategies, aims to 'empower' students. Empowerment is generally seen in liberal democratic terms, giving students a voice, creating an awareness of inequality and offering participatory practices for social justice and change. The institutional power that produces differences between groups of pupils, such as the ways in which 4Z and 3Y were perceived by teachers, is rarely recognised by literature that speaks of injustice as a monolithic force and liberation as a counter-force.

Ellsworth (1994 [1989]) refers to the assumptions, goals and practices of critical pedagogy as 'repressive myths that perpetuate relations of domination' (1994: 301). Her critique draws attention to the ahistorical and depoliticised context of critical pedagogic practices where an overwhelming rationalism suggests that equality can be created within the classroom while school relations remain hierarchical. From this perspective power imbalances can be seen to exist within and between students and teachers. My story, however, suggests that as a practitioner wanting to be 'radical' and 'critical', I was not driven by the rationalism of the project. Rather, my 'ideas into practice' can be seen as a form of idealism, a personal and political vision I had emotionally invested in and was reluctant to lose. Recognising the impossibility of the vision would signify the loss of self and the pain of redefinition. The notion that 'I thought it (radical pedagogic practice) could work with this class and I needed it to work' indicates that I was not ready for the psychic struggle involved in disengagement and loss. In retrospect, I realise that the romanticism was also imbued with a residual moralism. This was about what was *right* and what was *wrong* in a fundamental way; my rights and their wrongs, a powerful, self-righteous and ultimately self-serving notion of what is 'better' and what can be.

With 3Y 'I was keen to risk radical pedagogic practices' to maintain the emotional investment I had made. The use of the word 'risk' suggests that this decision, although compelling, involved an element of insecurity where the process and the outcome could not be predicted. Developing radical pedagogic practices involved a range of 'student centred approaches, discovery learning, small group discussion, less teacher led material'. Ellsworth (1994: 307–8) identifies three strategies for critical pedagogic practice: 'empowerment' of students through skills sharing and reflection; 'dialogic teaching' where the teacher becomes a second stage learner through sharing knowledge with students; and 'emancipatory authority' where power imbalances are accepted in the quest for democratic practices and shared human interest. These clearly outlined strategies contrast sharply with my 'approaches' which appear underdeveloped and ill-defined. My attempt at radical pedagogy was a more haphazard 'have a go, hope and let's see what happens' endeavour, where the long-term implications for myself and students had not been fully considered.

Furthermore, in pursuing radical pedagogies I did not consider the context of the school which shaped and gave meaning to these activities. Issues of democracy, equality and justice, as developed by radical educators, were not apparent when other teachers in the school spoke about their classroom practice. Neither did they surface during departmental discussions, parents' evenings or staff meetings. Within this context my attempt to bring about change can be seen as a marginal and isolated activity, unlikely to make sense to pupils (or other teachers) at the level of everyday experience. The disputes and conflicts that ensued among pupils indicate that changes in pedagogic practice need to be planned and co-ordinated to harmonise with other school-based practices. The naivete of my attempt at social change illustrates my lack of understanding of schools as networks of social relations where competing discourses and institutional arrangements provide a mediating context for possibilities as well as constraints.

Investing in radical pedagogy involves a commitment to changing consciousness and a belief that students can achieve full consciousness through developing an awareness of the 'banking concept of education' (Freire 1972: 46). In this critical engagement 'the project of liberatory pedagogy requires a subject who is an object of our emancipatory desires' (Lather 1991: 141). My idea that 'education was also about liberation' articulated a desire to change the consciousness of pupils, while I remained unwilling/resistant to shift my own consciousness as framed by the Freirean vision. This one-way dialogue within the classroom conflates many complex issues regarding the concerns and possibilities of liberatory education in a mass education system. Radical pedagogy can be seen in two ways: as an educational ideology, a way of thinking about education, and also a practice concerned with the micropolitics of teaching and learning. The conflation of these two themes within my conceptualisation of the emancipatory education agenda confused aims and practices in a personalised and overarching idealism. James Donald (1985) suggests that the process of schooling is incapable of producing the specific and identifiable social and political outcomes cited by educational ideologies:

> It is the *failure* of education to be functional to any one strategy that not only explains the rise and fall of educational ideologies, but also provokes shifts in policies, new strategies for organising schools and learning, new (or recycled) visions of what education might utopianly do.
>
> (Donald 1985: 216, italics as original)

My pursuit of the ideal, however, did not consider the broader limitations of emancipatory education. I was more concerned with the immediate and direct classroom responses where student centred approaches seemed to provoke widespread intra-pupil rivalry and discontent.

The desire to be a radical educator and to simultaneously establish myself as a competent teacher in the school contributed to the contradictory consciousness I identify in the story. The key contradiction at this time hinged around the issue of *control* that I perceived as the external imposition of a dominant will over a subordinate one. This surveillance did not sit comfortably with my ideological investment in emancipatory education. As Donald (1985: 217) points out, many of the rituals and routines of schooling 'cannot always be explained in terms of ideology'. Drawing on Foucaultian theory, Donald illustrates the ways in which the nineteenth-century monitorial school system employed the disciplinary technologies of hierarchical observation and surveillance to regulate and control pupils. This had the normalising effect of producing regimented, self-policing subjects or 'docile bodies' (Foucault 1977). The policing of pupils by schools, where the education of the working class is combined with specific forms of disciplining, moralising and dispensing welfare, can be seen as the exercise of 'bio-power' (ibid.), a modern technology for the organisation of the population. From a Foucaultian perspective the daily organisational routines of school – assembly, the timetable, bells, rules governing spaces such as corridors and playground – can be seen as mechanisms for the control of pupils. However, as a teacher with an alternative agenda, I felt these mechanisms also served to control and regulate me, to define my place within the school and to establish my responsibilities in relation to teachers and pupils.

Within the context of the story, *control* can be seen to operate on many levels: the dominant ideologies controlling the pupils, school hierarchies controlling me, me controlling the pupils, the pupils controlling me and the pupils controlling each other. By contrast, my fantasy of the radical vision was to see schools as sites for the development of *self control*, boundaries created by individuals for the protection of themselves and others and formed in dialogue with collective decision-making processes. I experienced the multiple and competing forms of control as a contradiction between what I wanted to achieve and what seemed possible. As I was emotionally invested in the desire rather than the ontological reality, the contradiction could not be sustained for very long. This psychic splitting manifested itself in my 'preoccupation' with control where losing control and maintaining control, the thought and the eventuality, became loaded with symbolic significance. The psychic dynamics involved in my anxieties around control indicate how school contributes to the production of subjectivities where unconscious structures can be played out and realised. My investment in the 'unitary' identity of teacher, the radical pedagogue who can be part of the system and work against the system at the same time, was a delicately balanced fantasy where the 'fear of losing control' can be seen as a fixation, the locus of anxieties, revealing the coming into consciousness of psychic struggle. Within the story I identify the fear as concerned with 'a form of psychic damage, a personal loss, an abandonment of Self'. At the level of external social relations, this can be interpreted as my fear of losing my place in a structure which places me and in which I place myself. However, it can also be seen as an internal dynamic engaged in the attempt to achieve a coherent identity. The vulnerability and exposure signified by the fear of losing control indicates that coherence is unattainable due to the workings of the unconscious. Losing control of 3Y and having 'order restored' in the classroom by the Deputy Head I defined myself against became a moment of recognition for me that the contradiction I thought I could 'resolve' through radical pedagogic practice was also a tension *within* myself. The 'theory into practice' contradiction was inextricably intertwined with the burden of contradictory subjectivities, the investment in a particular identity and the struggle to maintain and promote it against other aspects of the Self. Here there was no identifiable 'solution'.

Kehily is a bitch

This story comes from my second year as a teacher. Having failed in spectacular fashion to develop my ideas and resolve contradictions, I embarked on a series of compromises. Control was paramount to me and radical content could be fed into a formal structure. Radical pedagogic practice, though still desirable, was not possible at the moment. I didn't know when it would be possible but I was happy to get through every day and keep the nightmare at bay.

This year I was given an English class that were to be entered for a public examination. I was also given a list of exam board regulations concerning required reading, coursework and standards to be met to gain the qualification. I spent many hours working out how to make the course interesting and capable of incorporating oppositional politics, while meeting the regulations. Video material and drama were permissible if documented in certain ways. Creative writing could count as course-work. Devising new and exciting approaches became a personal project. A way of compensating for the earlier failures perhaps? Well, anyway, I didn't have time to worry about all that now. This was fine, it was going well in fact. Then one day I walked into the classroom to find the message KEHILY IS A BITCH in letters so large they covered one wall of the room. This was followed by a note on my car which said 'FOOK OFF'. What was wrong now? Had I meted out some terrible injustice to one of them, some of them or all of them? Or was I so preoccupied with the 'success' of the course that I hadn't noticed the groundswell of resentment and dissatisfaction? Or was I a bitch who should just fuck off?

This story presents my deferral and containment of the contradiction(s) as a temporary, if inadequate, coping strategy. I was very busy, under pressure, I had to go to school every day and do the best I could. Under such circumstances it was understandable that I should settle for survival as 'a series of compromises'. These compromises manifest themselves as a commitment to the subject specialism of English. Within the context of the late 1970s and early 1980s, the teaching of English was promoted as a liberal and potentially liberating activity by practitioners and educational theorists (see Searle 1974). This broadly radical framework was reflected in the literature of professional bodies such as the National Association of Teachers of English (NATE) and the Association of Teachers of African, Caribbean and Associated Literature (ATCAL). It was also apparent in the textbooks, anthologies and educational materials of the time.

The Penguin English Project (first published 1973), for example, produced anthologies of literature, contemporary writing and art aimed at secondary school pupils. The books were organised around themes such as 'Work' and 'Identity' and were presented in three stages appropriate to age and level of experience. A reviewer of the series commented:

> Unhappy the teacher who cannot structure the teaching situation so that oral and written expression springs spontaneously from the challenge to the mind, the kindling of the senses and the heightening of the emotions that these books provide.
> (Saxby, H.M., *Reading Time*, quoted in Barrs, M. (ed.)
> *Identity* 1973: back cover)

As a collection the books presented the diverse and often disembodied writings of poets, novelists and cultural critics, without comment or contextualisation, as a resource for teachers and pupils to explore. As the reviewer indicates, it is the responsibility of the teacher to organise the teaching in order to bring the pupils to a heightened awareness of their senses and emotions. Another popular anthology of poetry, *Touchstones*, compiled by Michael and Peter Benton (1971) was published in five volumes and widely used in secondary schools. In *Touchstones 5* the editors' preface for teachers states:

> We regard it as essential that pupils should not only read poems but try to write their own and come to grips with their own feelings and experiences in this way . . . we have suggested topics for discussion and writing which give children the chance either to show a wider social awareness or to come to terms with more complicated ideas and feelings; the sections on love and war should help here.
>
> (Benton, M. and P. 1971, ix–xi)

English teachers were encouraged to view their teaching as a creative endeavour where giving pupils the 'tools' to articulate their experiences was seen as empowering *in itself* and a key step in the development of critical awareness. This awareness, however, was framed by a teacher-mediated set of cultural values which actively promoted a literary canon and defined responses to, and appreciation of, the work. As a philosophy underpinning the teaching of English, it is possible to see these practices as working with a more progressive Leavisite notion of culture being 'good for you', a humanising and civilising force.

Working within this framework as an English teacher committed to liberatory education, I began to see the subject specialism of English as the means by which radical pedagogic aims could be achieved. As Perlstein (1995) points out, it is possible to see this reorientation as an example of the discipline regulating and *disciplining* those who work within its boundaries:

> The disciplinary gaze sees but cannot be seen; it is panoptical, and thus is assumed to be transcendent and not to issue *from* anywhere . . . All discipline becomes a version of self-discipline; those who transgress discipline's codes have no voice through which to speak.
>
> (Perlstein 1995: 132)

However, at the level of the subject inscribed in discourse, I did not experience disciplinarity as a pervasive, regulatory force; rather it represented something I was searching for, a framework giving my practice meaning and a way of looking that I actively and willingly embraced. The teaching of English gave legitimacy to my ideas of radical pedagogy by facilitating the incorporation of 'progressive' material into an established structure. This way of working appealed to me as a practice which was possible, a 'do-able' alternative to the unattainable dream. The project, though attractive to me, did not capture the imagination of the pupils in the way I assumed it would. The graffiti and the note on my car illustrate the tensions and differences between pupil and teacher perceptions. From the perspective of pupils I was a teacher with specific expectations of them, making demands and producing an agenda for them to follow. The radical content of the syllabus, which made such a difference to me, made seemingly little difference to their experience of the lessons or the curriculum subject. The possible was becoming impossible again.

The following story also comes from my second year of teaching and illustrates some of the gaps between the curriculum and the lived experience of pupils.

The girl in the toilet

One day in my class a girl said she didn't feel very well and asked if she could go to the toilet. In the toilet she gave birth to a baby. The event shocked everyone in the school. It wasn't long before teachers were constructing their own version of the incident – a version that usually made some pronouncement on the girl and her actions. These included: 'She was irresponsible'; 'She didn't know she was pregnant'; 'She didn't want to admit she was pregnant'; 'She thought that if she ignored the pregnancy it would go away and now she's got more than she bargained for hasn't she?' and, finally, 'How did she get away with it?' None of the teachers, including myself, made a link between the event and the school.

I'm not sure when I became aware of the connection, if indeed there was a moment of awareness. However, I developed a growing interest in the teaching of sex education, ways of learning about sex in and out of the curriculum and gender politics among teacher and pupil cultures. If a girl gives birth

in the school loo, the school must have something to do with
it, I thought.

This incident really happened. I have to keep telling myself this
as the longer I am away from teaching, the more it feels like a
mythic tale, a story often repeated by teachers in the staff room to
demonstrate the depravity and Otherness of young women in the
school. As I indicate in the story, teachers did not regard the sexuality of pupils as within their jurisdiction. Neither was it perceived
as part of the 'hidden curriculum', the unofficial and unacknowledged teaching and learning of the school. Rather, sexuality and
the sexual behaviour of pupils were seen as a social issue that pro-
liferated *beyond* the boundaries of the school. *It* happened elsewhere and was not linked to the curriculum or the ways in which
teachers related to sexual issues. This way of looking contained
and concealed contradiction; teachers *knew* at the level of everyday experience that sexuality infused and informed many social
exchanges.

Within the classroom words such as 'shaggy' and 'knob' could
produce enough hilarity to disrupt the classroom order for the
duration of the lesson. I recall scanning all teaching materials in
advance so that such moments of disruption could be avoided.
A colleague of mine, concerned to illustrate some grammatical
point, wrote 'Your pen is red' on the chalkboard. Seeing the
words 'pen' and 'is' next to each other produced mass laughter
and all hopes of grammatical correctness had to be abandoned.
The 'Carry On' style humour of the classroom, where innuendo
and double entendres became a source of shared mirth (Epstein
and Johnson 1994), was also present in the staff room. Allusions
to sexual activity – having sex, thinking about sex, associations
with sex – also made teachers laugh, about each other and with
each other. This seemed especially salient at certain times such as
Friday afternoons and the end of term, when a period of intense
pressure was drawing to a close. Invoking sexual matters as a way
of 'letting off steam' and as a source of humour indicates that
teachers and pupils operated within a framework where sexuality
was regarded and related to as cultural taboo; a deeply 'private'
matter to be dealt with publicly at the level of a 'joke'.

In the story I identify the girl giving birth in the school toilet as
a starting point in the development of my interest in sex education. The connections between the event and the school can be

seen in different ways; firstly, as having implications for the teaching and learning of sex education, secondly, as a moment of recognition that teachers and pupils occupy separate 'cultures' and finally, as a potential site for the restructuring of a political agenda. My interest in these strategies appeared, at the time, as a continuation of my concern with emancipatory pedagogy. Sex education offered the potential to develop relationships with pupils and 'make a difference' to their lives. It did not lead to a formal qualification and, therefore, was not subject to the regulatory requirements and constraints of an external examination board. This aspect appealed to me as I thought I would have autonomy over classroom content and teaching methods. In retrospect I realise I was busy reshaping the education-for-liberation agenda within a different political arena – sex education rather than English teaching. Although the shift begins to acknowledge and work with a different notion of politics, my commitment to the 'dream' appears as unshakeable as ever. My reluctance to relinquish an internalised vision reveals the extent of the emotional investment in a particular identity and the psychic struggle involved in 'letting go'.

The link between *The girl in the toilet* and the other stories included in this chapter can be seen in terms of my concern to recuperate the sex education curriculum within my personal version of critical pedagogic practice. In this respect the narratives represent an attempt to create a linear progression through time where my career as a teacher can be articulated within the context of the development of certain historically specific teaching and learning strategies. Collectively the narratives present incidents and events in sequences that become infused with moments of drama. The narratives can be conceptualised as dealing with moments of heightened dramatic action where unusual events contribute to the 'tellability' of the tale. Labov (1972) refers to such narrative structures as seeking to ward off the question 'So what?' (Labov 1972: 370). The 'So what?' question provides listeners with a way of evaluating and interacting with the story through active engagement with the point of view presented by the narrative form. This question also haunts my own evaluation of my fading career where the fragments can be seen as part of a process to explore this period in my life in terms of aims and intentions. The lingering of the 'So what?' question in relation to the stories presented in this chapter suggests that such attempts at self-exposition are ever partial and incomplete, selective fragments in accounts which simultaneously reveal and conceal.

Concluding comments

In this chapter I have used memory-work to generate a selection of personal narratives from my first two years of teaching. In the production of personal narratives, time and memory become key agents in the shaping and telling of the tale. Often seen as a selective process, memory is capable of huge lapses and almost visionary moments of clarity (Centre for Contemporary Cultural Studies 1982). Memory frequently takes on the role of 'fixing' events in the past. However, this stasis can be seen as temporary state, since memory is an active process, constantly working and reworking personal experiences. Hollway (1989) comments on the contextual contingency of personal narratives:

> People's accounts are always contingent: upon available time and discourses (the regimes of truth which govern the way one's thinking can go), upon the relationships within which the accounts are produced and upon context.
>
> (Hollway 1989: 39)

Different memories can be triggered by different contexts. In my own stories I realise I have focused on the dramatic tales of oppression, censure and failure and presented them as a linear quest for an ideal. The narrative accounts can be seen to move through the formulation and redefinition of a personal vision: change the school, change the English curriculum and pupils' experience of English teaching and finally, change personal relationships through sex education. The stories draw upon those moments of pain and humiliation where the contradictions associated with radical pedagogic practice are exposed. Collectively, the narratives present the desire for the ideal fused with the impossibility of this being realised. This selective remembering overlooks the moments of success and recognition (yes, this happened also) and the many other events which enhanced, disrupted and fragmented my career as a teacher. The prioritisation of certain accounts over others involves an active engagement in the process of identity construction, a way of making sense of the past within the context of the present. The shaping of experience in this way can be seen as a dialogue between identity, sense of self, and identities, those aspects of the self that seek social recognition (Kehily 1995). Finally, I feel that it is important to note that the personal narratives I recount are, of necessity, representations constructed for the sake of my argument. The stories are, literally and metaphorically, fragments that create a certain *version of identity* reflexively concerned with ways of understanding my career as a teacher. I do not want to suggest that there is an essential 'truth' about myself in relation to teaching and learning which can be recovered through memory-work. Rather, I hope to suggest that there is a relationship between subjective investment(s) and pedagogic discourses which speaks to us, in disparate voices, of who we are and who we want to be.

This chapter has sought to provide an account of my early interest in sex education as a secondary school teacher with investments in critical pedagogy. Memory-work is utilised to offer a glimpse into biographical experiences that I regard as formative moments in the genesis of this study. The following chapters deal specifically with my experiences as a researcher. Chapter 2 aims to provide a theoretical overview of literature that relates to issues of sexuality and schooling.

Ways of conceptualising sexuality, gender and schooling

This chapter aims to provide an overview of key debates and issues in the field of sexuality, gender and schooling. As such the chapter brings together different bodies of literature relating to sexuality, gender and society. Firstly, the impact of social constructionism and secondly, socio-historical approaches to sexuality are considered, particularly in relation to the work of Jeffrey Weeks and Michel Foucault. Thirdly, psychoanalytic approaches to sexuality are drawn upon and discussed, particularly Freudian and Lacanian theories. These different bodies of literature are cited and utilised, respectively, to provide a specific context for the empirical work and as a way of exploring issues of subjectivity and psychic processes. Finally, the chapter considers literature on sexuality and gender in the educational sphere. Researchers working more directly in the field of sexuality and schooling are discussed here and throughout the book. This study is in dialogue with the literature concerned with sexuality and relations of schooling (see for example: Epstein and Johnson 1994, 1998; Holland *et al.* 1998; Mac an Ghaill 1994; Redman 1994; Sears 1992; Thorogood 2000; Trudell 1993). An aim of the study is to develop an analysis of sexuality and contemporary schooling in ways that aid our understanding of heterosexuality as a dominant category. Such an analysis inevitably has implications for policy and practice in the area of sexuality education. While policy perspectives are not the main focus of this study, some of the practical implications for teaching and learning are discussed in subsequent chapters.

The impact of social constructionism

Contemporary perspectives on gender and sexuality often point to a dichotomy between essentialist and social constructionist ways of looking. Essentialism is commonly understood to rest upon biological arguments to posit that gender difference is genetically determined and that each gender carries with it a set of physical, emotional and psychological characteristics. Social constructionist perspectives on the other hand suggest that gender is shaped by and through the society in which we live. There are many different social constructionist perspectives on gender; however, they all share the idea that becoming male or female is a social process that is learned through culture – in the family, in school and in social interactions more generally. Viewing gender as culturally specific also suggests that notions of gender are not fixed but may in fact change over time and place. Social constructionist perspectives frequently point to the ways in which gender can be understood as relational. In other words, what it is to be male is often defined in relation to what it is to be female and vice versa. Correspondingly, the gendered identities of masculinity and femininity can be seen in terms of a mutually defining and mutually exclusive relationship. In this respect the relational aspect of gender categories produces and sustains binary opposites that may be invoked in stereotypical ways: masculinity/femininity; strong/weak; active/passive; hard/soft; rational/emotional.

Dualisms such as those above may be seen as part of a tradition of Western thought which has many consequences for us as gendered human beings. One often unacknowledged consequence has a direct bearing on sexuality and sexual identity. Sexual desire invoked through gender arrangements is premised upon the widely held assumption that if you are a man you will inevitably be attracted to a woman and if you are a woman you will inevitably be attracted to a man. Adrienne Rich (1980) refers to this as 'compulsory heterosexuality'; the largely unspoken policing of sexual desire in culture which makes same sex relationships marginal and even taboo. The assumed dominance of a heterosexual order in societies places heterosexual relationships at the centre as 'normal' and normalising and thereby indicates that all other forms of sexual relationship remain 'deviant' and 'abnormal'. The impact of social constructionist ideas upon contemporary analyses of sexuality and gender, particularly in the field of feminist research, is discussed in more detail below.

Socio-historical approaches

Among authors who take a socio-historical perspective to the study of sexuality, the work of Jeffrey Weeks (1977, 1981, 1985, 1986) has been significant in shaping the ways in which sexuality can be viewed and studied. His influential study, *Sex, Politics and Society* (1981) provides a comprehensive and scholarly analysis of sexuality as a historical concept which has been formed by many different forces and has been subject to complex historical transformations. Weeks (1986) points to some of the difficulties of understanding sexuality in contemporary culture, suggesting it has become:

> a transmission belt for a wide variety of needs and desire: love and anger, tenderness and aggression, intimacy and adventure, romance and predatoriness, pleasure and pain, empathy and power.
>
> (Weeks 1986: 11)

For Weeks the powerful feelings produced by sexuality indicate that the realm of the sexual is laden with assumptions which are deeply embedded in Western culture. These assumptions convey notions that sex is a natural force, takes place between members of the opposite sex and that through sex we are 'expected to find ourselves and our place in the world' (1986: 12). The cultural assumptions surrounding sexuality suggest that the term 'sex' can define both an act and a category of person. This approach to sexuality as natural and naturalised is one that, according to Weeks, has been endorsed by modern sexologists who have codified and thereby regulated the ways in which sexualities are lived and organised. Weeks postulates that the sexual traditions of the West offers two ways of looking at sexuality: sex as dangerous and needing to be channelled by society into appropriate forms; and sex as healthy and good but repressed and distorted by society. Weeks poses an alternative to the regulatory versus the libertarian positions:

> that sex only attains meaning in social relations, which implies that we can only make appropriate choices around sexuality by understanding its social and political context. This involves a decisive move away from the morality of 'acts' which has

dominated sexual theorising for hundreds of years and in the direction of a new relational perspective which takes into account context and meanings.

(Weeks 1986: 81)

In this formulation Weeks suggests that sexual practices can be understood in relation to and, as part of, wider social relations in an exploration of the contexts in which acts become meaningful. Weeks' body of work has applied this framework productively to the study of homosexuality. In tracing the socio-historical specificities which define the 'act' and thereby the identity, the 'sodomite' *becomes* the 'homosexual' and, more recently, 'gay'. Weeks' analysis points out the powerful ways in which the delineation of sexual behaviour and sexual identity creates sexual categories that can be defined in relation to each other. Weeks (1998) specifically acknowledges the influence of Foucault and McIntosh in the development of his approach to modern homosexuality. McIntosh's (1968) essay *The Homosexual Role*, in particular, is discussed by Weeks as a landmark study which innovatively proposed that, 'identities are made in history not in nature' (Weeks 1998: 140).

The adoption of a historical perspective in analyses of sexuality is characteristic of a number of studies which elaborate upon and utilise Foucaultian themes in this field (e.g. Bland 1995; Mort 1987; Hawkes 1996; Bristow 1997). Foucault's use of history to study ideas and institutions is, in itself, creative and unconventional (Dreyfus and Rabinow 1982). Foucault's (1976) *History of Sexuality, Volume 1* begins with a striking counter-narrative to the Freudian-influenced 'repressive hypothesis' which posits that the Victorian era was associated with sexual repression and inhibition. Foucault, by contrast, suggests that there has been a 'discursive explosion' on sexual matters since the seventeenth century. Discourses, in the Foucaultian sense, can be defined as ways of knowing and understanding the world. Foucault proposes that sexuality is a historical construct that is brought into being by and through discourses in fields such as medicine, religion, law and education. Discourses evolve patterns, processes and ways of operating or, in Foucaultian terms 'discursive practices' which can be deployed to observe and define individuals and groups. Within this framework psychoanalysis can be seen as an example of a discursive practice which has emerged within a medical discourse to study and define the psychic lives of individuals. Discourses also function as 'regimes of truth', a phrase which captures the cumulative power of discursive formations in the realm of the social. From a Foucaultian perspective discourses actively create specific sexualities by turning subjects into objects of knowledge. The creation of the 'homosexual subject' (Foucault 1976; Weeks 1981, 1986) enables certain disciplinary strategies to emerge in relation to sexual desire and personal relationships. Foucault suggests that the aim of the 'discursive explosion' of sexuality is to incorporate the sexual into the field of state rationality where power can be exercised to reinforce the state itself (Foucault 1988b: 150). The power of the state, exercised through forms of governmentality, should not be seen, however, as simply repressive. Rather, power in Foucaultian terms is productive and relational; it can be administrative and regulatory but, importantly, it can also be generated from below in forms of creative appropriation and resistance.

The Foucaultian insights discussed above have informed my thinking in significant ways. Central to my analysis is the conceptualisation of education as a discursive field in which a number of discourses are in play. These discourses offer competing and sometimes contradictory ways of understanding the aims and purpose of education in contemporary society. In the domain of the sexual, for example, the discourse of the official school assumes that students are sexually innocent and in need of protection while the discourse of the informal school assumes an active and knowing sexuality manifest in peer relations and exchanges between pupils and teachers. Following Foucault I conceptualise the school as a site of discursive practices relating to sexuality which I identify as active in three areas: the curriculum; the teaching of sex education; and the informal cultures of teachers and students. These discursive practices bring into being 'the pupil'; schoolchildren who can be observed, known and categorised according to their orientation to the learning process. In keeping with a Foucaultian framework, I employ a notion of power-as-everywhere in my analysis of school relations. I want to acknowledge that the hierarchical structure of schools create relations of domination and subordination in specific ways: teacher/pupil; adult/child; male/female; head-teacher/classroom teacher. However, my study also indicates that the realm of the sexual offers scope for the creative reworking of power in moments of activity and agency. The following section considers psychoanalytic approaches to sexuality and the ways in which they can be used to complement and elaborate upon socio-historical analyses.

Psychoanalytic approaches

A contrasting approach to understanding sexuality is through psychoanalytic ideas and practices. Psychoanalysis assumes the existence of an active and insistent unconscious in which repressed desires speak through the subject regardless of taboo or pro-hibition. Psychoanalytic theorists such as Freud and Lacan offer a framework for understanding the interior landscape of the uncon-scious that provides a particular perspective on human sexuality and gendered subjectivity. While it is not possible here to develop a comprehensive account of psychoanalytic theories on sexuality, I aim to outline and discuss particular ideas and insights from this body of literature that have influenced me during the course of the research process. These ideas are discussed further throughout the study (see Chapters 4, 5 and 6).

Freud points to the significance of unconscious 'events' in the emergent sexuality of individuals as lived and practised in the rela-tionships they seek and become involved in. Freud looks to the early life of individuals to provide explanations of human sexu-ality. In *Three Essays on the Theory of Sexuality* (1977 [1905]) Freud postulates that child development is marked by specific psycho-sexual stages which individuals negotiate their way through on the road to adulthood. These stages from sexually amorphous baby to gendered adult can be difficult and precarious. Further-more, Freud's notion of 'polymorphous perversity' suggests that practices which are usually seen as deviations from the sexual norm can be viewed more precisely as stages in the development of human sexuality. According to Freud the child's resolution of the psychic dramas with key adults, characterised as the 'Oedipal' and 'castration complexes', has a direct bearing on the shaping of sexual subjectivity. Freud's analysis of child development proposes a gendered model of sexual subjectivity that is biologically marked and psychically significant as it centres around the possession or lack of a penis. Boys' resolution of the Oedipal drama involves, Freud suggests, giving up desire for the mother due to fear of castration by the father. In contrast girls' resolution of the Oedipal drama involves relinquishing desire for the mother and replacing it with desire for the father. This process of transition from female to male love object involves girls in the recognition that they do not have a penis and, therefore, have been castrated. Freud suggests that this may have psychic implications for girls that he characterises, somewhat controversially, as 'penis envy' (1977: 186). Freud's analysis of child development and human sexuality has been both generatively received and heavily critiqued by subsequent theorists. While Lacan and Kristeva, for example, developed Freud's ideas, second wave feminists such as Friedan (1974), Firestone (1972) and Millett (1970) took issue with the biologism that they considered to be inherent in Freudian accounts and also the lack of a perspective that appreciated differences of power and social status in gender relations. Juliet Mitchell (1974), however, attempted a feminist reworking of Freudian themes, particularly the Oedipus complex. Mitchell's (1974) analysis suggests that psychosexual development, in the Freudian sense, can be understood as the social interpretation of biology rather than the inevitable fulfilment of biological destiny. Mitchell's reinterpretation of Freud gives the concept of patriarchy a psychic dimension by suggesting that societal laws for the exchange of women in marriage also constitute an unconscious dynamic of the Oedipus resolution. Mitchell's contribution to analyses of sexuality lies in the insight that women's subordination in sex-gender relations is not only ideological but is also reproduced at the level of the psyche.

Lacan elaborated upon Freud's ideas and also drew upon the work of structuralist anthropologist Levi-Strauss (1966, 1969) to suggest that the unconscious is structured like a language. Lacan (1977a) uses the term 'Symbolic Order' to refer to the ways in which society is regulated by a system of codes, signs and rituals which individuals internalise through language in order to take their place in society. Rosemarie Tong (1989) provides a succinct definition of this process in operation:

> The Symbolic Order regulates society through the regulation of individuals; so long as individuals speak the language of the Symbolic Order – internalizing its gender roles and class roles – society will reproduce itself in fairly constant form.
>
> (Tong 1989: 220)

Lacan proposes a process of psychosexual development which falls into three stages: the pre-Oedipal phase where the child experiences itself as fluid and boundariless; the mirror phase where the child begins to recognise boundaries between Self and Other; finally the Oedipal phase which is marked by separation from the mother and entry into the world of language and rationality which Lacan terms the 'Law of the Father'. Lacan suggests a gendered asymmetry in the internalisation of the Symbolic Order; while boys *become* subjects through the taking on of dominant codes and values, girls' relationship to the Symbolic Order is more difficult to assimilate and places them at the periphery of this system. Lacanian insights have been utilised in productive ways by feminist theorists who have further explored issues of sexuality and the unconscious (see Mitchell and Rose 1982). As Mitchell and Rose (1982) point out, the concept of the phallocentric order and the status of the phallus and the 'feminine' within the Symbolic continue to be abiding concerns in literary and psychoanalytic approaches to feminine sexuality.

Using psychoanalysis alongside a Foucaultian analysis may, at first sight, appear problematic; the cultural and historical specificity of discourses may be seen as in opposition to the generalised principles of subjectivity in psychoanalysis, often postulated in terms of infant development and family dynamics. Foucault demonstrates that discourses shape our knowledge of the self and notions of 'self' can be seen as subjectively constituted by theories of the self. Foucault further suggests that the psyche is transparent and that meanings of the self are less important than the methods used to understand it (Hutton 1988). A Freudian framework, by contrast, suggests that the self and the psyche can be known and understood through therapeutic practices and, furthermore, that knowledge of one's sexuality can be empowering for individuals. These seemingly contradictory ways of looking at individuals and society are brought together in aspects of my study as a way of developing issues of subjectivity within discourse analysis. My use of psychoanalytic ideas indicates that unconscious dynamics and associations at the level of the psyche may be important to our understanding of social relationships. In adopting this approach I am drawing upon the work of Henriques *et al.* (1984) and Walkerdine (1990) in which poststructuralist understandings and psychoanalytic insights are successfully combined in order to theorise issues of subjectivity and desire. In *Changing the Subject* (Henriques *et al.* 1984) the notion of 'investment' is used to offer ways of theorising subjective affiliations – that is to say, ways of understanding what makes an individual take up a position in one discourse rather than another. This approach encouraged me to consider further the realm of subjectivity and the relationship between internal relations of the self and the world of social relations. Jacqueline Rose asserts that psychoanalysis examines what '*insists* on being spoken rather than what is *allowed* to be said' (1986: 86, *italics as original*). The recognition that repressed desires speak through the subject provided me with a valuable insight that could be utilised on occasions as a further resource in thinking about the layers of analysis involved in empirical data. Finally, psychoanalytic theories offer a purchase on subjectivity that I find instructive in many ways. Psychoanalytic theories suggest that gendered subjectivity is central to identity, and that the process is precarious, not easily achieved and ever incomplete. The work of Valerie Walkerdine in this respect has had a significant impact on my thinking and is discussed in more detail below. The following section of this chapter considers some contemporary approaches to sexuality from a social science perspective. This section outlines some salient features in contemporary analyses of sexuality as well as highlighting points in the literature where these features come under scrutiny in moments of debate and contestation.

Contemporary approaches

Contemporary approaches to sexuality have been concerned to apply poststructural, psychoanalytic and postmodern perspectives to the domain of the sexual. The application of recent social theory to the realm of sexuality has produced a vast body of literature, ever expanding and diversifying, which indicates that this field of academic enquiry can be seen as a burgeoning and productive area of debate and analysis. Feminist thinking on sexuality, as Stevi Jackson (1996) points out, has conceptualised the sexual domain as a site of male power in which the erotic can be understood in cultural terms as a product of gendered patterns of domination and submission. The work of theorists such as Dworkin (1981) and MacKinnon (1983) on sexual violence and pornography can be seen from this perspective as grounded in feminist political activism and invested in social change.

Carol Vance (1995) assesses the impact of understanding sexuality from feminist perspectives as culturally mediated rather than biologically given. Vance suggests that social construction theory has been important to analyses of sexuality in the following way:

> Social construction work has been valuable in exploring
> human agency and creativity in sexuality, moving away from
> unidirectional models of social change to describe complex
> and dynamic relationships among the state, professional experts
> and sexual subcultures.
>
> (Vance 1995: 42)

A key feature of contemporary analyses has been a concern to
explore the relationship between gender and sexuality in social
spheres. Vance suggests that social constructionism offered a way
of uncoupling gender and sexuality which, she postulates, began
with Gayle Rubin's (1975) pathbreaking essay, 'The traffic in
women: notes on the "political economy" of sex'. Rubin's account
demonstrates the ways in which fraternal interest groups have
historically exercised control over women's sexuality through
patterns of kinship and reproduction. Rubin's analysis suggests
that gender and sexuality become linked through patriarchal
systems that commodify women's bodies as carriers of a biological
sexuality. Within this schema women's capacity to reproduce
becomes a recognisable part of the 'sex/gender system' whereby
women can be exchanged between fathers and husbands in ways
that prescribe female sexuality and gender relations. Rubin concludes her analysis by postulating that while sexual systems take
place in the context of gender relations, gender and sexuality are
not the same thing. Rubin calls for the need to separate gender
and sexuality analytically in order to accurately reflect upon the
ways in which sexuality is socially organised. In a later essay
Rubin (1984) elaborates upon the social organisation of sexuality
and the discontinuities between kinship based systems that fused
gender and sexuality and modern forms of sexuality. In 'Thinking
sex: notes for a radical theory of the politics of sexuality' (1984)
Rubin asserts that human sexuality is not comprehensible in
purely biological terms as biological explanations cannot account
for the variety of human sexualities. Like Weeks (1977), Rubin
(1984) acknowledges the centrality of social specificities to contemporary analyses of gender, sexuality and embodiment: 'any
encounter with the body is mediated by meanings that culture gives
to it' (Rubin 1984: 276).
   Carole Vance (1984) further explores the analytic separation of
gender and sexuality in her work on female sexuality and desire.
Vance postulates that gender systems have traditionally urged

women to make a bargain with men; being sexually 'good' in order to be protected. The social and psychic effects of this bargain place pleasure and safety in opposition to each other and act as an internalised control on female desire. Vance suggests that the domain of sexuality presents a challenge to feminist enquiry as it involves recognising and dealing with difference. For Vance, female sexuality is diverse, life-affirming and potentially empowering. Vance recognises and points to the relationship between fantasy, behaviour and the development of an agenda for social change. Finally, Vance's analysis of sexual pleasure and danger emphasises the political potential of the sexual domain by indicating that sexuality can be understood as a site of struggle wherein sexual pleasure can be regarded as a fundamental right where women play an active part as sexual subjects and agents. The following section discusses a paradigm shift in contemporary analyses of sexuality which has been referred to as the 'queer turn' (Seidman 1998).

Turning queer

A key shift in contemporary analyses of sexuality can be seen in the impact of queer theory, commonly associated with the writing of Sedgwick (1990, 1994); Dollimore (1991) and Butler (1990, 1993). Tim Edwards (1998) defines queer as:

> an attempt to undermine an overall discourse of sexual categorisation and, more particularly, the limitations of the heterosexual–homosexual divide as an identity.
>
> (Edwards 1998: 47)

Queer theory employs poststructuralist and postmodern insights to the field of sexuality to indicate that the heterosexual/homosexual binary, pervasive in activism and analysis, can be deconstructed in ways that suggest creative possibilities for sexual politics and practice. As Ann Brooks (1997) points out queer theory involves the political and theoretical rejection of Western liberal homosexuality as a form of constraining difference premised on notions of rights and identity. The move from identity politics to queer involves shifting the focus from sexual minorities to a consideration of sexual majorities, specifically the politics and practice of heterosexuality. Looking at the dominant rather than the decentred involves an analysis of the power and fragility of heterosexuality as a sexual category that exists only in relation to that which it opposes. Jeff Weeks (1998) discusses the queer turn in the following way:

> the perverse is the worm at the centre of the normal which gives rise to sexual and cultural dissidence and a transgressive ethic which constantly works to unsettle binarism and to suggest alternatives.
>
> (Weeks 1998: 146)

Butler (1990) and Sedgwick (1990, 1994) suggest that homophobia is intrinsic to contemporary heterosexual masculinities. Sedgwick (1990) develops an analysis based upon the premise that the 'closet' can be seen as an 'epistemology'; a way of organising knowledge/ignorance in relation to the sexual which gives shape to the centrality of heterosexual–homosexual relations. Butler's (1990) analysis focuses upon gendered identity and develops a critique of the modernist notion of identity and its associations with rational, developed forms of selfhood. Butler (1990) proposes a less tangible conceptualisation of identity as gendered 'performance' which gives the illusion of substance but does not exist outside of the performed act. For Butler there is no pre-given subject or, to use her terms, no 'doer behind the deed' (1990: 25). Rather, gender identity achieves the *appearance* of subjective personhood through the sustained enactment of performances. The notion of performance, however, does not necessarily imply depoliticisation; Butler uses the example of cross-dressing to suggest that queer theory can be connected with activism and specifically with the politics of transgression. The emergence of queer theory is also associated with new modes of analysis, in particular the move away from historicism, empiricism and sociological methods and the embracing of other theoretical approaches such as literary criticism, linguistics-based semiotics and psychoanalysis. While queer theory has been commended for its contribution to theoretical debate (Seidman 1998), it has also been critiqued for its lack of political engagement with the social world (Adam 1998; Edwards 1998). Despite Butler's claims for transgressive political acts, Edwards (1998) postulates that queer theory offers little potential for the development of communitarian politics and fails to make links with other forms of discrimination or, indeed, other forms of radical activism. Despite Seidman's (1998) assertion that British researchers have not taken the queer turn, some UK based studies have been informed by queer theory in significant ways (see for example Hird 2000; Hood-Williams 1996). In an earlier study (Nayak and Kehily 1996) we applied Butler's notion of performativity to an analysis of the peer group practices of young males. Our study argued that the homophobic practices of young men in school can be seen as a psychosocial performance which is enacted and repeated to create the illusion of a coherent heterosexual masculinity. Our analysis illustrated the ways in which the fraught exhibition demonstrated in homophobic performances can be understood as a technique for the expulsion of homoerotic desire from the Self onto Others. Through such performances, we argued, young men in school sought to conceal fears of being gay and assert themselves as heterosexual and masculine. In this study I draw upon Butler's ideas more generally to suggest that gender can be seen as performative in the context of student sexual culture. Chapter 5 in particular develops an analysis which argues that female friendship groups provide a performative space for *gender displays* which can be seen as constitutive of a collectively negotiated femininity. Chapter 6 develops this argument in relation to male peer group cultures to explore further links between gender, sexuality and embodiment. Furthermore, the study as a whole has been influenced by the queer imperative to deconstruct the heterosexual–homosexual binary in ways that explore relations of power in the domain of the sexual. In this respect the focus of the study is upon the school as a site for the production of heterosexualities which, I suggest, can be seen as both powerful and fragile in the ongoing struggle to achieve and maintain a dominant sexual category.

The work of Valerie Walkerdine

While contemporary approaches to sexuality discussed above have formed the backdrop to my work in this field, the writing of Valerie Walkerdine has had a particularly direct impact on my thinking and on the ways in which this study is shaped. Walkerdine's body of writing from 1981 to 1989, collected in *Schoolgirl Fictions* (1990), explores many of the themes I have been concerned with throughout this ethnographic study. Subjects such as child development, the relationship of sexuality to pedagogy, practices of femininity and popular culture are explored and analysed by Walkerdine in creative and original ways. Walkerdine's body of work is also concerned with the academic mode of production in reflections upon the ways in which subjects are researched and written about. Central to Walkerdine's work is a compelling mode of reflexivity, creatively employed in the inter-weaving of autobiographical reflections and social research. As a working-class woman Walkerdine is keen to hold onto a notion of social class that exists not only as taxonomy for the location of position and status but also as a psychic location for the forma-tion of gendered subjectivity. Walkerdine's use of contemporary social theory and psychoanalysis contributed to the ways in which I thought about and researched issues of sexuality and schooling. I viewed Walkerdine's body of work as politically informed writing and thinking which was generative in its analysis and inno-vative in its method; as such it provided me with inspiration and desire.

In 'Sex, power and pedagogy' (1981) Walkerdine discusses the transformative dynamics of power in a nursery school classroom. Walkerdine's analysis indicates that 'male sexual discourse' can be seen as a resource that boys can draw upon and use against female teachers. In the now famous exchange between Mrs Baxter and two four-year old boys, the boys enter into a discourse that gives them the power to disrupt pedagogic discourses predicated on 'universals' of child development and female nurturance. Walkerdine's analysis points to the contradictions inherent in peda-gogic strategies and practice where male power can be recuperated as 'natural' rather than oppressive or problematic.

Pedagogic themes and their relationship to femininity are further explored in 'On the regulation of speaking and silence: subjectivity, class and gender in contemporary schooling' (1985). Drawing on Foucault's *Discipline and Punish* (1977), Walkerdine suggests that schools can be seen as sites for the production and regulation of the modern concept of the individual where logo-centric discourses of rationality set up the irrational (female) other as its opposite. Through such discourses schools define what knowledge is and what the 'child' is, in ways which produce systems of categorisation, individuation and self-regulation. How-ever, these processes are mediated through the presence and practice of female teachers. Walkerdine concludes that, 'the self-regulating citizen depends upon the facilitating nurturance, caring and servicing of femininity' (1985: 237). 'Post-structuralist theory and everyday social practices: the family and the school' (1986a) discusses further contradictions to be found in contemporary schooling. In this essay Walkerdine explores the ways in which girls can be pejoratively defined and pathologised by pedagogic discourses. Turning her attention to childhood sexuality, Walkerdine suggests that dominant discourses produce a fiction of 'the child' as sexually sanitised and safe from the contaminating world of the sexual:

> The 'universal and natural' child is the one for whom sexuality is central but left behind on the path toward rationality. In later formulations, neither gender nor sexuality is mentioned and we are left with a de-sexualized, safe, self-disciplined child on the road to autonomy. But the desexualized child is constructed as a fiction in the fantasies and desires of adults for safety.
>
> (Walkerdine 1986a: 73)

As Walkerdine points out, this fantasy overlooks or, rather, displaces the sexual desire of adults for children onto an image of childhood innocence. Walkerdine suggests that, in particular, it is female sexuality, manifest in girls' engagements with popular culture, that is seen to constitute a threat to the moral order of school and a disruption of the rational educative process. The recourse to notions of childhood innocence in pedagogic discourses has the effect of turning displays of sexuality into something which is 'forbidden, hidden and subverted' (1986a: 73). Girls' relationship to the erotic and the eroticisation of girls in Western culture is further developed by Walkerdine in a subsequent study, *Daddy's Girl* (1997).

In 'Femininity as performance' (1987) Walkerdine pursues the rationality/femininity opposition in relation to specific features of gendered subjectivity. Walkerdine discusses women's troubled relationship with achievement and femininity as a psychic struggle in which women frequently equate success/ability in the academic domain with a loss of femininity at the level of the Subject. Drawing on poststructural and psychoanalytic theories, Walkerdine suggests that women develop complex conscious and unconscious configurations for dealing with the 'unbearable contradiction' (1990 [1987]: 144) of performing academically and performing as feminine. Elsewhere in the book I discuss Walkerdine's analysis of girls' engagement with popular cultural forms through the *Bunty* comic [see Chapter 5]. Walkerdine's account of the methodological implications of social research developed in the study 'Video replay: families, film and fantasy' (1986b) provide an interesting fusion of auto/biographical method and social research. In this study Walkerdine chronicled her growing involvement with a working-class family she was researching. Her inextricable involvement in aspects of the family's interaction led Walkerdine to argue persuasively for reflexivity in ethnographic study, specifically for an identification of 'the ethnographer's own position in [the] complex web of power/knowledge/desire' (Walkerdine 1990: 196). In this particular case, that involvement included identification with, and positioning by, a fantasy held by the father of the family. The research encounter triggered Walkerdine's identification in fantasy with a vulnerable form of femininity connected to a certain moment in childhood when her own father positioned her as the Tinkerbelle fairy. As I have indicated, the work of Valerie Walkerdine has had a generative effect on my thinking and writing during the course of this study. The issues raised in 'Video replay' inspired me to develop the reflexive auto/biographical account used in Chapter 1 in which I combine memory-work with personal reflections of the early years of my career as a teacher.

As discussed above, Walkerdine's body of work has been particularly generative for my research as it is concerned with the exploration of similar themes and approaches to sexuality, schooling and popular culture. Unlike the body of literature on sexuality discussed in the early sections of this chapter, Walkerdine's analysis is frequently based upon an 'in-school' account of social and psychic processes. This engagement with children and teachers in school provides Walkerdine with a specifically grounded insight into educational discourses and pedagogic practice. A further point of identification for me is Walkerdine's biographical reflections on her working-class childhood and the experience of social mobility through educational achievement. The pain and desire associated with this trajectory has particular resonance for me as a working-class girl who has followed a similar path. In the following sub-section of this chapter I discuss other school-based approaches to sexuality which have had a significant impact on my thinking and, in turn, have shaped the contours of this study.

Sexuality, gender and the domain of the school

How do the ideas about sexuality and gender outlined above relate to schools? The concept of the 'hidden curriculum' has been used by educationalists to acknowledge that learning extends the boundaries of the official curriculum and may have inadvertent effects. What is learned by pupils may not fit with the intended aims of teachers and educational policy makers (see Hammersley and Woods 1976; Whitty 1985 for a discussion of these themes). A body of educational research suggests that through participation in school routines, pupils learn to conform or resist the official culture of the school (see for example Rosser and Harre 1976; Willis 1977; Apple 1982; Curry 2001). Like other feminist educationalists, I would like to suggest that the 'hidden curriculum' can also be seen in terms of the regulation of sex–gender categories. Within the context of the school much informal learning takes place concerning issues of gender and sexuality; the homophobia of young men, the sexual reputations of young women, and the pervasive presence of heterosexuality as an 'ideal' and a practice mark out the terrain for the production of gendered and sexualised identities. Furthermore, such social learning is overt and explicit rather than hidden.

A rich vein of research on gender and schooling has exposed the gender inequalities that exist between young men and women and the implications for school-based policy and practice (e.g. Griffin 1985; Lees 1986; Connell 1987; Weiner and Arnot 1987; Arnot and Weiler 1993; Kenway and Willis 1998; Gordon et al. 2000). This body of work has the effect of 'making visible' the experience of girls within the schooling process and points to the need to account for gender inequalities in school. Gordon et al. (2000) explore issues of inequality as a spatial dynamic as well as an effect of power relations. Their innovative approach to themes of marginalisation and participation demonstrates the complexity of gender arrangements and the need for a reformulated notion of 'citizenship' to be taken up in schools. Further research has drawn attention to sexuality and particularly the heterosexist structure of school relations by acknowledging gay and lesbian identities in school (e.g. Trenchard and Warren 1984; Sears 1992; Mac an Ghaill 1994; Britzman 1995; Epstein and Johnson 1998). This literature provides us with valuable insights and ways of understanding gendered and sexual hierarchies in schools. Within

sex–gender structures in school homosexuality may be marginalised and stigmatised through the curriculum, pedagogic practices
and pupil cultures. This literature indicates that sexual identities
are not biologically given but are created through institutional and
lived practices. Moreover, schools can be seen as sites for the
production of gendered/sexualised identities rather than agencies
that passively reflect dominant power relations. More recent work
on masculinities has contributed to the literature on sexuality and
gender by exploring the recognition that boys too are gendered
subjects, engaged in the struggle for masculine identities both
within schools and in social relations more generally (e.g. Mac an
Ghaill 1994; Connell 1995; Epstein *et al.* 1998; Gilbert and Gilbert
1998; Pattman *et al.* 1998; Lingard and Douglas 1999; Frosh *et al.*
2002; Martino and Meyenn 2001; Skelton 2001). Mac an Ghaill's
study in particular illustrates the ways in which diverse sexualities
can be spoken through the various masculinities young men come
to inhabit. Being a lad may involve the cultivation of a hyper-
heterosexual identity, while being a 'wimp' implies occupying a
feminised or asexual identity that may easily translate into being
called 'gay'. In this sense sexuality underpins the location of
young men's masculinities within the schooling system and can be
seen to structure gender arrangements more generally.

As noted above, my approach to researching issues of sexuality
and schooling draws upon an emergent body of literature in this
field (e.g. Britzman 1995; Epstein 1994; Epstein and Johnson 1994,
1998; Haywood 1996; Mac an Ghaill 1991, 1994; Moran 2001;
Redman 1994; Sears 1992; Thorogood 2000; Trudell 1993). While
much of this literature is discussed throughout the book, here I
want to highlight some features of this work that provide a starting point for my analysis.

The conceptualisation of schools as sites for the *production* of
gendered/sexualised identities represents a break with earlier
approaches that viewed schools as *reproducers* of dominant modes
of class, gender and racial formations. The theoretical shift from
reproduction to production takes into account Foucaultian
insights into relations of power in which social categories are
produced in the interplay of culture and power. Power, moreover,
is discursively produced and cannot be seen only as a 'top-down'
dynamic. It is also created locally in sites such as schools. Within
this framework school cultures can be seen as active in producing
social relations that are contextually specific and productive of

social identities. Another concern of contemporary analyses in this field is the uncoupling of sex/gender. In this respect there is a recognition that school policies and practices traditionally treat gender and sexuality as if they are inextricably linked where one bespeaks the other. The prising apart of the sex–gender couplet in recent research allows for a more nuanced analysis of masculinities, femininities and their relationship to sexuality. The growth of work on masculinities has been important in this respect and suggests new ways of looking at schools as productive of sex–gender hierarchies.

Contemporary analyses of sexuality and schooling in the UK have taken place within the context of rapid and far-reaching educational change referred to in the introductory chapter of this book. These changes, associated with the success of New Right legislation of the 1980s and 90s, affected the organisation of schools and the implementation of the curriculum. The changing political climate in school is discussed in more detail in Chapter 7. Here, however, I want to note that within the framework of educational change, schools, teachers and teaching have become the object of public critique and accountability. The climate of blame and exposure pervasive in the field of education during this period has been referred to by researchers as productive of 'discourses of derision' (Ball 1990). As noted in the introduction, this notion of teachers and schools as culpable has provided the context in which this study has taken place. Inevitably this dominant discourse has had an impact on the research, even though I was not focusing directly upon issues of policy or school effectiveness.

The subsequent chapters draw upon and discuss ethnographic material gathered during the course of the fieldwork period. The following chapter seeks to provide an approach to ways of understanding the school as a social site. Based upon a close reading of Foucault's (1976) *History of Sexuality, Volume 1*, Chapter 3 aims to provide a framework through which subsequent chapters can be read and interpreted.

Producing heterosexualities: the school as a site of discursive practices

It would be less than exact to say that the pedagogical institution has imposed a ponderous silence on the sex of children and adolescents. On the contrary, since the eighteenth century it has multiplied the forms of discourse on the subject; it has established various points of implantation for sex; it has coded contents and qualified speakers . . . the sex of children and adolescents has become an important area of contention around which innumerable institutional devices and discursive strategies have been deployed.

(Foucault 1976: 29–30)

Modern sexuality, from a Foucaultian perspective, can be understood as a historical construct; the product of particular discourses which are articulated around a cluster of power relations. Foucault counterposes the Freudian notion of sexual repression by suggesting that modern Western societies have developed numerous ways of talking about sex and regulating sexual activity. The development of mechanisms to talk about sex in fields such as religion, medicine, criminal justice and education was underpinned by a notion that sexuality was a thing to be known and spoken in the 'public interest'. Foucault links this shift from taboo to 'discursive explosion' in the sexual domain as central to the emergence of 'population' as an economic and political problem. From this perspective the sexual conduct of a population becomes an object of classification, administration and regulation. The deployment of discursive strategies in relation to sexuality can be seen to demarcate the terrain for the production of sexual identities. In this schema the hysterical woman, the homosexual, the masturbating child, the sex worker can be viewed as actively generated by discourses of sexuality. In the modern era, discourses of sexuality offer a complex means of policing the person, whereby individuals are represented as containing a sexually constituted internality that can be accessed and monitored. Central to a Foucaultian analysis is the position of the family and, particularly, the heterosexual married couple as a site for the recognition and regulation of sexual activity.

Schooling and the domain of the sexual

Looking at Foucaultian ideas within the context of contemporary schooling, what can we say about issues of sexuality and schooling? This chapter is concerned with the application of a Foucaultian perspective in order to identify the discursive strategies that may be deployed within the school setting. Here the school can be understood as a site where a nexus of discourses in relation to sexuality are articulated and struggled over; moral/religious, medical, political and cultural. The chapter is particularly concerned with the ways in which these discursive formations produce sexual identities within school settings. The chapter argues that sexualities are produced within the school and inscribed in discursive practices that are normatively heterosexual. In this respect the interest is in the *processes* which are constitutive of dominant practice; school routines and procedures situated within the curriculum and pedagogic practice that serve to shape and consolidate heterosexual relations. The chapter identifies and explores three areas of discursive practice that serve to shape sexualities in school settings: the official curriculum; pedagogic practice; and pupil cultures.

School practices create a particular context for the production of sexualities and sexual identities (Epstein and Johnson 1994, 1998; Mac an Ghaill 1994). As I indicated in the introductory chapter, the everyday social practices that constitute school culture create boundaries in relation to issues of sexuality: teacher/pupil; public/private; adult/child; male/female (see Kehily and Nayak 1996 for a further discussion of schooling and symbolic boundaries). These boundaries demarcate the terrain for sexualities where certain features appear visible and acceptable while others remain inadmissible and even deviant or offensive. The establishment of boundaries in the domain of the sexual provides for the possibility of multiple transgressions. In the social arena of the school, sexuality can be seen as a *playground* for pupils to negotiate and resist the dominant values of the school. Pupil sexual cultures, often defined in opposition to teachers and the official curriculum, frequently utilise sexualised themes as a vehicle for humour in situations where teachers can be humiliated and school authority flouted. Pupil sexual cultures also offer a site for the production of masculinities and femininities, whereby sex–gender identities can be displayed, contested, made and remade. The following section considers some key features that emerge in different literatures on heterosexuality in order to provide a context for focusing on heterosexuality in school.

Approaches to heterosexuality

The normative power of heterosexuality referred to by many writers points to some of the difficulties that arise when research-ing a dominant sexual category. The 'natural' status of hetero-sexuality makes it a slippery topic to grasp for critical inquiry and focused analysis. Given the taken-for-grantedness of heterosexu-ality, it is perhaps unsurprising that the challenge to the dominant sexual category has come from those who do not circumscribe to its regulatory boundaries. Stevi Jackson (1996) suggests that feminist approaches to heterosexuality can be defined in terms of three main strands of thinking and writing: patriarchal approaches which stress the centrality of male dominance; historical approaches which foreground the variability and plasticity of sexu-ality; and finally, approaches which emphasise subjectivity and the formation of individual desires. The dominant and structuring presence of heterosexuality has encouraged Adrienne Rich (1980) to identify it as a political institution with the coercive power to make male–female fucking a part of 'compulsory' existence for women. From a similar lesbian-feminist perspective, other writers have discussed the relationship between male violence and hetero-sexual practices in educational arenas (see Jones and Mahony 1989). The focus of this work has been upon the structural connec-tions between heterosexuality and patriarchy, and the oppressive effects this has upon the lives of women and girls.

From a different viewpoint, other writers have considered the relationship between masculinities and heterosexuality (Herek 1987), and applied this to the English state schooling system (Haywood 1996; Mac an Ghaill 1994). Connell (1995: 104) has used life history case studies to illustrate that 'compulsory heterosexuality is also enforced on men'. In this reading heterosexual relations of power may carry costs for men as well as women, in an acknowledgement that 'the male body has to be disciplined to heterosexuality' (ibid.). In an article about heterosexual practices, Wendy Hollway (1988) deploys discourse analysis to address masculine experiences of heterosexual relationships. In a frank and fascinating account Hollway considers, firstly, why she has been able to feel powerful in heterosexual relationships and, secondly, why men have experienced her as powerful. Consequently, she goes on to explore 'why men feel similarly intense, irrational and vulnerable' in heterosexual relationships (1988: 125). More recently, Hollway (1995) has discussed the positive possibilities of reconfiguring heterosexuality, and the potentiality for such a project to become a site for the pleasure and empowerment of women.

A complex approach to questioning contemporary heterosexuality can be found in some psychoanalytic inflected studies drawing on Freud's notion of the human subject as neither gay nor straight but 'polymorphously perverse'. The language of psychoanalysis has provided a new vocabulary for thinking through the formation of heterosexual identities by engaging with concepts such as projection, splitting and internalisation in order to understand homophobia as an internal and external dynamic (Nayak and Kehily 1996). The psychoanalytic term 'homophobia', has itself helped problematise the oppressive styling of masculine heterosexualities by shifting the focus from 'Other' to 'Self'. Richard Johnson explains:

> Heterosexual identity is constituted by an imaginary expulsion of homosexual desire which is externalised as Other, as Not Me. Imagined, actively held at bay as well is some version of the 'feminine'. But this is not the end of the story, for expulsion is, in one sense, in vain, because heterosexual male identity needs an internalised version of the feminine and must handle the confusions of the homosexual in order to preserve the ongoing sense of difference.
>
> (Johnson 1996: 183)

So, the homosexual is not only the deviant 'out there' but is also 'in here' creating troubling anxieties for heterosexual male identities. The ebb and flow that occurs within this psychodynamic nexus suggest that heterosexuality is always worked at and struggled over in a relentless effort to be 'kept safe' from the enemy within.

In recent analyses contemporary writers have sought out new ways of understanding heterosexuality as simultaneously an institution and a set of specific situated practices (Richardson 1996; Wilkinson and Kitzinger 1993). Wilkinson and Kitzinger's (1993: 25) collection aims for 'more rigorous and sophisticated analyses of heterosexuality' in an attempt to theorise how heterosexual relations shape women's lives, gay and straight. By 'making explicit the silent term' (1993: 5) heterosexuality, the editors see this analysis as necessary to the development of feminist politics, and a key move in the field of psychology. Meanwhile, Mac an Ghaill (1996) has applied a deconstructive method to the study of heterosexualities in an understanding that 'in English schools there is a tendency to see questions of sexuality as something primarily to do with gays and lesbians' (1996: 193). This mode of deconstruction is used to dismantle the normative position of heterosexuality by 'shifting from a focus on sexual minorities to a critical engagement with sexual majorities' (1996: 204). Haywood (1996) similarly writes of heterosexualities in the plural, paying careful attention to the multiple discursive positions that different young men attempt to occupy when styling their sexual identities. Richard Johnson (1997) further explores approaches to heterosexuality in his introduction to the work of the Politics of Sexuality Group, University of Birmingham. Johnson's analysis of discussions within this group trace the critique of heterosexuality 'from power-invested differences, to their instabilities and policing, to defensive, recuperative or transformative strategies' (Johnson 1997: 15). The shifting ways of viewing heterosexuality in the group point to the enduring and ever-changing nature of this sexual category.

A third strand in the contemporary critique of sexuality, referred to by Jackson (1996), has come from 'queer theorists' working to decentre the normative presence, privilege and practice of heterosexuality. Judith Butler has written about the 'performativity' of gender and 'the regulatory fiction of heterosexual coherence' (1990: 137). In Butler's analysis gendered/sexualised identities are consolidated through a 'heterosexual matrix' of power in the effort to evade 'gender trouble'. These diverse approaches to the study of heterosexuality are not always empirically distinct but may combine a variety of perspectives and approaches. As part of the recent encompassing of heterosexuality within academic debates outlined above, this study has been influenced by a need to understand both the power and the fragility of sexual majorities by focusing on the processes that are constitutive of dominant practice in educational settings. The analysis synthesises many insights from the approaches outlined above to offer an ethnographic interpretation of heterosexualities within different discursive spaces in school.

Discursive practice: the official curriculum

> Heterosexuality as a social reality seems to be invisible to those that benefit from it. In part this is because of the remorseless construction of heterosexuality as natural. If things are natural they cannot really be questioned or scrutinised and so they fade from view. Such naturalisation often characterises how we see, and don't see, the powerful, how they see, and don't see themselves.
>
> (Dyer 1993: 133–4)

Heterosexuality is largely assumed and unnamed within the context of the school. When teachers and pupils talk about sex they are implicitly talking about heterosex. The pervasive presence of heterosexual relations and the simultaneous invisibility of its structure makes heterosexuality normatively powerful in the lives of teachers and pupils (Epstein and Johnson 1994). Its 'natural' status as a dominant sexual category gives it a taken-for-granted quality referred to by Richard Dyer. School relations are organised around the assumption that heterosexuality is the 'natural order of things'. One effect of the naturalisation of heterosexual relations is widespread homophobia, with homophobic practices often treated as routine everyday activities, particularly among male peer groups. Unlike other discriminatory practices (e.g. sexism, racism), homophobic abuse has not been treated as an equal opportunities issue in school and, until recently, has not been seen as a disciplinary offence nor found its way into school policy documents.

Within the school the naturalisation of heterosexuality provides an *absent centre* in relation to the curriculum. The structuring yet invisible presence of heterosexuality as a category and a practice can be seen in school policy documents. As noted above, Clarke

School is a non-selective Church of England secondary school for boys and girls aged 11–16 in the East Midlands area of England. The school population is predominantly white working class, with a small percentage of students from middle-class (usually church) backgrounds. There was also a small number of African Caribbean, South Asian and mixed heritage students at the school. The Church of England affiliation described in the school's statement aims 'to provide a high quality education in a committed Christian environment, in which the love of God is central and young people are valued and nurtured to achieve maximum potential'. This broad Christian ethos permeates most school policy documents relating to curriculum content and social issues such as bullying. In the sex education policy this is articulated in the following way:

> As a Church of England school, particular emphasis and consideration will be placed on the views of the Church towards teaching in this area. Our sex education will be appropriate to the pupils' age, experience and special needs. It will emphasise that personal and family values are important. The moral, ethical, religious and cultural dimensions of young people's lives should influence all approaches to Sex Education which will be presented within a moral, family oriented and Christian framework.
>
> (Clarke School Sex Education Policy, October 1994)

The wording of Clarke School's Sex Education Policy can be seen to echo and reflect themes found in legislative documents. The 1986 Education [No. 2] Act required teachers and school governors to ensure that sex education was presented in a manner that encouraged pupils to have 'due regard to moral considerations and the value of family life' (Section 46). The same Act removed responsibility for sex education from Local Education Authorities and placed it under the auspices of school governing bodies. This move invested in parents and teachers in individual schools as the agents of control in the development of an approach to issues of sexuality and the pedagogic practice of sex education.

The discursive strategies deployed at the level of the Clarke School policy document inscribe heterosexual relations within societal institutions of the Church and the family. The mobilisation of moral/religious discourses in relation to sex education are cited as an 'ideal' overarching framework which allows sex to be thought about and spoken about in particular ways. Within this schema legitimate sexuality is confined to the heterosexual married couple, the conjugal family where certain 'values' can be regulated and reproduced. More specifically, the parents' bedroom becomes the 'single locus of sexuality' (Foucault 1976: 3), the one place where sexual activity is recognised as permissible. The Christian perspective embraced by Clarke School at the level of the official curriculum links 'the love of God' with the care and nurture of young people where the purity of ascetic devotion is connected to a concern for the protection of the young. The stated aim that 'our sex education will be appropriate to the pupils' age, experience and special needs' indicates that sexual learning is premised on a notion of physical and emotional development, an adult-formulated taxonomy of what pupils need to know and when. As Sears (1992) points out, official school discourses on sex education, the delivery of programmes and criteria for effectiveness often reflect a techno-rational worldview which rarely relates to the world of adolescent sexual activity.

Foucault's analysis points to the many ways in which discourses aimed at restriction in the field of sexuality frequently have the unintended effect of producing the opposite. The Christian pastoral tradition sought to produce specific effects on desire; in confessing to the weakness of the flesh one achieved spiritual reconversion, 'turning back to God, a physical effect of blissful suffering from feeling in one's body the pangs of temptation and the love that resists it' (Foucault 1976: 23). Such practices, Foucault suggests, extend the boundaries of sexual discourse through the public disclosure of hitherto unspoken desires. In this way acts of prohibition and censorship produce and enlarge the very things they seek to deny. It could also be argued that such acts of confession play a significant part in the constitution of the Other within oneself, heightening desire by producing the 'forbidden' internally within the Subject and revealing it in an attempt to overcome it. It is possible to see the homophobic practices of young men and the concern with sexual reputation among young women and men as part of this economy of desire where social regulation and internal struggles are enacted in contextually specific discriminatory rituals.

At the level of the official curriculum, school policy documents can also be read through the lens of institutional anxieties. Here, it is possible to see the concerns associated with assembling large numbers of young people in one place as a 'problem' to be managed. From this perspective the school population becomes a body to be controlled and regulated. In a site where large numbers of young people interact, the sexual conduct of pupils becomes a matter for surveillance and intervention. Foucault outlines the ways in which secondary schools of the eighteenth century were preoccupied with sex, as displayed in the architectural layout of the buildings, disciplinary procedures and organisational structures. Here, the sexuality of children was addressed directly:

> the internal discourse of the institution – the one it employed to address itself, and which circulated among those that made it function – was largely based on the assumption that this sexuality existed, that it was precocious, active and ever present.
>
> (Foucault 1976: 28)

In particular, Foucault suggests, the sex of schoolboys was regarded as a public problem requiring vigilance, moral guidance and medical intervention. The proliferation of discourses aimed at sex and specifically the sexuality of adolescents, although aimed at restriction and confinement, can be seen to increase awareness of sexual matters and thereby serve as a further incentive to talk about sex. At the level of the official curriculum in Clarke School, the incitement to discourse in relation to issues of sexuality can be understood as a strongly imaginary project involving investments in an ideal of heterosexual coupledom and Christian guardianship which can be shared and taught. The ideal is, of course, a statement of how things should be, the approved and preferred form, and also a projection of how school officials would like things to be, a fantasy of virtue and holiness.

Discursive practice: pedagogy

This section will consider the ways in which school policy documents are translated into everyday practice through pedagogic strategies employed by individual teachers. The religious inflection of school policies was publicly supported by the staff and school governors, many of whom were involved in churches in the locality. Specifically, this section will focus upon the teaching of Personal and Social Education (PSE) at Clarke School. Responsibility for this area of the curriculum was undertaken by one senior member of staff who planned the syllabus and taught eighteen of the twenty-two PSE classes timetabled each week. The remaining four classes were taught by two other members of the senior management team. PSE was a compulsory part of the curriculum for all classes from Year 8 onwards and occupied one forty-five minute period per week. Mrs Evans, the teacher responsible for (PSE) at Clarke School, was a practising Christian. She had worked at the school for many years as a Physical Education teacher and more recently had taken responsibility for the co-ordination of PSE throughout the school.

In an early meeting I had with Mrs Evans she explained that the PSE curriculum adopted a Christian perspective. During this discussion she spoke favourably of a teaching pack called *Make Love Last*, produced by a Christian organisation to impart the message that it is acceptable to 'say no' to sex.[1] Mrs Evans commented that it is important for young people to realise that they could 'say no' and that choice in contraception did not necessarily involve engagement in sexual activity (Fieldnotes 9.10.95). Mrs Evans saw this as an 'empowering' message for young women and her use of the notion of 'empowerment for girls' suggests that she is also aware of this as a particular feminist message where saying no to male advances can be understood as a positive, self-affirming act. For Mrs Evans it seemed that at the level of personal practice, discourses of Christianity and feminism could be creatively interpreted and interwoven in a way which was specifically intended to address young women. Here, the notion of girls' empowerment can be seen to have both productive and restrictive effects. While girls were encouraged to exercise choice in sexual activity, the fact that the practice of PSE invariably focuses on young women and particularly on their reproductive capacities, reinforces their definition in terms of sexuality (Thorne 1993). This approach to sex education places being female within the asymmetric power relations inscribed in heterosexual practice where female sexuality is often regarded as potentially dangerous and the object of male sexual desire.

Within the US context issues of sexuality and morality have had a dramatic impact upon the teaching of sex education (Fine 1988; Whatley 1991; Trudell 1993). Like studies of sexuality education in the UK, this body of literature illustrates the asymmetrical power relations and lack of female agency in the domain of the sexual, succinctly framed by Fine as the 'missing discourse of desire'. Federal sponsorship of 'abstinence only' sex education programmes over abstinence-based programmes suggests to young people that sexual activity has negative consequences and offers little support or advice on issues of sexuality that may be pertinent to the experiences and dilemmas faced by young people themselves. Within the dominant discourse of abstinence, however, it is possible to achieve progressive ends. Weiss and Carbonell-Medina's (2000) discussion of an abstinence-based sexuality education initiative at an Arts Academy school in Buffalo, New York, points to the radical potential of such programmes. Their analysis indicates that sexuality education can provide a space for personal and collective identity work in ways that empower and enrich the lives of young women. The issue of agency in relation to the domain of the sexual remains a central theme of this study and is further explored in the following two chapters.

In many respects the ways in which Mrs Evans spoke of the PSE programme at Clarke School can be seen within a radical or progressive pedagogic framework outlined by Weiss and Carbonell-Medina. Mrs Evans endeavoured to give PSE a high profile within the school and, crucially, had gained the support and respect of other teachers and school governors. As part of her ardent search for the recognition of PSE within the school, Mrs Evans had asked the headteacher for a noticeboard in the reception area of the school that could be used to display information and helplines on social issues and local facilities such as drug use, child abuse, contraception and sexually transmitted diseases. Other teachers commented on this as a 'brave' and 'up-front' move. It is an indication of Mrs Evans' success as a teacher of PSE that she maintained the support of senior teachers and governors in the school and was singled out for commendation by government appointed inspectors from the Office for Standards in Education (Ofsted) during an evaluation of the school carried out while I was conducting fieldwork. Mrs Evans described her teaching methods as 'pupil centred' where the emphasis is on pupils' awareness and understanding. Mrs Evans indicated that pupils could be regarded as a resource for learning, generating issues for discussion and exploring ideas among themselves. Her preferred teaching methods involved group-work discussion and interactive tasks with the class divided into small friendship groups for a range of activities. Mrs Evans also stressed the importance of giving pupils information and access to agencies through the use of guest speakers, videos and public health leaflets. This mode of organisation formed a central part of the PSE programme. Mrs Evans' approach to the teaching of PSE can be seen to be innovative and pioneering. She felt strongly that PSE should have the same status as other subjects in the school; like other areas of the curriculum, PSE should have a clearly planned and taught syllabus and should not be regarded by teachers and pupils as a 'doss'. Mrs Evans spoke disparagingly of 'sitting pupils on bean-bags and having a chat'; doing PSE involved engagement in important social learning and should be taken seriously.

In outlining her pedagogic practice, Mrs Evans draws upon different (and sometimes contradictory) discourses to give PSE a coherent structure that she felt happy with. Her approach can be seen as a fine balancing act between official school policy, teacher directives and pupil-centredness. Pedagogic approaches that value pupil perspectives are often fused with points of tension and contradiction (see Chapter 1 for a discussion of these themes). The adoption of aspects of progressive pedagogy inevitably involves some degree of imposition whereby teachers define the learning environment by saying to pupils 'this is how *I* want it to be, it's for the benefit of *us all*'. In the sex education programme at Clarke School, this feature of pedagogic practice is illustrated in relation to issues of language and the expression of sexual themes. In examples where teachers and pupils discuss sexuality, the message to pupils is 'please feel free to speak openly as long as you use the proper terms'. This insistence on correct terminology can be understood as a discursive manoeuvre which legitimises sexuality and, simultaneously, prescribes the boundaries within which it can be spoken. The use of an officially sanctioned vocabulary conveys a particular notion of sexuality which, in this case, represents an adult world of heterosexual sex spoken in 'proper' terms and preferably with reference to, and mindful of, religious and moral discourses. In such instances, language can be seen as a site of discursive struggle where certain ways of speaking and looking attempt to displace other ways of speaking and looking (see Chapter 7 for a further discussion of language in sex education teaching). Here pedagogic practice in relation to language provides a site whereby pupil perspectives and adolescent sexual cultures can be displaced and silenced. As Foucault points out, silences and acts of silencing are active processes which form an 'integral part of the strategies that underlie and permeate discourses' (Foucault 1976: 27). However, the regulation of language in formal spaces such as sex education classes does not necessarily inhibit the language used within pupil sexual cultures. On the contrary, ways of speaking about sex among pupils may proliferate in particular ways, in part as a response to restriction in other spheres (see Chapter 8).

Other aspects of Mrs Evans' pedagogic practice suggested that she had a well-developed personal vision concerning the aims and outcome of sex education. Within this personal vision was a strong pragmatic purpose which can be seen in terms of the promotion of sexual health. Mrs Evans indicated that she saw a direct connection between the PSE programme and rates of pregnancy in the school:

> Mrs Evans: When I first took over this course I was walking round town and I saw five of our girls either pregnant or pushing prams, *five of them*. Now there is only one girl in Year 11 who is pregnant so we must be doing something right . . . The worst year for teenage pregnancies in this school was the year of the Victoria Gillick case.[2] We were warned off giving advice on contraception and several girls fell pregnant.

For Mrs Evans, the proliferation of discourses of sexuality within pedagogic practice produced sexual awareness and responsibility; the repression of discourses in this area led to pregnancy. Within this framework the pregnancy rate in the school could be seen as a signifier for the success or failure of the PSE programme. At this level medical discourses and moral imperatives were working together and located on the bodies of adolescent girls.

Mrs Evans' approach to PSE indicates the many ways in which pedagogic practice can be seen to produce new knowledges with potentially expansive and restrictive effects. As a practising Christian Mrs Evans is supportive of the moral and religious standpoint found in school policy documents. However, as a teacher she is committed to making the PSE syllabus relevant to the pupils in the school. Mrs Evans' concern with sexual health can be seen as a significant move in the translation of policy into practice. In the utilisation of a sexual health model for the teaching of PSE, issues such as methods of contraception, pregnancy and sexually transmitted diseases can be communicated directly to students to impart information in ways that may connect with their needs. The gendered implications of this practice can be seen to make young women visible in ways that are not reflected in school policy documents or official discourses. The concern to communicate sexual health messages to pupils in practice assumes and bespeaks a normative gender order where the female body is conceptualised as saturated with a sexuality which can be pathologised, regulated and reproduced. The targeting of young women through sexual health clearly produces a double discursive formation; females as sexual and females who need to know about the sexual. This construction of female sexuality as embodied and in need of regulation connects with pupil cultures in ways that reinforce heterosexual relations, while male sexuality is assumed as dominant and remains unchallenged. The effects of PSE as a practice would support Alison Jones' (1993) argument that the subject positions available to girls in school are inevitably inflected with gendered power relations in which dominant gender narratives remain uninterrupted. Other researchers have commented on the contradiction between conservative traditionalism and discourses of public health in work on sex education policy (Johnson 1996; Redman 1994; Thomson 1994). Within this literature tensions can be identified in the recourse to moralism of traditional conservative approaches which are continually interposed with the need for information and discussion in the interests of sexual health. Mrs Evans' approach to sex education suggests that these tensions may also be identified at the level of everyday practice where moral perspectives and public health imperatives co-exist in the teaching of PSE. Within the domain of sex education, 'public' and 'private' issues are struggled over at the level of policy and interpretively interwoven at the level of practice.

Discursive practice: student cultures

In this section the focus is upon the informal learning that takes place within pupil cultures and the ways in which the PSE curriculum is *received* by pupils. In this setting I am interested in the social meanings that pupils ascribe to events and the ways in which these meanings contrast and overlap with sexual learning in formal spaces such as PSE lessons. Barrie Thorne's (1993) US study of gender relations in school has commented on the ways in which adolescence can be understood as a period of entry into the institution of heterosexuality. Viewed from the perspective of pupils, adolescent relationships form part of a *sexual economy* where features such as physical attractiveness, desirability and status are commodified and played out in rituals of dating and dumping. Within the arena of these cultural practices same-sex peer groups play an important part in the mediation of ideas and exchanges which constitute these processes.

The following extracts are from a Year 10 PSE lesson where the classroom task was for pupils to complete a quiz sheet on different forms of contraceptives. I am sitting at a table with five girls – Vicky, Sophie, Naomi, Sara and Sarah – and Nathan, a boy in the class. Nathan usually sat at a table near the door with a group of boys. However, for this lesson he has moved to sit by Louise who is sitting directly behind Naomi. The reason for Nathan's change of location become clear as the lesson progresses. During the course of the lesson Nathan asks Naomi a series of questions, verbally and in the form of notes, passed via Louise who appears to be acting as an intermediary.

Vicky: (to me) Naomi is having boy trouble.

Vicky: (to Naomi) You told me earlier that you can't stand him, what are you sending messages to him for? (in loud authoritative voice) You're playing with his emotions my dear.

[*girls on table work through the questions in the quiz in fairly haphazard fashion*].

Vicky: (reading) 'It is easy to teach yourself to use the natural method'. I don't know. Can you? True? (reading) 'Baby oil is good for lubricating condoms' is it? (reading) 'Hormone injections interfere with a woman's menstrual cycle' yes they do don't they?

Sophie: (reading) 'All male condoms prevent against sexually transmitted diseases'? I don't know. Is this a test? Do female condoms prevent against sexually transmitted diseases? I don't know.

Vicky: I don't know. I don't know any of this, we haven't been taught all this. (reading) 'IUDs are ideal for' – IUDs, what's IUDs? (reading) 'Condom splits on you, you can take emergency contraception'. Yeah you can.

Sophie: Yeah, 72 hours after, up to three days.

Naomi: Yeah. Louise [unclear message to Nathan].
Vicky: (to Naomi) So are you going to go out with him? You
           like him then? Just tell him you don't wanna go out with
           him if you don't wanna go out with him. Oh, (in exasper-
           ated tone) I don't wanna get involved.

In this interaction ethnographic account suggests that there are
two different agendas operating in the classroom; the set task for
the lesson, the contraceptive quiz, and the dialogue between
Naomi and Nathan. Pupils are engaged and occupied by both
activities, though there are seemingly no points of connection
between the two. The exchange illustrates the ways in which two
contrasting approaches to the power–knowledge couplet are being
deployed and negotiated within the same educative space. The
official classroom task sees sex education in terms of technical
knowledge, details of biology and sexual health to be learned and
accumulated, while pupil interactions stress the importance of the
experiential and the instrumental role of the peer group in key
aspects of social learning. The 'dialogue' between Naomi and
Nathan indicates that, for them, negotiating the sexual is strongly
gendered. Asking to go out with someone and agreeing to go out
with someone entails engagement with normative sex–gender categories that in turn involve identity work and imperatives to act.
These issues of sex–gender conformity are commonly cast in terms
of binaries such as: male/female, pursuer/pursued, assertive/sub-
missive, demanding/conciliatory. In this exchange Nathan appears
to be enacting boy-who-wants-girl while Naomi's responses involve
her in a performance of the opposite, girl-being-chased-by-boy.
Their 'relationship' is mediated by a go-between, Louise, and
under the scrutiny of the female peer group. There is a strong
sense of Naomi and Nathan's 'business' being public property,
requiring discussion and intervention in the female peer group.
This sense of collective ownership and negotiation in relation to
male–female relationships contrasts with the construction of sex
in PSE classes as 'private', involving two people in matters of
personal choice, intimate relations and medical knowledge. The
activities of the peer group indicate that sexual relations offer a
sphere for the negotiation and regulation of gender appropriate
behaviour in school. The role of Vicky, in particular, illustrates
the multiple dimensions of peer group activities. In this exchange
Vicky can be seen to expose and monitor Naomi's actions and

intentions, orchestrate peer group responses, adopt different voices, liaise with me and be actively involved while claiming to desire non-involvement. The activities of the peer group suggest that sex–gender identities are not fixed but, rather, are shaped by and through social exchanges that offer possibilities for expansion and regulation.

As the lesson proceeds the two activities continue with the details of the quiz being attended to intermittently, interspersed with dialogue and commentary concerning developments between Naomi and Nathan:

Vicky: She's (Naomi) just getting another note. What does it say Sara?

Sara: It says, 'So you want to go out with me in two weeks?' ***De De Derr***!

Vicky: She's told Nathan she'll go out with him in two weeks. Why d'you say you'll go out with him in two weeks?

Naomi: 'Cos Jonathan will be back then.

Vicky: You're not even going out with him though.

Naomi: I am!

Naomi: (to me) I like Jonathan you see, but Nathan likes me.

MJK: So what are you going to do about it? Do you feel that Jonathan isn't so interested in you as you are in him?

Naomi: Um yeah, that's right.

Vicky: What's a matter? Why d'you tell him (Nathan) you'd go out with him in two weeks?

Naomi: I don't want to tell you. It's private.

Vicky: You tell me everything else [laughs].

Here, the interest in Naomi's affairs comes to a tentative and temporary closure. Naomi's concern to make herself available to Jonathan while holding Nathan in abeyance is a strategy which involves distancing herself from her female peer group while responding in favourable, though non-committal tones to Nathan's advances. Naomi's actions incur direct disapproval and censorship from Vicky who believes that Naomi has misplaced investments in Jonathan and is deliberating misleading Nathan. For Naomi, in this instance, maintaining girlfriends and having a boyfriend is a difficult balancing act and her discomfort can be seen in terse replies and the retreat into 'privacy'. In courting femininity and heterosexuality Naomi finds herself positioned by two different discourses as loyal female friend and compliant would-be girl-friend. In such moments heterosexual relations may be consolidated through girl–boy encounters that involve a disruption of same-sex alliances. The link between heterosexuality and the management of social relations can be seen in Naomi's circumscribed and protracted negotiations with Nathan, Louise and Vicky in which notes, declarations, explanations and calls for privacy become symbolic signifiers in the paraphernalia of heterosexual practice.

At the end of the lesson Naomi told me in more detail that she feared her relationship with Jonathan may be over when he returns from his holiday and she may then consider a relationship with Ryan as he 'likes her'. She, however, likes Jonathan. Naomi's attempts to exercise control in this situation illustrate the limitations of sex education practice which do not engage with the 'lived' version of sexual relationships within pupil cultures. The 'just say no' message of the sex education video and the clinical knowledge of the contraceptive quiz do not address the feelings of power and vulnerability experienced by young women in the negotiation of femininity and heterosexual relationships. Naomi wants to be recognised as sexually attractive, wants to be 'liked' and wants a relationship, preferably with Jonathan. Her desire to be desired places her in the uncomfortable position of being pressured by Nathan and policed by her female peer group. As Beverley Skeggs (1997) points out, the concern of young women to validate themselves through dynamics of desirability requires the confirmation of men. Over the following weeks the dalliance between Naomi and Nathan escalated to the point where Naomi's mother came into school to speak to Mrs Evans. Mrs Evans reported to me that Naomi's mother expressed concern about Naomi as she was being 'pestered' by Nathan and they (the family) had a terrible weekend and even had their Sunday lunch disturbed. Apparently, Nathan had been telephoning their house persistently, putting lots of money in the telephone and then when Naomi tried to end the conversation he would say, 'Not yet, don't make me waste my money'. Nathan had also followed Naomi around over the weekend when she went into town with her girl-friends. When Naomi told Nathan she wanted to spend time with her friends, he threatened to get some other girls to beat her up. Naomi's mother had told Naomi to have nothing to do with Nathan, was worried that the boy had an obsession with her daughter and that Naomi was secretly enjoying the attention. Mrs Evans also added that Nathan was sitting near to Naomi in lessons and had asked to change groups for some subjects in order to be in the same class as Naomi on all occasions. Mrs Evans decided to speak to Nathan and his mother about his behaviour and hoped that this intervention would resolve the situation. However, Mrs Evans' comments to me focused upon Naomi's burgeoning sexuality,

> Mrs Evans: Last year, you know, she (Naomi) wore her hair scraped back into a pony-tail and this year she's got it in tresses all over her face, she's always flicking it back and playing with it and then there's all the make-up and the [*flutters her eyes*].

Mrs Evans also commented that Naomi's mother appears to be very strict, does not allow her to have boyfriends and is clearly not someone Naomi could talk to about relationships or sexual matters. This example illustrates the ways in which embodied femininity is read in terms of sexuality and thus becomes the object of attention, rather than the sexual harassment and threatening behaviour of the young man. Naomi's sexualised femininity, expressed through her physical appearance, bodily styles and gestures is interpreted by adults as worrying and potentially dangerous. Naomi's mother appears to wish to repress and deny the sexual in the strict prohibition of boyfriends and her disapproval of domestic disruption. Mrs Evans' preoccupation with Naomi's appearance rather than Nathan's actions echoes elements of the 'she-asked-for-it' argument, popularly employed in commonsense discourses to account for incidents of sexual harassment and, in some cases, assault. The suggestion here is that Naomi's demeanour displays sexuality in ways that provoke the male sex drive into action. Both adults indicate an awareness of the dangers ascribed to female sexuality, particularly the power of sexuality to disrupt the rational educative process (Walkerdine and Lucey 1989). From the perspective of the adults, Naomi is 'playing with fire', promoting her sexuality at the risk of damaging her reputation and her chances of academic success. It is interesting to note that Naomi's behaviour incurs recrimination from all of the social spheres she has contact with: Nathan's advances, her peer group's regulatory exclamations, her mother's concern and her teacher's disapproval. The collective reproachment of Naomi during the course of this experience illustrates the many ways in which female sexuality can be seen as culpable. My fieldnotes, written-up after the discussion with Mrs Evans underline the gendered inter-pretation of the incident in which femininity is seen to bespeak a potentially dangerous form of sexuality,

> I'm sure that Catrina (Mrs Evans) does feel that Nathan's behaviour is a form of harassment but find it strange, in retro-spect, that she made hardly any comment on his behaviour and focused almost entirely on Naomi.
>
> (Fieldnotes 25.3.96)

Concluding comments

This chapter has focused upon the school as a site for the produc-tion of discourses in relation to sexuality. While the school can be seen as one site, the proliferation of discourses can be seen to occur in different spaces *within* the school. The chapter argues that heterosexuality remains the dominant sexual category invoked and produced by school-based practices. Versions of heterosexuality can be produced within the school through the different discursive practices in three areas of school life: the official curriculum, peda-gogic practice and pupil cultures. At the level of the official curri-culum heterosexuality is inscribed in school policy documents as a religious and moral ideal; the preferred form of sexual activity anchored in 'family values' and heterosexual coupledom. This view of legitimate sexuality is mediated by pedagogic practice. In sex education lessons at Clarke School, young women become the focus for sexual learning in ways that emphasise their reproductive capacities and their ability to exercise 'choice'. The final section of the chapter explored the ways in which issues of sexuality feature in pupil cultures. Here the emphasis is upon the social learning that takes place within peer groups and student interactions more generally. In this context we see that young people make sense of sexuality within their immediate social world and that this form of meaning-making may appear far removed from the teaching of sex education. My observations support the findings of other researchers that point to a gap between the teaching of sex educa-tion and the 'lived' experience of sexuality among pupils in school (Holland *et al.* 1991; Wolpe 1988). Finally, the chapter suggests that the domain of the sexual is inextricably bound up with, and reflective of, the asymmetrical power relations inscribed in a sex-gender order where female sexuality can be viewed as dangerous and disruptive.

This chapter has illustrated the ways in which different discourses in relation to issues of sexuality can be drawn upon in spaces within the school and become naturalised in the everyday practices and routines of the school. An analysis of the different discursive practices in the school indicates that heterosexuality is not a singular category. Heterosexual ideas and practice exist in plurality, invoked in many different forms: at the level of the institution through policy documents; at the level of pedagogic practice; and in the realm of lived social relations in informal spaces within the school. The following chapters look, in more detail, at the informal sphere of pupil cultures and issues of sexuality. 'Agony Aunts and Absences' is based upon a closely worked analysis of one sex education lesson. The aim of the chapter is to explore the connections and fissures between the practice of sex education and the interests and concerns of the student body.

Chapter 4

Agony aunts and absences: an analysis of a sex education class[1]

> Gender is the repeated stylisation of the body, a set of repeated acts within a highly rigid regulatory frame that congeal over time to produce the appearance of substance, of a natural sort of being. A political genealogy of gender ontologies, if it is successful will deconstruct the substantive appearance of gender into its constitutive acts and locate and account for those acts within the compulsory frames set by the various forces that police the social appearance of gender.
>
> (Butler 1990: 33)

This chapter develops themes and issues introduced in Chapter 3 through a discussion of student cultures and the teaching strategies employed by Mrs Evans. The focus for this chapter is upon the proceedings of one sex education lesson for Year 10 pupils (age 14–15) at Clarke School. The lesson, in which pupils were asked to write and discuss fictional problems, formed part of a ten-week course on sex education. This lesson constitutes session eight of the course. The course is taught to all Year 10 pupils in the school and forms part of a broader PSE programme that is planned and taught over four years. By developing an analysis of one lesson I aim to illustrate some of the complexities involved in the teaching and learning of sex education. The analysis indicates that sex education offers a space where competing discourses meet and are played out within the classroom arena. The chapter suggests that young women, in particular, draw upon popular culture as a resource to articulate aspects of sexuality while young men feel less comfortable with such discussions. Finally, the chapter indicates that the use of popular cultural forms such as agony aunts provide students with the opportunity to discuss several themes

which are generally underdeveloped within sex education programmes such as: sexual abuse; pleasure and danger in sexual relations; constancy and betrayal; homosexuality.

The difficulties of sex education as a practice have been documented by many researchers (Johnson 1996; Lees 1993; Redman
1994; Sears 1992; Thomson 1994; Trudell 1993; Wolpe 1988).
Within this body of work the competing demands of politicians,
parents, public health policy makers and students work together
to create 'impossible' conditions for practitioners. The pedagogic
practice of sex education is frequently marked by a series of
constraints and adversity, often under the gaze of a critical and
scandal-hungry tabloid press (see Epstein and Johnson 1998). It is
anticipated that this analysis of sex education at Clarke School
will contribute to our understanding of sex education by exploring
factors which make it a difficult, if not, 'impossible practice'
(Johnson 1996: 163).

The lesson

The teacher responsible for the ten-week PSE course was
Mrs Evans. As noted in the previous chapter, Mrs Evans was a
practising Christian and a senior teacher at Clarke School. She
had a good relationship with most students in the school, many of
whom saw her as someone to confide in and share problems with.
In this respect Mrs Evans can be seen as the school's unofficial
agony aunt, where counselling becomes part of her recognised and
informally sanctioned role as PSE co-ordinator. In many cases
Mrs Evans was familiar with the home backgrounds of students
and had built up relationships with parents and siblings.

In this sex education lesson, which was concerned with discussing problems in relation to issues of sexuality, Year 10 students
were asked by the teacher to write a fictional 'problem' to a
fictional agony aunt. Mrs Evans described the class to me as 'able,
good at discussion and supportive of each other'. The class activity involved students volunteering to read their 'problems' to the
class. This was followed by a discussion of the 'problem' with the
class, facilitated by Mrs Evans. Sessions prior to the 'agony aunt'
activity included the viewing of videos on marriage and relationships in the 1950s and 1960s and a lesson on contraceptive
methods given by the school nurse. In the sex education lesson of
the previous week, students watched a video entitled *Agony Aunts*

where two adults (one male, one female) offered advice to young people using three examples: asking someone out; deciding to have sex; and relationship breakdown. After viewing the video students were asked to write their own 'problem' to an agony aunt. Mrs Evans suggested to the class that they could perhaps draw upon the themes of the PSE course.

The agony aunt activity was enjoyed by many members of the class. My fieldnotes, written up after the lesson, contain the following observations:

> All problems aroused great interest from the class who seemed to be more animated than in other lessons. 'Agony aunt' seemed to be a popular format for voicing issues – vicarious pleasure of discussing other's problems, curiosity, or a way of making safe one's own fears and anxieties?
>
> (Fieldnotes 11.3.96)

Like the problem pages of teenage magazines, the agony aunt format can be seen as a facility for discussion of sensitive and controversial issues. Otherwise unspoken topics can be written, read and discussed within this approach to sex education. This clearly has an appeal for young people where 'daring' to speak about certain issues can be legitimated within the scope of a classroom task.

Everything was perfect but . . .

Mrs Evans began the session by asking for students to offer their 'problems' for discussion. The first 'problem' was written and read by Vicky:

Vicky: (reading) I have a very serious problem. I have recently slept with my boyfriend and everything was perfect. I thought he really loved me but one week later I found out that he has got a long string of one night stands. He has slept with them all without contraception. He even admitted it to me and said it was all in the past and I believed him. What if he is still doing it? I have also missed my last period by one week and I do not know what to do. If my boyfriend has contracted HIV by having unprotected sex I will have it because we did not use any form of contraception and if I have it so will my child. From a desperate E17 fan.

This letter combines the themes of romantic love, pregnancy and HIV and presents them as one problem. The articulation of such a 'problem' may point to some of the ways in which young women experience and relate to issues of sexuality. As a letter to an agony aunt it is similar in style and tone to letters found in the problem pages of contemporary teenage magazines such as *More!* and *Sugar*. Teenage magazines and their readership are explored in more detail in the following chapter. Vicky's letter uses short sentences to present a linear narrative sequence, told in stark terms that can be seen as an attempt to emulate the language and style of popular cultural forms. All superfluous details are stripped away to present the 'core' of the 'problem' as a 'desperate' dilemma based on personal pain which combines knowledge and inexperience. The knowledge of menstrual cycles, pregnancy and the ways in which HIV is contracted contrasts sharply with the naivete of Vicky's emotional investments in the rituals and symbolic representations of romantic love. In the letter romantic ideals are expressed in many ways: sex for the first time in the relationship is presented as the 'perfect' sexual union; the search for constancy follows, 'he has a long string of one night stands . . . [he] said it was all in the past and I believed him'; and finally there is the fear of betrayal, 'what if he is still doing it?' Vicky's letter can be read in terms of her ability, as a good student, to take on a role through the deployment of a sophisticated literary competence in the emulation of a popular cultural form. However, Vicky's letter can also be interpreted psychoanalytically as a projection of her concerns regarding sexual relationships where emotional anxieties are interwoven with practical details of sexual health and reproduction. My use of the term 'projection' draws upon the recognition within Freudian theory of the process whereby individuals refuse unpleasant accusations of the self by projecting them onto others. Although, as far as we know, Vicky is not directly experiencing the problems of the young woman in the letter, the agony aunt activity allows her the opportunity for imaginative identification within the domain of the sexual which may imply unconscious investments. Under the guise of writing to a problem page, Vicky can risk the expression of personal pain and prohibited subjects within a context where social recognition can be conferred on individuals who produce interesting 'problems' for the class to discuss. Furthermore, the reading and discussing of problems can be seen as a pleasurable act, arousing interest and excitement in a similar way to the consumption of problem pages in teenage magazines (see Chapter 5).

The class discussion of Vicky's letter was concerned with offering advice and support in relation to the issues of sexual health presented by the writer:

Mrs Evans: How would we help? What are the issues? What's the advice? How would you start off? This person is desperate . . .

Boy 1:   Get a pregnancy test and a HIV test.

Mrs Evans: Well hang on, that's essential, but how are you going to start off? What do you think you might say before you even say that?

Girl 1:   Calm down.

Mrs Evans: Calm down. Yes, anybody done any first aid training? The first thing you're supposed to do is keep reassuring the victim, the person that's hurt isn't it? You reassure them, 'It's OK, it's going to be alright, calm down' . . . Any other advice?

Girl 2:   HIV test and contact your GP.

Girl 3:   Brook Centre.

Girl 4:   I think they (staff at the Brook) should speak to the boyfriend as well so that he's not putting it on someone else.

Mrs Evans: Yes, any other advice? Have we covered the main issues of advice and support?

Emma: What about contraceptives for the future?

Mrs Evans: What about some advice for the future? Yes, do you think it would be a good place to include some advice for the future? 'I'm sorry to hear you didn't make clear, this is something you need to talk over with your boyfriend in the future. Perhaps you could look around for advice centres in your area.'

In this discussion the help and advice offered to the writer is couched in terms of a medical discourse where the physical body can be seen to manifest symptoms of ill health which can be 'reassured' and recuperated. The collective recommendation of a pregnancy test, HIV test, consultation with health agencies and contraceptives for the future, present the young woman with a sexual health package as a panacea for the 'problem'. Although a fictional account, this replicates the conventions of actual problem pages. Discussing the problem within the terrain of a medical discourse overlooks the lived experience of sexuality as presented by the writer. Vicky's letter articulates a 'problem' arising from an imagined sexual relationship where sexual health knowledge is intermeshed with emotional uncertainty. The expressions of anxiety and entreaties in relation to emotional investments in the ideology and practice of heterosexual romance are not addressed by the discussion which is framed by imperatives to act in the interests of an individualised, and non-gendered, sexual healthcare programme. The presence of some themes concerning knowledge of sexual health and the absences of other themes concerning emotional experience suggest that the practice of sex education, in this case, can be located within a medical discourse which is familiar to teacher and students. The ways in which knowledge of sexual health interacts with emotional experience in the lives of young women is seemingly more difficult to discuss within the context of the sex education class.

Late period: girls and reputation

The following 'problem' discussed in the sex education class is written and read by Sophie:

Sophie: (reading) Dear Agony Aunt, I'm 19 years old and I made a stupid mistake. I went out with my mates one night to a local night club. I got drunk quite easily and I had unprotected sex with a boy I hardly know. Now I'm worried sick. My period is six days late and the boy has been going round telling everyone that I'm easy. I now have a bad reputation and everybody is lecturing me. Help. How quickly can I have a pregnancy test to tell if you are pregnant or not and is it always accurate?

In this letter Sophie outlines a concern over 'reputation' as a salient feature of social experience in the lives of young women. Her letter indicates that young women must be ever vigilant in the protection of their reputation as a momentary lapse in responsibility may be regarded as regrettable and damaging or, as Sophie puts it, 'a stupid mistake'. Sophie's 'problem' makes a direct link between reputation and sexual behaviour; having sex with someone you 'hardly know' inevitably leads to a 'bad reputation' and social admonishment from female friends, 'everybody is lecturing me'. In this situation it is young males who are invested with the power to define the sexual reputation of young women as 'easy'. Sophie's letter finds points of resonance with researchers in this field where the experience of sexism, misogynistic labelling and a concern with female sexual reputations have been seen as key markers in the construction of young women's identities (McRobbie and Garber 1982; Griffin 1982; Lees 1986, 1993; Canaan 1986; Cowie and Lees 1987). In this body of literature the presence of the 'slag/drag' dichotomy used by males in the sexual appraisal of women, has the ideological effect of transforming unequal gender relations into sexual differences which can be treated as 'natural' and inherently given. In the class discussion which followed Sophie's letter, the gendered dynamics of the situation are articulated in a particular way:

Mrs Evans: Well, she's asked a lot of questions. It must be a difficult one because you've got the problem and you've got the direct questions as well. How are you going to start this one off? It's quite tiring being an agony aunt I think. How are we going to write back? OK, some advice for this letter then? I guess that the name-calling part and the reputation is bothering her. That seemed to come across quite strongly.

Girl 1:   Well it wasn't her fault because she was taken advantage of. That's what she's got to say now, 'It's not my fault, it's something that's happened' and she's got to tell her friends about what happened.

Mrs Evans: This one of reputation, how other people think of you, what other people say about you is – we usually care quite a lot how we come across and how people view us and it's very special and unique to you and it's usually quite precious and if someone dents or damages your reputation it causes quite a lot of hurt. I think they need reassuring. Go on, what else?

Girl 2:   She should talk to the boy, I mean he's –
Blake: He won't wanna know though.
Mrs Evans: He won't wanna know. You're absolutely right
              Blake, he is not gonna want to know is he? He's
              either not gonna want to know, say he was drunk,
              he's not going to remember.

   In this discussion the notion of 'reputation' is seen as 'special',
'unique' and 'precious' to the individual. The words used by
Mrs Evans to convey the importance of 'reputation' suggest that it
can be viewed as part of an 'inner self' concerned with self-worth
and social presentation of self. This conceptualisation is not
extended to the ways in which 'reputation' may be gender differentiated and mediated through social interaction. The discussion,
then, explores the 'problem' within the parameters of dominant
gender/sex categories where predatory males are able to abdicate
responsibility for sexual activity ('he won't wanna know'), while
vulnerable females must take responsibility for themselves and
their reputation. Alcohol plays a significant part in the remembering and forgetting of the sexual activity which, again, is viewed in
gender specific terms. For the young women being drunk creates
the context for a temporary loss of control that she is constantly
reminded of in the fixing of her 'bad reputation' and fear of pregnancy. For the young man, however, being drunk allows for a
moment of forgetting where the memory can simply be erased and
disavowed.

A boy and his friend: the homosocial or the homoerotic heterosexual?

The next agony aunt letter to be discussed by the Year 10 class
was written and read by Neil:

Neil: (reading) I've been with my best friend for many years and
         we do a lot of things together. I also have a girlfriend that
         I've been going out with and she wants me to spend more
         time with her than with my friend, I want to spend time
         with my friend and not lose my girlfriend. What should
         I do?

Neil's letter provides a point of contrast with the letter written and read earlier by Vicky. Neil offers the class a 'problem' for discussion but does not display any of the personal pain and self-revelation of Vicky's letter. The 'problem' as expressed in Neil's letter is one of divided loyalties, how to split his time between his friend and his girlfriend and maintain his relationship with both parties. While male friendship can be seen as a key site of emotions, it is seldom commented on explicitly outside of 'Buddy' movies. Neil's letter works within conventional assumptions of gender relations where males and females are located within separate and mutually exclusive social spheres, where notions of independence and dependence are played out in particular ways. From this perspective women can be positioned as possessive of their partners' time and may attempt to monitor the relationship in this respect, 'she wants me to spend more time with her than with my friend'. The pervasive assumptions relating to males, on the other hand, concern their investments in the exclusivity of male peer group friendships and resistance to any perceived attempt to encroach on this space. The gendered dynamics of this situation, within the context of heterosexual relationships, place males as guardians of their independence and females as pursuers of their own dependence.

Whereas Vicky's letter utilises the language and themes of popular culture, particularly the problem pages of teenage magazines, Neil's letter does not demonstrate such a sophisticated familiarity with these popular cultural forms. It is possible that these forms are coded as feminine (see Chapter 5) and, therefore, inappropriate for Neil to deploy them even if he knows them. Neil's letter does not 'risk' any projection of the 'problem' into areas of fantasy and sexual interest such as: in what way is the relationship with his girlfriend sexual; in what ways does sex present additional responsibilities/problems; is his desire to spend time with his friend homoerotic or 'natural'? Neil's 'problem' as articulated in the letter is a brief, starkly presented 'fact' of heterosexual romance ('I want to spend time with my friend and not lose my girlfriend. What should I do?') that makes no attempt at dramatic presentation or elaboration. The contrast between Vicky's letter and Neil's letter suggests that gender differences are further played out within the context of the classroom where the discourse of popular culture can be used by young women to articulate sexual issues and areas of interest and curiosity. Neil's letter, however, suggests that young men do not utilise this discourse in the same way and appear reluctant to use the exercise as a space for the projection of fantasies and anxieties.

In the brief discussion of Neil's letter, Mrs Evans and members of the class suggested that it was important to make time for his friend and his girlfriend and in some situations it may be possible to bring them together.

The Flasher: the gaze and its object

Laura: (reading) I don't know what to do. It happened a few weeks ago. I'm worried it might ruin my relationship. I went with my little sister and my Mum to the High Street to do some shopping. When we got there I decided to stay in the car. Mum told me to lock all the doors. As she left the car I locked all the doors and turned on the radio. I found a magazine and sat and read it. I was engrossed in reading my magazine and noticed out of the corner of my eye a man standing there. He was in his late 30s and smartly dressed in a coat and raincoat. The way he looked at me I assumed he was waiting for someone so I carried on reading. After a minute or two I heard a noise. I looked up and he was standing right in front of me. Transfixed by the weird look in his eyes, it was a few seconds before I realised he was doing something to the fly of his trousers. Suddenly I lowered my eyes and to my horror the man [smothered laugh] was masturbating. Staying there as I was I wanted someone to hide me. I thought that if this pervert couldn't see me he might go away. I lowered myself into the front of the passenger seat and waited for my Mum to come back. Lying there in that small place, panic set in. What if he banged the car door? What if he smashed the windows? Every foot-step outside was amplified. I jumped when I heard the key in the car door but to my relief it was Mum.

'What are you doing down there love?'

'Er, um, I'm just sleeping' I lied.

When we got home I went straight to bed but every time I closed my eyes I could see that man with the beady stare and I was helpless to stop the panic rising to my

stomach all over again. It's two weeks later and I still
haven't spoken to anyone. I haven't told my boyfriend
and I'm sure he must know that something's up. I'm
afraid that if I tell him he'll leave me and I won't be
able to cope with that as well as that man. Please help.
A dedicated fan.

Laura's letter presents a case of indecent exposure that is rich in
its detailing of the incident and the sensibilities of the experience.
The narrative is carefully structured, setting up the context
whereby such an event could occur, 'I decided to stay in the car';
recalling the experience, 'to my horror the man was masturbating'
and drawing upon cultural signifiers to document pertinent details
and feelings. The description of the man uses visual imagery such
as the 'raincoat' and 'the beady stare' to portray a stereotypical
picture of the flasher as an older man ('pervert') who lurks around
in public places. The narrative closure creates a powerful well of
post-traumatic emotions expressed in terms of having to live and
relive the experience, 'the panic rising to my stomach all over
again' and a subsequent inability to speak to anyone about the
event.

The presentation of this 'problem' as a powerful and dramatic
scene of exposure and vulnerability draws upon the language and
style of popular cultural forms, particularly the problem pages of
teen magazines. The use of teen magazines within the presentation
of the 'problem' can be seen to work at different levels. At the
level of cultural representation, the narrative structure of Laura's
letter emulates the problem page format in direct and specific
ways. Within this context a dilemma is presented and recounted as
a linear sequence of cause and effect. A damaged and dysfunc-
tional persona presents a crisis and makes an impassioned plea for
help that can be seen as a desire for validation of self through the
experience. The response from the agony aunt provides a moment
of recognition and affirmation which operates regardless of the
content of the advice offered, and represents an attempted 'solution' to the crisis by suggesting an explanation and/or action. The
process of writing to an agony aunt and gaining a response can be
seen as a therapeutic relationship in itself where both parties are
engaged in an act of 'speaking out'. At another level the magazine
is also present within the experience itself as the recreational
activity engaged in while alone in the car, 'I found a magazine

and sat and read it. I was engrossed in reading my magazine
when I noticed out of the corner of my eye a man standing'. The
appearance of the man at this point may not be entirely acci-
dental. In a groupwork discussion with girls from this class, many
of the girls I spoke with referred to *Sugar* magazine as a particular
favourite of their peer group. The girls suggested to me that *Sugar*
gained this place in their affections as it contained 'interesting
stories such as *I was terrorised by a flasher*'. The discussion of this
story, which may have been read by Laura, and the availability of
a social space for the projection of fantasies and anxieties may
have created the conditions whereby an enactment of the story can
be staged. Within the context of the classroom this enactment is
both safe and risky; the area of safety lies in the exercise itself
which allows experiences to be created without them really
happening and, risky, in the sense that issues such as masturbation, indecent exposure and sexual threat are rarely discussed in
the classroom.

Viewing the 'problem' psychoanalytically as a projection of
Laura's fantasies and anxieties gives us an insight into some of her
concerns in relation to issues of sexuality. As the author of the
'problem', Laura brings into being both the flasher and herself as
the victim of an act of indecent exposure. Within this scenario
Laura's imaginative identification with the victim is also in relation to the male exhibitionist or 'pervert' as she terms him. Freud's
(1977) discussion of sexual perversions regard the perversions of
scopophilia and exhibitionism as psychical opposites which may
be embodied within an individual:

> Every active perversion is thus accompanied by its passive
> counterpart: anyone who is an exhibitionist in his unconscious
> is also at the same time a voyeur.
>
> (Freud 1977: 81)

The demonstration of this relationship within Laura's letter
positions her as both exhibitionist and voyeur in Freudian theory
where such perversions are conceptualised as fixations of pre-
liminary sexual aims. The associative link between scopophilia
and exhibitionism can be seen in the act of looking where the eye
corresponds to an erotogenic zone, a site of pleasure and desire
'subordinate to the genitals and as substitute(s) for them' (Freud
1977: 84). Acts of *looking* and being *looked at* permeate Laura's

letter: 'the way he looked at me' in the initial encounter; witnessing the man masturbating, 'I looked up and there he was . . . transfixed by the weird look in his eyes'; and finally the distress of constantly reliving the experience, 'every time I closed my eyes I could see the man with the beady stare'. In Laura's articulation of this experience the pleasure of looking is intimately related to the danger of being looked at in which the threat of violence and further sexual violation is present (Kelly 1988). In the Freudian framework the activity engaged in by exhibitionists involves 'exhibiting their own genitals in order to obtain a reciprocal view of the genitals of the other person' (Freud 1977: 70). In this reading, the exposure of the genitals *becomes* the act of intercourse where sexual pleasure is located in the gaze. In the context of Laura's letter the pleasure and danger involved in looking and being looked at exist in a closely bound relationship which bespeaks both a desire for sexual experience and a fear of it. The sight of the man masturbating is immediately followed by the response, 'Staying there as I was [in the car] I wanted something to hide me'. The appeal for 'something to hide me' can be interpreted in different ways as an attempt to escape the sexual threat and also a desire to experience sex without being seen to experience it. The concealment involved in these expressions of desire is indicative of the absences within sex education classes, particularly the missing discourse of desire identified by Fine (1988) which operates to police the boundaries of the speakable and the unspeakable in relation to female sexuality. Laura's 'problem' further suggests that the absence of desire in such contexts may also be related to the internal repressions of sexuality where sexual activity can become a site of struggle between desire and revulsion.

Psychoanalytic insights drawing upon frameworks other than the Freudian suggest further ways of reading Laura's letter in terms of pleasure/danger posed by the sexual. Using Lacanian theory it is possible to suggest that there is some playing around with the 'I'/'not I' identifications of the Symbolic, the world of language and the social which pre-exists the Subject (see below for a further discussion of the Lacanian Symbolic). Although Laura is not obviously powerful in the story, she does create the 'I' and the 'eye' of the exhibitionist and imagines the power of his position. It is possible to see the car itself in sexual terms as a *receptacle* for her and her experience and, hence, a maternal body. In the Lacanian sense the primary loss or 'lack' is that of the maternal

as threatening and a source of problems is a salient feature of this discussion and many others during the course of the lesson. This discourse allows for dangers to be revealed and spoken while issues of pleasure and desire remain concealed and unspoken. The pleasure of discussing sexual events such as the one presented by Laura is similarly hidden, though it is clearly present in the willingness of the girls to discuss the 'problem' and Laura's stifled laughter as she reads the words, 'to my horror he was masturbating'.

'I feel so dirty . . .': discussing sexual abuse

Clare: (reading) Dear Agony Aunt, I haven't spoken to anyone since this happened but I just need to tell someone. Last week my mum's boyfriend raped me. I was so scared I had no-one to talk to and I felt if I told my Mum she wouldn't believe me. I can't face my mum's boyfriend when he comes round. But to make matters worse I think I might be pregnant. I haven't been to school because I think everyone can tell what's happened. I feel so dirty and I spend hours in the bath trying to scrub away the bad memories. Please help, a dedicated Vanilla Ice fan.

In this letter of pain, hurt and violation Clare writes to an agony aunt to share the secret of sexual abuse within the family, a secret which, until now, she has not been able to tell anyone. The fear of speaking about sexual abuse in the family is a theme echoed by survivors of rape and incest in feminist literature in this field (see, for example, Gordon 1988; Kelly 1988). In Clare's letter this fear is articulated in terms of isolation, 'I had no-one to talk to' and a concern that her mother would not believe her. The pressure to keep child sexual abuse and incest hidden from view is indicative of the cultural taboo surrounding these issues which makes 'breaking the silence' a difficult and oppositional strategy. This taboo co-exists with a public discourse in relation to sexuality that seeks to naturalise the heterosexual nuclear family as an 'ideal' for the organisation of gender relations and parenting practices.[2] Clare's letter describes the distress and lasting shock of sexual abuse in the family in terms of feeling 'dirty', despoiled and in need of self-purgation which is both physical and psychological, 'I spend hours in the bath trying to scrub away the bad memories'.

The 'bad memories' and feelings of uncleanliness expressed in the letter suggests that the subject position adopted by the author is one of 'victim' where fear of male sexual violation and blame for it is internalised by the woman who experiences it. This theme is a feature of feminist analyses from different perspectives which see rape and sexual violence as a 'symbolic expression of male power' (Segal 1990: 232). Deborah Cameron and Elizabeth Frazer (1996) comment on the ways in which notions of male sexuality and female responsibility structure contemporary gender relations:

> a powerful incentive exists for us to police our own behaviour and acquiesce in the idea that men's sexuality is 'naturally' predatory, only to be contained by female circumspection.
>
> (Cameron and Frazer 1990: 208)

From this perspective the problem is *men*; masculine sexuality becomes emblematic of male power and is expressed through the motifs of '*performance, penetration, conquest*' (ibid.: 211, italics as original).

The responses from members of the class which followed the reading of Clare's letter illustrate some of the strengths and limitations of sex education programmes where issues of rape and child sexual abuse are discussed in ways which incorporate some aspects of feminist analysis while excluding other aspects:

Voices:	[in low tones] Oooh, wooh, woo-ooh.
Mrs Evans:	Well Blake, what do you make of that?
Blake:	I reckon she should move house.
	[all laugh]
Mrs Evans:	As you would expect from Blake, a good piece of practical advice there. Go on Blake.
Blake:	She should tell someone ... yeah she should, because –
Mrs Evans:	That's great. Thanks for starting us off. What other advice do we have?
Girl 1:	Tell the police.
Girl 2:	Ring Childline.
Mrs Evans:	What do you think about some of the things the person's included in her letter? Can you just go back over the bit about, Clare, have you got the letter there still? Can you read the bit about unclean?

Clare:	(reading) I feel so dirty I spend hours in the bath scrubbing away the bad memories.
Mrs Evans:	Yes, who'd like to make any comment on what the writer has said?
Girl 3:	She thinks it's her fault.
Girl 2:	Yeah, she probably thinks it's her fault.
Mrs Evans:	Feels that it's her fault, feels guilty, dirty, literally dirty. The other thing was she says she hasn't been going to school because she feels the others can tell what's happened.
Girl 4:	She knows it's there and she feels she can project it to everyone else around as if it's a mark on her body.
Mrs Evans:	Absolutely . . . Again it's a very perceptive letter, you've written them with a lot of thought, with what actually people do feel . . . What other advice would you give this person?
Girl 5:	Talk to a counsellor.
Boy 1:	Go back to school.
Mrs Evans:	Go back to school, yes, try to get your life back into as normal – and then what about once you're there?
Girl 3:	Speak to your friends or somebody at school.
Girl 6:	Find out whether you're pregnant or not.
Mrs Evans:	Yes, that's another issue she raised, pregnancy issue. So you're not just giving one piece of advice, you're giving several leads aren't you?

In this discussion of Clare's letter the engagement with the issues demonstrates a high level of awareness, sensitivity and empathy for the individual who has been sexually abused. The 'ooh' sounds from members of the class which immediately follow the reading of the letter suggests that there is a recognition of rape as a transgressive act the letter dares to name. The discussion focuses on the emotional distress of the writer's predicament and what she can do about it. The feelings of blame, guilt and responsibility articulated in feminist literature on rape and sexual abuse clearly find points of resonance in the discussion in the reiteration of the comment, 'She thinks it's her fault'. In this respect the experience of rape comes to be understood by the class as 'a mark on her body' which is both real and symbolic. The assimilation of this aspect of feminist analysis in the class discussion works within a feminist discourse which aims to discredit the myth that women are, in some way, to blame for (male) acts of sexual violation. In other respects, however, the class discussion omits important features of a feminist perspective such as a consideration of gender difference, power relations and heterosexuality. Within a feminist framework there is an acknowledgement that women and children occupy positions of powerlessness in nuclear families. This lack of power in the family and the social construction of masculinity in terms of a demanding and forceful sexuality[3] create the conditions whereby sexual abuse involving heterosexual men and young girls in the family accounts for the majority of cases of child sexual abuse (see Segal 1990: 160). In the class discussion of Vicky's letter, the familial context of the rape (occurring at home with her mother's boyfriend) is not mentioned and the term *sexual abuse* is not named. These absences serve to perpetuate some features of the pre-feminist story of rape where sexual abuse may be viewed as the rare and aberrant behaviour of some individuals. In the class discussion there is an assimilation of feminist perspectives in relation to females as victims of male sexual violation while broader social issues of gender and power are not embraced. This partial and selective appropriation of aspects of dominant ways of looking at sexual abuse combined with some feminist themes suggests that the school, as a site for the production of sexuality, is active in creating sexual stories of its own.

Ken Plummer (1995) offers an analysis of the ways in which the sexual stories that can be told are dependent upon a social context where they can be heard. Plummer documents the emergence of narratives telling of women's experiences of rape from the 1970s. These new stories of rape challenged the old story of male entitlement and privilege by placing women's experiences of fear, subordination and violation at the centre of the new narrative structure. This shift in emphasis in the telling of the rape story found a community of listeners and supporters in the collective activities of the second-wave women's movement. Plummer's analysis considers the ways in which the old story marks out the terrain for the new story, where the emergent narrative frequently becomes an inversion of the older form. Plummer outlines three strategies in the emergence of new narrative forms: the debunking of myths; the creation of a history and the writing of a political plot (1995: 67). The class discussion of Clare's letter indicates that her narrative is read within the context of challenging some myths concerning rape but does not move to a consideration of the other two strategies. There is no suggestion that Clare's experience could be a common one which may enable women to create a sense of history based upon shared recognition of the links between personal experience and social structures. Neither is there an acknowledgement that collective experience can form the basis for the development of a political agenda or transformative practice. The ways in which Clare's story is told and heard by the class suggests that the school story in relation to rape and child sexual abuse is an individualised one, calling for specific and singular action such as, 'tell the police', 'call Childline', 'talk to a counsellor' and 'go back to school'. The individualisation of sexual issues can be seen to work with dominant assumptions of gender categories and relations of power which take on a 'fixed' quality in the story-telling community. In this respect the school story echoes the treatment of sexual themes in popular cultural forms such as soaps and chat shows where story 'overload' may provide a context for the depoliticisation of narratives (Plummer 1995: 78). In the generation of new narratives, 'authors' do not necessarily have any purchase on the ways in which stories are appropriated, disseminated and used.

Scared to be gay: homophobia and the power of girls

The following 'problem' to be discussed by the class is written and read by Sara.

Sara:	(reading) I'm a fifteen year old boy with a really serious problem. I've recently split up with my girlfriend and at the same time I realise I'm attracted to my best friend Simon. I don't want to be gay. I'm really scared of being gay and I don't think I am. Please help.
Voices:	[with disgust] Urghh Uuurrghhh Yuk [laughter and cries of derision] [temporary breakdown in social order of the classroom with everyone talking and laughing at once]
Helen:	Ask some more boys Miss! [more laughter]

Mrs Evans:	[*struggling to make herself heard above noise of the class*] That's clearly the sort of thing. All the letters have been written – the ground rules of this are – we ask everyone to join in with the task, yes. Don't be identifying with the letters. We've only actually had, so far, one boy's letter but here's somebody writing what is a very typical boy's problem.
Boys:	[chorusing] Is it? Is it?
	[laughter]
Mrs Evans:	Isn't it?
Boys:	[talking and shouting at once] No it isn't.
	Not likely!
	Not with me it's not.
	Nor me.

Sara's articulation of the boy's 'problem' and the ensuing responses of the class illustrate some of the difficulties involved in discussing issues of homosexuality in school. Sara's letter expresses an explicit and impassioned fear and denial of homosexuality, 'I don't want to be gay. I'm scared of being gay and I don't think I am'. The breakdown in social order that follows Sara's disclosure suggests that this fear may be shared by members of the class in a context where voicing same sex attraction in itself becomes an act of severe disruption. Mrs Evans' attempt to restore classroom order recognises the anxiety involved in young people discussing homosexuality and tries to allay the panic by inviting students to participate in a rational discussion where ground-rules are adhered to. Her endeavour to 'normalise' homosexuality through discussion meets with further disruption and group denial by many of the boys in the class. In this context the 'really serious problem' can be seen as a dread of being gay which encourages young men to engage in homophobic performances (Nayak and Kehily 1996). The disruption and disavowal involved in the young men's responses to Sara's letter and Mrs Evans' attempt at discussion suggests that young men in school are concerned to display a masculine identity that is directly linked to a heterosexual identity. The pervasive presence of homophobias in school point to the instability of gender categories where masculinity is repeatedly struggled over within male peer groups. Homophobic performance can be seen as an attempt to display a coherent masculinity through the dramatic enactment of heterosexual desire that disclaims and derides any relationship to homosexuality. At the level of the individual, homophobic performance expels homoerotic desire from the Self onto Others in a public display which serves as a 'self-convincing ritual' in the denial of homosexual desire through the conspicuous demonstration of a heterosexual masculine ideal. The repetition of homophobic performances in school indicates that heterosexual masculine identities are sustained through fraught exhibition, where the enactment itself can be seen as evidence of the insecurities and splittings within the male psyche.

It is interesting to note the position of young women in this exchange. It is, of course, Sara who initiates the subject of homosexuality in the letter which she writes from the subject position of a fifteen year old boy. She does not speak of lesbianism or imaginatively identify as a young woman who is sexually attracted to a female friend. Sara's letter, followed by the comment from another girl urging Mrs Evans to, 'Ask some more boys Miss!' suggests that young women are aware of the power of homosexuality to tap into points of vulnerability in the enactment of masculine heterosexual identities. The discussion proceeds in the following way:

Sara:	First of all you should calm him down and say a lot of people go through this.
Girls:	[chorusing] Yeah, all the boys. Yeah, the boys.
Sara:	Not me though.
Mrs Evans:	[directing her comments to two tables of predominantly boys] I think we must press back over here for some extra opinion there. Perhaps I, I, yes I did deliberately say that to see what reaction there would be when I said that's a very typical problem and you said, very strongly, 'No, no it isn't'. Go on, take us from there – you don't think it's a very common situation?
Boy:	Not at this age anyway.
Mrs Evans:	Not at this age. What, d'you mean you've been there already and been through it? [laughter and momentary disruption]
Girls:	[chorusing] They're embarrassed – the embarrassment! Look, look! Next question Miss!

The development of the discussion in this way illustrates the polarisation of gender categories which occurs in relation to issues of homosexuality. In this exchange males and females take up positions in opposing and closely bounded categories which do not allow for moments of alliance or ambivalence. The identity work involved in discussing homosexuality in school indicates that young men engage in defensive strategies to preserve the fiction of heterosexual coherence while young women clearly enjoy a collective identity premised upon the exposure and subsequent humiliation of young males. This opens up the question of where young women can be positioned in relation to issues of homosexuality and homophobic performance. Can the deliberate delight in the exposure of young men be seen as an indication that young women are more comfortable with homosexuality? Or is it, rather, a counter indication that the homophobia of young women is played out in different ways? In order to explore these questions I draw upon a Lacanian framework to offer an account of the acquisition of gender identity and, in particular, the development of female subjectivity.[4]

In Lacanian psychoanalysis gendered subjectivity is acquired at the end of a long period of infant development through the splitting of the Ego and the resolution of the Oedipal and castration complexes. These processes mark the transition of the Subject from the pre-discursive domain of the Imaginary into the Symbolic order. The domain of the Symbolic is constituted through language and the social organisation of signs and symbols which pre-exist the Subject. Entry into the Symbolic order enables the subject to take up a position within the realm of the social through the use of language which bespeaks a gender identified and gendered subject. Lacan describes the gendered 'I' as constructed through the opposition of the masculine which is positively signified and the feminine which is negatively signified. Within the Symbolic order the opposition of positive/negative, masculine/feminine is dependent on the possession or non-possession of the phallus. Here, the phallus can be understood as a signifier which is central to the organisation of the Symbolic order. The position of masculinity within the Symbolic can therefore be seen as one of inclusion where masculine subjects can assume the 'I' of patriarchal culture. Femininity, by contrast, can be viewed in Lacanian terms as a position of exclusion within the Symbolic, where female subjects are constructed into an identity as 'not-I' or Other *as against* the masculine 'I'. The 'not-I' of feminine subjectivity indicates that, within this schema, a woman can never have the phallus though she may, at times, *be* it (Lacan 1977b).

I would like to suggest that Lacanian insights can help us to explore why girls may enjoy teasing boys in the context of a sex education class where the challenge to young men is organised around an implied homosexuality. The development of female subjectivity can be seen as a process marked by moments of accommodation and resistance to the domain of the Symbolic. In moments of accommodation women make investments in discourses of femininity which confirm their 'not-I' status. As will be seen in the next chapter, the reading of teenage magazines such as *More!* and *Sugar* can be viewed as a practice which operates within the bounds of discourses of femininity where patriarchal culture is assumed and remains largely unchallenged. In moments of resistance to the Symbolic order, women reject the 'not-I' position through acts of power/mastery which enable an enactment and identification with the 'I' of patriarchal discourse. In using the language of popular culture in the context of the classroom rather than in friendship groups, young women are able to demonstrate a knowledge and familiarity with sexual themes which offers them a sense of personal power in relation to young men in the class. This shift in relations of power suggests the instability of gender categories where 'I' and 'not-I' subject positions can be contested. The articulation of boy-to-boy attraction voiced in Sara's letter and the responses of other young women in the class present a challenge to the coherence of masculine subjectivity through the re-appropriation of discourses of femininity. This momentary inversion of the Symbolic order indicates that the exchange between males and females in the class represents a struggle over gendered subjectivity where homosexuality becomes a strategy for rupturing the gendered 'I' and a point of resistance to the 'not-I'. Seeing the exchange in terms of gender and power suggests the fragility of gendered subjectivities where homosexuality may be constructed as Other for male and female subjects. This can be seen in the 'not me' voices and expressions of disgust from boys and girls in the class. The breakdown in social order in the classroom and the treatment of homosexuality as a difference to be expelled and denied indicates that, for some participants in this discussion, the search for the consolidation of a coherent identity is premised upon heterosexuality and the regulation of desire.

Concluding comments

By conducting an analysis of one sex education class my intention
was to explore, firstly, the ways in which sexualities can be lived
out within the context of the school and, secondly, the difficulties
involved in the practice of sex education. The 'problems' written
by members of this Year 10 class and the subsequent discussion of
them within a sex education programme offers us an insight into
these areas. Many of the letters suggest that sexualities are
developed and experienced in relation to dominant sex/gender
categories where a strong link is made between gender appropriate
behaviour and sexual identities. Thus, we see a concern with
heterosexual relationships articulated differently in terms of gender
where issues of time and independence become features of a male
perspective while health issues, emotional uncertainty and powerlessness feature in accounts from young women.

Contribution and participation in the class can also be read as
gender inflected with young women taking the initiative in the
reading and discussion of the 'problems'. Six out of the seven
letters discussed in the lesson were written by young women, who
also featured more prominently in the follow-up discussions than
male members of the class. Deborah Lupton and John Tulloch
(1996) and Lynda Measor et al. (1996) comment on the non-
participation of boys in sex education classes that can be variously
interpreted as bravado, anxiety and resistance. The marginalisation of boys' voices in the 'agony aunt' lesson can be seen in terms
of their lack of familiarity with the problem page format and a
seeming reluctance to appropriate the language and themes of
popular cultural forms in ways that relate to their concerns,
experiences and notions of gender identity. The recourse to dominant sex/gender categories in the 'problems' and discussion of
them points to the productive possibilities of problematising such
categories in educational settings. Lynn Segal (1990) suggests
intensive, anti-sexist consciousness raising for young people in
schools and youth organisations as a way of developing awareness
of sexual power, especially in relation to date rape. The sex education lessons I observed indicate that such an approach could be
usefully extended to include a critical take on gender and gender
appropriate behaviour where some of the insecurities and contradictions of gender identity could be broached.

Letters written by young women suggest that sexuality is a site for the playing out of fears and desires where aspects of popular culture can be utilised as referents and resources in the articulation of sexual themes. The agony aunt format offers students the opportunity to respond creatively to the identification of sexual themes and issues that can be seen as a projection of their internal and external concerns in the domain of the sexual. Their letters find ways of speaking the unspeakable which are both imaginative and revealing in their identification of issues that constitute significant absences in the sex education programme. The agony aunt format facilitates discussion of issues that were not part of the sex education programme such as rape/sexual abuse, homosexuality and masturbation/indecent exposure. The expression of these 'problems' often contrasts sexual knowledge with emotional insecurity suggesting that the experience of sexuality for young women may be located within competing discourses of sexual health and romantic love. Here, fear of pregnancy and HIV is interwoven with concerns regarding sexual reputation, constancy and betrayal. Laura's letter, further suggests a link between desire for, and fear of, sexual intercourse which is intimately bound up with internal repressions and external relations. The complexity of these lived relations have implications for our understanding of sex education as a difficult, even 'impossible', practice.

The ways in which the letters are discussed in the class offer an insight into sex education as a practice where approaches to sexuality are outlined in particular ways. Within the pedagogic practice of sex education, sexuality can be seen as a site for the construction of boundaries which demarcates the terrain for the articulation of sexual themes. Michelle Fine (1988) identifies three discourses which characterise debates over sex education: sexuality as violence; sexuality as victimisation and sexuality as individual morality. These discourses are also present, in disparate ways, in the Class 10 lesson where the discussion is constructed around issues of sexual threat and personal responsibility. The 'agony aunt' task indicates that sex-as-danger and a source of problems offers a 'safe' way of discussing sexuality which is appropriate to the genre of problem pages and the sex education class. Within this format teacher and pupils can utilise the language of popular culture and medical/sexual health discourses to create a school story of sexuality which offers an individualised and decontextualised approach to sexual issues. The construction of boundaries in

Chapter 5

More Sugar? Teenage magazines, gender displays and sexual learning[1]

My Dreams Show Me My Sexuality
The strongest tradition that the girls observed in the school
had to do with friendship. Any girl who had any intelligence
and self-respect searched for the smartest, most beautiful and
powerful girl who would have her. These two then made the
following pact: they vowed to devote themselves to each other
forever and to protect each other against all the machinations
and treacheries of the others. If any girl was powerful enough
and properly protected, one was the same as the other, she
could be chosen for a second game, which was also nameless.
   In this game, all the remaining girls in the class for one
week had nothing to do, either in speech or in any other way,
with the child who had been chosen. If at any time during the
week of silence, silence reaching into nothingness, the child
broke down crying or complained or ran to a teacher, she
would no longer be worth the attention and respect of any
other girls for the rest of her life. Her life in this school. If she
did survive torture which seemed too mild to be called 'torture',
torture by girls of girls, she could again enter the magic circle
of power.
                    Kathy Acker (1995: 47–8) *Pussycat Fever*

   This chapter will look at the ways in which magazines aimed at
an adolescent female market can be seen as a cultural resource for
learning about issues of gender and sexuality. The chapter will
explore the ways in which sexual issues are presented for young
women through the magazine format. This is followed by an
analysis of the ways in which young women and young men read,
discuss and negotiate these media messages. Using ethnographic

material combined with textual analysis of teenage magazines, the chapter outlines a complex process of negotiation through which young people *read* the material and the messages within the social context of friendship groups and personal experiences. The chapter argues that acts of readership within the school context produce enactments of femininity and masculinity which can be seen as *gender displays* that provide a space for the constitution and public exhibition of sex-gender identities.

It is not uncommon for teen magazines to get a bad press. They have been variously viewed as poor quality dross for the undiscerning masses (Alderson 1968) and as 'ideology purveyors' producing and reproducing a culture of femininity which provides young women with limited and limiting ways of making sense of their experiences (McRobbie 1978a, 1978b, 1981, 1991; Tinkler, 1995). Magazine scholarship has explored the enduring popularity of magazines for women and the ways in which the magazine can be seen to provide a space for the construction of normative femininity (McRobbie 1996). Through this extensive literature it is possible to trace key themes in feminist scholarship more generally: a concern with issues of power and subordination; a consideration of the pleasures of femininities; and, more recently, a recognition of the 'failure' of identity and the impossibility of coherence at the level of the Subject. Studies of magazines have been marked by two distinct methodological approaches; textual analysis focusing on the magazine and its associative meanings, and audience ethnography exploring the ways in which readers make sense of the text. Studies of magazines aimed at a female readership initially pointed to the many ways in which the stories and features of the magazine format could be *bad-for-you*, directly connecting the femininity represented in the pages with the oppressive structures and practices of patriarchal society (McRobbie 1978a, 1978b; Winship 1985; Coward 1984; Tinkler 1995). Further work has indicated the complexity and agency involved in reading practices where pleasure and fantasy can become strategies for the organisation and verification of domestic routines and lived experience (Radway 1984; Hermes 1995). Psychoanalytically inflected studies point to the internal fracturing of the psyche and the conceptualisation of subjectivity as a site of struggle, suggesting that ideological messages can never be fully conveyed. Valerie Walkerdine's (1984) study of girls' comics explores the relationship of cultural products to the psychic production and resolution of desire. Walkerdine's analysis of *Bunty* indicates that reading practices involve formations of fantasy wherein desires take shape and conflicts can be resolved. From this perspective the consolidation of heterosexual relations can be seen as a product of the complex interplay of conscious and unconscious dynamics involved in the constitution of femininity.

From the perspective of educational research, it is possible to detect a disjuncture between education and popular culture. Earlier studies of pupil culture describe incidents where magazine readership is regarded as an inherently counter-school activity. Viv Furlong's (1976) study of interaction sets in the classroom recounts an example of a girl reading 'comics' that are subsequently removed by the teacher. Similarly, in Fuller's (1984) study of black girls in a London comprehensive school, the reading of magazines in class is generally understood, by teachers and pupils alike, as an 'illegitimate activity' (1984: 83) to be ranked alongside chatting and avoiding work as strategies of opposition. Such strategies could be utilised by pupils at certain moments to register their intolerance of school routines. These incidents are suggestive of the ways in which dominant educational discourses have traditionally eschewed 'the popular' as intellectually impoverished and unworthy of critical attention. By contrast, the official school curriculum has occupied a reified status which bespeaks notions of erudition, refinement and self-improvement while concealing the 'inherited selections of interests' (Williams 1965: 172) which constitute it.

Educationalists have documented the ways in which the 'new' sociology of education of the 1960s began to ask critical questions about educational values and the role of the school (see, for example, Hammersley and Woods 1976; Whitty 1985 for a discussion of these themes). This emergent body of work was directly concerned with children's learning in relation to issues of social class and educational achievement and drew upon ethnographic methods to explore such themes. Educational researchers of this period focused their attention on processes within the school to address issues of *what* was learned and *how* it was learned (e.g. Hargreaves 1967; Lacey 1970). The concept of 'hidden curriculum' came to be widely used to describe how the world of learning appeared from the perspective of the learner. As Hammersley and Woods (1976) articulated it,

Instead of school achievement being taken to be the product of some mysterious 'intelligence', people began to ask, What exactly are pupils required to learn in school? The obverse of this was also posed at the same time: Is there something else besides the official curriculum that is learned?

(Hammersley and Woods 1976: 2)

Here, there was an acknowledgement that 'learning' extended the boundaries of the official curriculum and may have inadvertent effects; what is learned by pupils is not necessarily what is intended by teachers and educational policy makers. Hammersley and Woods further suggest that *what* pupils learn, as gleaned from research of the period, can be seen in terms of conformity to school values. Through participation in school routines, pupils 'learn' to conform or resist the official culture of the school as elaborated in the identification of pro-school and anti-school groupings in studies such as Rosser and Harre (1976) 'The meaning of trouble' and Willis (1977) *Learning to Labour*.

This chapter focuses upon 'conformity' and 'learning' of a different sort. I would like to suggest that the 'hidden curriculum' can also be seen in terms of the regulation of sex–gender categories. Within the context of school much informal learning takes place concerning issues of gender and sexuality: the homophobia of young men; the sexual reputations of young women; and the pervasive presence of heterosexuality as an 'ideal' and a practice mark out the terrain for the production of gendered and sexualised identities. Furthermore, such social learning is overt and explicit rather than 'hidden'. Specifically, this chapter explores the ways in which magazines aimed at an adolescent female market can be seen as cultural resources for learning about issues of sexuality. In focusing on magazine readership in school I am interested in investigating the following research questions: In what way is the school a site for learning in relation to issues of gender and sexuality? What do young people learn about gender and sexuality in this context? My analysis suggests that, through engagement with popular cultural forms, young people produce sex–gender identities that provide an arena for the negotiation of peer group friendships and the consolidation of heterosexual relations. My conversations with young people in school suggest that they are *critical* readers of popular culture who engage with text in productive ways. They are aware of the ways in which sexual issues are presented to them through the magazine format; this awareness contrasts and occasionally overlaps with sexual learning in more formal contexts such as sex education classes. Moreover, the comments of young people I spoke with suggest that they have developed a range of strategies for reading, discussing and negotiating these media messages.

Magazines in context

Recently, in the UK context, there has been some debate concerning appropriate reading material for adolescent girls. Teenage magazines such as *More!* and *Sugar* have been at the centre of this controversy. Media attention in the form of news items on television and in the tabloid press have suggested that these teen magazines are too sexually explicit for young women. Concerns over the 'corruption' of adolescent girls have found voice in governmental debates and legislative proposals with one Member of Parliament, Peter Luff, declaring that the magazines 'rob girls of their innocence'.[2] Concerns expressed at this level can be seen, in part, as the articulation of a broader 'moral panic' relating to teenage pregnancy, single motherhood and the provision of state benefits.

During my fieldwork period I found that young people frequently used popular cultural forms as a resource and a framework for discussing issues of sexuality. Plots from the soaps such as *Brookside* and *Eastenders*, characters such as Hannah in *Neighbours*, episodes of *Byker Grove* and TV personalities such as Barrymore were cited and used as reference points in discussions of sexual relationships, physical attraction, parental constraints and homosexuality. These cultural references acted like roadmaps whereby students could negotiate the hazardous terrain of sexual taboo. They also provided a frame, or way of looking at sexuality through which students could juxtapose their personal experiences with media constructions. Teen magazines can be seen as part of this broader social context; they are a popular, mass produced and publicly shared media form which speaks to young people in particular ways and enables them to talk back. In this way teen magazines can be seen as a cultural resource for young people that they can, at different moments, 'talk with' and 'think with'.

All the young women I spoke to, and some of the young men, were regular readers of magazines aimed at an adolescent female market. The young people frequently mentioned magazines such as *Bliss, Mizz, More!, Sugar, Just Seventeen* and *Nineteen*, with *Sugar* being the most popular and *More!* the most controversial. The young women were aware that the magazines played a part in a developmental process that was guided by age and gender.

Sophie: I think that *More!* is for older girls really. Like the younger ones (magazines) where you've got, you've got ponies and stuff.
Naomi: And pictures of kittens.
Sophie: Yeah, there's like *Girltalk* and *Chatterbox* and you go up and you get *Shout* and then you get *Sugar* and *Bliss* and then it's like *Just Seventeen, Nineteen* and then it's *More!* and then it's *Woman's Own* and stuff like that. So you got the range.

The 'going up' that Sophie refers to can be related to the gendered experience of moving from girlhood to adolescence and into womanhood in relation to particular magazines which may be seen as cultural markers in the developmental process. The reproduction of a specific class-cultural femininity is naturalised within the magazines through an appeal that is based on the seemingly 'natural' categories of age and gender. Angela McRobbie (1978a; 1978b; 1981; 1991) has commented on the ways in which *Jackie* magazine of the 1970s introduced the girl to adolescence by mapping out the personal terrain, 'outlining its landmarks and characteristics in detail and stressing the problematic features as well as fun' (1991: 83). McRobbie's analysis of the multiple ways in which *Jackie* worked demonstrates that the different features of the magazine are involved in reproducing a *culture of femininity* cohering around the concept of romance. From this perspective *Jackie* can be seen as preparatory literature for a feminine, rather than a feminist career; the search for a 'fella', the privileging of 'true love' and an induction into repetitive beauty routines which can be seen as an introduction to domestic labour. Penny Tinkler (1995) in her study of popular magazines for girls during the period 1920–1950 similarly suggests that these magazines actively 'construct girlhood' by according significance to age, social class and girls' position in the heterosexual career.

Martin Barker's (1989) research suggests other ways of looking at these magazines which problematise the feminist assumption that *Jackie* is 'bad for girls'. His analysis indicates that a knowledge of the history of the production of magazines can contribute to an understanding of the ways in which magazines can be seen as specific cultural products, produced within a context of technical and social compromises and constraints which change over time. Factors relating to the physical production of magazines such as machinery, resources, artistic input and marketing, complexify notions of 'reproduction' whereby simply seeing *Jackie* as an ideological purveyor of a culture of femininity overlooks many other factors which *make* the magazine what it is. Barker's reading of *Jackie* postulates that the magazine has an agenda that is based on 'living out an unwritten contract with its readers' (1989: 165). The 'contract' is premised on active engagement of the reader with the magazine – the magazine invites a reader to collaborate by reading in particular ways:

> The 'contract' involves an agreement that a text will talk to us in ways we recognise. It will enter into a dialogue with us. And that dialogue, with its dependable elements and form, will relate to some aspects of our lives in our society.
>
> (Barker 1989: 261)

Barker points out that the contractual understanding between magazine and implied reader is reliant on social context. The act of reading can be seen as a process that creates feelings of mutual recognition and familiarity between the reader and the features of the magazine. Barker's reading of *Jackie* and other magazines develops a textual analysis which emphasises the interactive engagement of the reader with the magazine, through which both parties are involved in a conversation premised on shared social experiences and expectations. By contrast, Joke Hermes' (1995) study of the readership of women's magazines proffers an analysis based on interviews with women who identify themselves as readers of women's magazines. Her audience research indicates that the reading practices of women are mediated by the context of their everyday lives. The 'pickupable' and 'putdownable' quality of magazines fits in with daily domestic routines women describe and participate in. This contributes to the magazines' popular appeal as an appropriate companion for women in moments of 'relaxation', signifying the demarcation of personal space within a busy day. I am indebted to feminist scholarship on magazines and in particular the insights of Barker and Hermes where the use of different methodological approaches contributes to our understanding of magazines and acts of readership. Barker (1989) and Hermes (1995) illustrate how the reading of magazines can be seen respectively as a contractual understanding between reader and magazine and an integral part of everyday routines in the lives of women. The ethnographic study I conducted develops this analysis by illustrating how the reading of magazines by students in school is shaped by the context of school relations where *gender displays* are enacted collectively through friendship groups and peer relations. This approach builds upon and develops the observations of the previous chapters which note the discursive strategies deployed in school settings in relation to issues of sexuality (see Chapter 3) and the ways in which these discursive strategies are translated into the curriculum at the level of pedagogic practice (as discussed in Chapters 3 and 4).

School-based reading practices and gender difference

My group-work discussions with young women and young men in school indicated that gender played a key role in shaping the attitudes and practices through which young people read magazines. This theme is further elaborated by researchers in this field where there is an acknowledgement of the significance of gender to reading patterns and levels of literacy among school-age students (see, for example, Alloway and Gilbert 1997; Davies 1997; Millard 1997). Within this literature the investments in particular reading practices by young women provide a point of contrast with the non-participation of young men. Many young women I talked with spoke of magazine reading as a regular collective practice. Within the context of the school day this involved the reading of magazines in breaks and lunchtime as well as in certain lessons such as drama, English and Personal and Social Education where the magazine features and format could inform discussions and classroom activities.

MJK: Do you read the magazines together?
Ruth: We used to, all the time . . .
Amy: Sometimes we do.

Ruth: When we've got a magazine we do, we have a good laugh.

Joanne: Like if one person buys it and brings it into school, we all look through it together, so we don't buy four separate copies.

Amy: Some of them make you laugh though, don't they?

For these young women reading magazines can be seen as a shared, school-based activity which female friendship groups draw upon as a resource for humour. Here the 'contract' between the magazine and the reader which Barker refers to has been extended to the friendship group where readership offers the group the opportunity for dialogue at the level of collective experience. McRobbie (1981) has commented on the way in which girls' collective reading of *Jackie* may be oppositional, citing an example of a group of girls truanting from lessons to do a *Jackie* quiz in the toilets. Within the school context such activities can be seen as a point of resistance to the organisational structure of the school day where magazine reading serves to disrupt and fracture everyday routines rather than fit in with them. However, as Walkerdine (1990) has pointed out, not all acts of resistance against school authority have revolutionary effects: they may have 'reactionary' effects too. In this case young women locate themselves within a class-cultural dynamic where they actively choose reading magazines and 'learning' femininity as an alternative to attending lessons (see also Nava 1984).

By contrast, the reading of magazines did not appear to occupy a similar social space among male peer groups. In a group-work session with boys, the suggestion that they might read magazines which speak to them of social/sexual issues appears to generate feelings of emasculation and suspicion.

MJK: Do you wish there was a boys' magazine?

Blake: Nah, you'd get called a sissy wouldn't you?
              (all laugh)

Christopher: Well there are some like *Loaded* and there's *Q* and *Maxim* as well with things like football, sex and clothes and –

Blake: You're an expert you are!
              (all laugh)

MJK:	If there were a magazine like that for your age group – what about that?
Andrew:	Yeah, I wouldn't mind buying a magazine like that sometimes but I wouldn't, like the girls do, buy it every week, that's just too – I wouldn't like that. I'd only buy it when there was something in it like an article or something. You know, sometimes like when you get into a situation and you don't know what you're doing it would help then if there was a magazine to tell you what to do then.

The responses of the boys indicate that their reading of magazines is more of an individual than a group activity, as it is for girls. The boys indicate that reading magazines risks being regarded as 'sissy', a derogatory term suggesting such practices could be less than manly. Eric Rofes (1995) documents the painful experiences of 'sissy' boys in the American school system where bullying and abuse become part of a process of Othering, establishing differences between dominant and subordinate groups of males (see also Haywood 1996; Mac an Ghaill 1996; and Kehily and Nayak 1997 for a further discussion of masculinities and the production of heterosexual hierarchies in educational settings). Rofes notes that, 'sissy boys have become contemporary youth's primary exposure to gay identity' (1995: 81). The shared laughter of Blake, Andrew and Christopher at Blake's connection of magazine readership for males with being a 'sissy' indicates that there is group recognition/surveillance relating to gender appropriate behaviour for young males.[3] Here, the reading of teen magazines comes dangerously close to falling beyond the bounds of publicly acceptable behaviour for male peer groups. Christopher's awareness of magazines aimed at a male readership and his willingness to name and discuss them is viewed by Blake as a form of 'expertise' that generates more laughter. In the context of male peer groups in school, Christopher's 'knowledge' may be hazardous to the presentation of a socially recognised male identity. Andrew's comments specifically locate magazines as a manual or reference book to be consulted as and when necessary to solve particular individual problems. His expressed distaste for regular readership 'like the girls do' is suggestive of the resonant interplay of internal anxieties and external policing where there may be a fear of dependency and a need to display an emotional self-sufficiency based on investments in an imagined masculine ideal.

Hermes (1995) notes the enjoyment of gossip magazines among certain gay men where a camp fantasy world of appearances, trivia and 'bad taste' is celebrated. Here pleasure in subversion turns the reading of gossip magazines into a 'performative art' (Hermes 1995: 137) and establishes points of difference between gay and dominant culture. This social practice contrasts sharply with the group of boys in school who articulate their ideas within a dominant culture of masculinity in which an unspoken desire to assert themselves as heterosexual structures the discussion (see also Chapter 6). The boys' attempt to distance themselves from the perceived reading practices of girls may be voicing a fear of camp, whereby to embrace magazines in the same way as girls would create internal anxieties about becoming gay/female or 'sissy' as Blake puts it. The boys' comments on magazine readership is suggestive of the complex dynamics involved in the relationship between cultural forms and the constitution of gendered subjectivities. For the young men in this group there is a collective investment in forms of masculinity premised upon heterosexual desire and the enactment of a gendered identity defined *as against* females and gay men (Connell 1989; Mac an Ghaill 1994; Nayak and Kehily 1996). In this exchange the concern to demonstrate competence, self-reliance and an independence from cultural products become signifiers for a particular publicly displayed and socially validated form of masculinity.

Treatment of homosexual themes by teen magazines such as *More!* and *Sugar* do little to challenge the homophobias present within pupil sexual cultures. A 'real-life drama' in *More!* publicised on the front cover as, 'My gay friend Ian stole my man!' illustrates some of the ways in which homosexuality is positioned as a deviant and marginal practice, existing at the fringes of a centred and normalising heterosexuality. Tina tells her story of meeting her 'soulmate', Jules, and discovering he is gay by reading his diary:

> I'll never forget the hideous, sick feeling that swept over me. As I turned each page, details of their secret liaisons leapt out . . . It described 'rolling around together' and kissing. Thank God there were no descriptions of full sex.
>
> (*More!* 1995: Issue 198)

Tina's description of the gay relationship between Jules and Ian reveals a strong sense of repulsion and disgust. The 'hideous, sick feeling' experienced when gay sexual practices are inferred contrasts sharply with the normalisation of heterosexual penetrative sex, visibly displayed on other pages of the magazine. Tina's narrative can be read teleologically, pathologising Jules' homosexuality and problematising their relationship in the light of her discovery. The realisation that Jules 'simply was gay' engages Tina in a reconstruction of their past in which a low sex drive, lack of excitement during sex, sexual conservatism and an absence of jealousy now become signifiers of a latent homosexuality. Tina's account moves towards narrative closure with her reflections on meeting her new partner, David:

> It was the best thing that ever happened to me. I'd forgotten what it was like to have sex more than once and not just in the missionary position. But I asked David early on, 'Are you sure you don't prefer men?' It's an odd question to ask, but I never want that to happen to me again. Now I feel lucky I didn't marry Jules, have two kids and find out the truth when I was 40.
>
> *(More!* 1995, Issue 198)

Tina's good fortune is seen as an escape from the inadequacies of gay masculinity where to marry someone who also enjoys same sex relationships would ultimately be a regrettable error and a waste of a life. The presence of homophobias in pupil cultures and teen magazines is illustrative of the different ways in which sexualities are regulated. Gendered differences in reading practices and the associated meanings generated collectively by boys and girls in school reveal that teen magazines are more likely to be a cultural resource for sexual learning among young women than among young men. This has implications for classroom practice and, particularly, the ways in which Personal and Social Education programmes relate to young men.

Sexual learning – problem pages

Problem pages in magazines can be seen as an interactive space specifically set up for producers of the magazine and readers to engage in dialogue. Rosalind Coward (1984) comments on the spectacle of public confession to be found in problem pages which encourage readers to view these pages as a distinct sub-genre of sexual fiction producing culturally specific ways of knowing oneself:

> Problem pages are themselves a historically specific symptom of the way in which sexuality and its emotional consequences have been catapulted to the foreground in our culture as the true expression of our intimate selves.
>
> (Coward 1984: 137)

The incitement to share problems, particularly sexual problems can be seen as constitutive of a sexualised subjectivity, a *technology* bringing into being a discursively produced 'deep' self that can be situated within a field of social regulation (Foucault 1976). My research findings suggest that young women *self-regulate* their use of magazines to enable discussion and informal learning of sexual issues. Problem pages in particular are read and discussed collectively by young women in school. Young women appropriate the discourse of teen magazines and demonstrate a confidence in this field as discussed in the previous chapter. Problem pages are viewed collectively by pupils as a 'laugh', not to be taken seriously, and, simultaneously, as a way of framing personal problems, emotional concerns and 'boy trouble'. Boys and girls in school shared a scepticism and enjoyment of problem pages, often mentioning the problem page as the first page they turn to when they open a magazine. The following extract demonstrates the ways in which young women distance themselves from the problem page and, at the same time, find the feature compelling.

Rebecca: Yeah, the agony aunts, they're good.

Sophie: They're good because a lot of people enjoy reading that sort of page, if you buy a magazine you go straight to the problems for the information.

Julia: Yeah!

Rebecca: Yeah you read the problem but not the advice.
(all laugh)

MJK: Why is the problem more interesting than the advice?

Rebecca: I don't know, it just is.

Sophie: Some people find it really . . . fascinating.

Julia: Yeah if the problem is to do with you then you read the advice but otherwise you just go on to the next one (problem).

Rebecca, Sophie and Julia suggest that the 'fascination' of the problem page lies primarily in reading about a problem where the 'information' to be gleaned is contained within the problem as the reader expresses it rather than in advice given by the experienced agony aunt (see Lee 1983: 80–91 for an interesting discussion of the difficulties of being an 'agony aunt'). However, if the problem is 'to do with you' and can be seen as an articulation of your own situation in some way, then advice may be read. McRobbie (1978a: 29) asserts that the problem page in *Jackie*, known as the 'Cathy and Claire' page, 'sums up the ideological content of the magazine' by giving girls culturally loaded messages in the form of guidance to be heeded by the sensible girl. Barker's (1989: 160) analysis of the Cathy and Claire page found most advice to be 'specific and commonsensical' where girls are encouraged to take a close look at themselves, their reasons for writing, their personality and self-confidence. He suggests that the significance of the Cathy and Claire page revolves around girls being asked to engage in a personal re-evaluation, to look at themselves in different ways and to see their feelings and emotions from other perspectives. My ethnographic study, however, suggests that the advice is of marginal interest and the focus of appeal for young people in schools is in *the problem itself* which may be read in friendship groups and discussed critically in terms of pleasure, humour, empathy and disbelief:

Andrew: Some of them (problems) are pretty terrible, I reckon some people just write for fun. When you're reading them – they can't possibly be for real.
Christopher: You can't take them seriously.
Tim: Yeah, you can't take them seriously.
Andrew: You can't imagine someone not knowing stuff like that.
MJK: So you think that some people, they haven't got a problem really but they just sit down and –
Andrew: Yeah, just write in for a joke, see if it gets published or not, just for something to do.

The views of the boys express a disdain of ignorance, 'you can't imagine people not knowing stuff like that' which is working with a sense of amusement and 'fun' where writing to problem pages can be seen as a practical joke to relieve boredom and generate humour. In this exchange Andrew, Christopher and Tim position themselves as knowledgeable and discerning readers able to detect the 'for real' problems from the wind-ups. Problems which do not appear credible are not worthy of being taken seriously. Viewing the problems with a sense of disbelief that can be explained in terms of ignorance or tomfoolery enables these young men to establish a distance from the feature and the problems. The incredulity of the boys was also shared by many of the girls I spoke with:

Clare: They (the problems) look as though they're made up.

Ruth: They do, some of them are really silly.

Joanne: Sometimes it's like really serious 'cos we have them in Drama when you're reading it and some of them are just, you know, really serious.

Amy: You wouldn't say that kind of thing or put it in a magazine or even write it –

Joanne: If you're desperate you would.

Ruth: Yeah!

Clare: Yeah!

Amy: You know, they don't sound real.

Clare: Half the time I think they're made up, people do it for a laugh and then they (staff at the magazine) take it seriously, or the editors make them up.

Ruth: At the start of, like, *Sugar*, when *Sugar* first came out there was a problem page in it and, like, how d'you know where to write to 'cos the magazine hasn't come out yet.

Clare: Well maybe they just make up the first ones.

In this discussion the group of girls work through their feelings of disbelief, empathy and deception which contribute to the contradictory appeal of problem pages. The 'silliness' of some problems and the 'seriousness' of others combine to create distrust of the feature, grounded in evidence that new magazines have problem pages in their first issue before a readership has been established. The deception involving readers and editors fabricating problems is punctured at one moment when Joanne asserts that if you were 'desperate' you would write to a problem page. This is echoed by the affirming voices of Ruth and Clare. Joanne, Ruth and Clare are responding to Amy's point that some problems as printed in magazines transgress certain boundaries by speaking the unspeakable, 'You wouldn't say that kind of thing or put it in a magazine or even write it'. The responses of the other girls indicate that, in cases of extreme distress, *you would* talk about taboo subjects. This understanding that the magazine can assist in difficulties by placing them 'out there' simultaneously gives girls licence to discuss these issues among themselves. From this perspective problem pages can be seen to open up areas for discussion by giving young women access to a particular discourse; ways of talking about issues and emotions, giving experiences a vocabulary within the language of the felt. My discussions with young men and women indicate that young people collectively negotiate their responses to problem page features within the context of friendship groups. Here, friends act as mediators and regulators of 'problems', determining whether they should be dismissed, humoured, taken seriously or discussed further. The activities of young men and women in this respect indicates that, within the context of the school, peer group relations play an important part in the social regulation of sexual discourse, offering a sphere for conveying sex–gender identities. The gendered dynamics of these exchanges illustrate the distancing displays of young men in relation to cultural products and sexual problems while young women appear more open to discussion in this area.

Sexual learning and cultures of femininity

The problem pages, like other regular features of the magazine such as the stories and fashion pages, present points of continuity for readers, providing them with a familiar format and set of expectations:

Sara: I find *Sugar* good value.
Laura: I like *Sugar*, I get *Sugar*.
Catherine: *Just Seventeen*, I get that every week.
Sara: In every issue of *Sugar* there's always something about sex, something involving sex.

Catherine: There's like good stories in there as well, really interesting stuff . . . Someone with really bad problems will write in and they get really helped and next month they write back and say 'Thank you' and a bit of their little note will be in there saying 'Thank you' and stuff like that.

Here, the agreement that *Sugar* is 'good value' and a good read is supported by Sara, Laura and Catherine. A salient feature of every issue is 'something involving sex' as Sara puts it. This 'something' could be expressed in the problem page or in the story feature. The comments of the girls suggest that problems and stories are read alongside one another and conform to their expectations of the magazine speaking to them about sex. The problem page in particular provides a direct link between the magazine and the reader by creating a cosy, interactive environment in which intimacies can be shared. Catherine's comments suggest that individuals can be 'helped' by the problem page which provides a linear trace of events through the problem, advice offered and expressions of gratitude.

Teen magazines containing features on sex and readers expecting to be informed and entertained by the sexual content of the magazine can be seen as partners in the contractual understanding that Barker (1989) refers to. However, the young women I spoke to indicated that this source of sexual knowledge is viewed critically by individuals and mediated by friendship groups. *More!* magazine in particular aroused controversy among the young women:

Clare: But that *More!* really goes into it. I mean some of the stories are, you know, you wouldn't want to tell anybody about 'em. Like, if you look in those other magazines they say, 'My boyfriend did this and what can I do?' and a story and there's other stories you would want to tell your friends at your age. But that *More!* magazine, it's more, you know, for seventeen year olds to read 'cos it goes too into depth with them.

Amy: In fairness to *More!* though, it aims at a higher age group, so, like, it's younger people's fault if they read it, or their mom and dads' fault.

MJK: But you'd find, like, things in, say, *Sugar*, you'd all talk about among yourselves?
Clare: Yeah.
Amy: Yeah we would.
Ruth: Yeah.
Amy: But you couldn't do the same with *More!* magazine.
MJK: Because of embarrassment?
Amy: It is yeah. You say, 'Oh I saw this in this magazine' and then everybody starts laughing at you.
Clare: Yeah, it just goes over the top really.

In this discussion Clare, Amy and Ruth suggest that *More!* breaks the contract between magazine and readers by being too sexually explicit. By printing stories 'you wouldn't want to tell anybody about' *More!* is placed beyond the collective reading practices of these young women. The embarrassment of the young women suggests that their reputations may be tainted by reading and embracing *More!* magazine. Amy's comments, particularly, indicate that to repeat features to friends may result in embarrassment and humiliation, 'everybody starts laughing at you'. This collective action which relies on humour to deride and 'other' a member of the group is illustrative of the ways in which these young women negotiate some subjects deemed appropriate for discussion and successfully marginalise others. This active engagement with issues arising from the reading of magazines suggests that female friendship groups provide a site for the enactment of particular cultures of femininity (Hey 1997; Skeggs 1997). This culture of femininity may, at moments, work to expel other cultures of femininity such as those contained in the pages of *More!* magazine and external to the friendship group. In this context the 'too in depth' and 'over the top' features of *More!* transgress the boundaries of legitimacy defined by these young women as suitable for their age group and feminine identities. Cindy Patton (1993) has commented on the ways in which identities carry with them a 'requirement to act which is felt as "what a person like me does"' (1993: 147). Clare, Amy and Ruth indicate that female friendship groups adopt a collective 'requirement to act' in relation to issues of sexuality which appears to be anchored in an agreed notion of 'what girls like us do'. This action can be seen to be concerned with the establishment and maintenance of a particular moral agenda that marks out the terrain for discussion and/or action. Female friendship groups, in moments of collective action, 'draw the line' (Canaan 1986: 193) to demarcate the acceptable from the unacceptable. In these moments female friendship groups incorporate spheres or practices they feel comfortable with and displace practices that do not concur with their collectively defined feminine identities. In Canaan's (1986) US study concerning middle-class young women and sexuality, young women who do not 'draw the line' incur a reputation as 'the other kinda girl' (1986: 190), the sexually promiscuous and much denigrated female figure whose lack of adherence to conventional morality serves as a 'cautionary tale' for young women to be ever vigilant in the maintenance of their reputation.[4] The collective activity of female friendship groups in relation to the reading of teenage magazines can be seen as part of a constant and sustained engagement in the production of school-based femininities. These processes involve the continual negotiation and delineation of acceptable and unacceptable forms of behaviour/action which bespeak and thereby bring into being feminine identities. The collective investment in particular feminine identities as expressed by the young women I spoke with reveals the associative link between magazine reading and identity work as mutually constitutive acts in their everyday social interactions in school. The creative energy involved in the constitutive enactment of a particular femininity points to the labour involved in the production of sex–gender identities and can be seen as an attempt to fix and consolidate continually shifting social and psychic locations.

More! is too much

More recently, McRobbie (1996) has commented on the ways in which contemporary teenage magazines such as *More!* embrace and display an intensification of interest in sexuality. She notes that this sexual material is marked by features such as exaggeration, self-parody and irony which suggest new forms of sexual conduct for young women:

> This sexual material marks a new moment in the construction of female sexual identities. It proposes boldness (even brazenness) in behaviour . . . Magazine discourse brings into being new female subjects through these incitations.
>
> (McRobbie 1996: 177–8)

My ethnographic evidence suggests that this 'new moment in the construction of female sexual identities' is actively resisted by the young women I spoke with. A closer look at the content of *More!* magazine may offer an insight into practices and behaviours which appear as points of concern for the young women. A regular feature of *More!* magazine is a two-page item called 'Sextalk'. This includes an assortment of information about sex such as answers to readers' questions, sex definitions, sex 'factoids', short 'news' items and 'position of the fortnight' – a line drawing and explanatory text on positions for heterosexual penetrative sex such as 'backwards bonk' and 'side by side'. The following are examples of a 'sex definition' and 'sex factoid' from two issues of *More!*:

Sex Factoid:
Once ejaculated, the typical sperm travels five-and-a-half inches an hour – that's about twice as fast as British Rail!

(*More!* 1995, Issue 198)

Sex definition:
Penis Captivus
The act of holding his penis tightly in your vaginal muscles during sex (hold it too tight and he can develop a castration complex).

(*More!*, 1996, Issue 208)

The combination of 'fact', definitions, drawings and advice found in 'Sextalk', expressed colloquially and with humour, points to a departure from the ideology of romance as expressed in teen magazines such as *Jackie* (McRobbie 1981; Winship 1985) and a move towards the *technology* of sex where consensual procedures organise and monitor human activity (Foucault 1976). From a Foucaultian perspective the proliferation of sexual material in teen magazines can be seen to demarcate a terrain for social regulation where the exercise of power is productive rather than repressive. Ways of having intercourse, things to try, things to ask 'your man' to try, ways of looking and thinking in relation to sex, privilege heterosexual penetrative intercourse as the cornerstone of sexual relationships. In the 'Sextalk' feature of *More!* magazine sexual activity is demystified through line drawings and instructive text, presented and discussed in ways that encode heterosexuality. This can be interpreted as the creation of a site where heterosex can be learned, desired and manipulated, where sexual experimentation and pleasure leads to a particular expertise. The link between sexual knowledge and pleasure established in the 'Sextalk' feature privileges sexual identity as a way of knowing our 'inner' selves and, of course, 'our man'. In this feature the magazine appropriates a discourse of sexual liberation as articulated in 1970's sex manuals such as the Alex Comfort collection, *The Joy of Sex* (Comfort 1974). Here, the language, style and diagrammatic mode of instruction suggests to young women that the route to sexual emancipation lies in the 'doing it' and talking about 'doing it' of male–female fucking. Meryl Altman's (1984) study of 1970's sex manuals demonstrates the way in which anecdotes and clinical case studies are used in these texts and act as devices to inscribe ideology within the sex manual format. Altman argues that the combination of the familiar with the medical gives the texts an authoritative tone that conceals the fiction of ideological constructs. The 'Sextalk' feature can be viewed in a similar way as 'information' that utilises 'medical' and 'personal' discourses to impart ideological messages. However, my ethnographic work with young people suggests that readers of the feature are not beguiled by the ideological content.

Many young women I spoke to regarded *More's* up-front, 'over the top' approach to sex as embarrassing, disgusting and 'too much' (Lara). The responses of many young women I spoke with indicate that *More!* literally is 'too much'; its sexual excesses denote that it is not being taken seriously and requires regulation at the level of peer group interaction. Some young women reported that their parents had banned them from buying *More!*, while another said she had bought it once and 'binned it' (Joanne). In discussions I conducted with young women, the regular feature 'position of the fortnight' was spoken about in ways that fused embarrassment with a moral discourse of censorship and self-censorship:

Catrina:	Oh, I saw that, totally –
Laura:	Yeah.
	(all laugh)
Sara:	Yes, well.
Catherine:	I don't think we should say anymore about that!
MJK:	Are we talking about position of the fortnight?
	(all laugh)

All:	Yeah.
Laura:	My sister has one and it had like the best positions or something [unclear]
All:	Ughhh.
	(muted laughter)
MJK:	What do you think of that then?
Catherine:	I think there should be age limits on that kind of thing.
Laura:	There should be a lock on the front!

In this discussion the embarrassment of the young women can be seen in the half sentences, laughter and exclamations of disgust which reveal a reluctance to name and acknowledge the topic they are speaking about, 'I don't think we should say any more about that!'. My attempt to name and explore the issue in the question, 'Are we talking about position of the fortnight?' produces more laughter and embarrassment that further suggests that *More!* transgresses the bounds of the speakable for these young women. Catherine and Laura's expression of censorship, 'I think there should be age limits on that kind of thing' and, 'There should be a lock on the front!' may indicate that the appropriation of moral, parental discourse, in this case, offers an unambiguous way of censoring 'position of the fortnight' to illustrate their distaste of the feature. For Catherine and Laura, explicit details of sex or as they put it, 'that kind of thing' is clearly not *their* kind of thing – a matter they feel comfortable with or wish to be associated with. In this exchange the young women discursively position them-selves as untouched by the sexual material of *More!* and resistant to the possibility of the new female sexual subjectivities/behaviour referred to by McRobbie (1996). The moralism of the young women and expressions of disgust in relation to issues of sexuality finds points of resonance with Freudian analysis where middle childhood is seen as a period of (relative) sexual latency producing shame, disgust and claims of aesthetic and moral ideals which impede the course of the sexual instinct (Freud 1905). In the transition from childhood to adulthood these negative associations can be expressed and reconciled in the consolidation of hetero-sexual relations. The adverse reactions to the sexual content of *More!* can be seen to produce a moment of collective psychic and social positioning where young women take refuge in childhood approaches to sexuality rather than the older and potentially threatening domain offered by *More!* Of course, this does not mean that young women do not enjoy talking about sex or engaging in sexual activity. Rather, it suggests the power and agency of female friendship groups wherein, at certain moments, a collective approach to sexuality can be shared, regulated and expressed.

The jigsaw puzzle of sexual learning

At other moments, however, the young women I spoke with did discuss issues of sex and sexuality in positive and affirming ways. In these discussions they suggested that some teen magazines such as *Sugar* and *Just Seventeen* were a useful source of information on sexual matters. Their comments in these examples indicate that magazines can serve as a supplement to formal sex education classes in school and other forms of communication on sex such as leaflets and discussions with parents and peers. Rachel Thomson and Sue Scott (1991) comment on the ways in which young women in their study pieced together information from different sources in their search for sexual knowledge:

> The young women we spoke to reported learning by 'picking things up' and 'just catching on' . . . [young women] would frequently search for sexual references in any available sources such as popular sex manuals, 'Jackie Collins' books and most commonly in magazines aimed at young women.
> (Thomson and Scott 1991: 27–31)

Hermes (1995) suggests that women read magazines through a range of different repertoires where acts of readership engage them in ways of making sense of their experiences in relation to the contents of the magazine. The repertoire of 'emotional learning and connected knowing' is identified by Hermes as a way of dealing with emotions, validating experience and developing understanding. In the following example young women 'connect' knowledge gained in a sex education class with pictorial advice in a magazine. In this case the sexual learning relates to a demonstration on the use of condoms:

MJK: What did you think of the putting the condoms on?

Ruth: That was good that was.

Clare: It was good actually 'cos, like, I didn't know how to put it on (laughs).

Ruth: At least you got a chance to try.

Joanne: It was in the magazines as well.

Ruth: You can see what they're like in real life rather than just pictures . . .

Joanne: Yeah, it was in that magazine wasn't it? The *Sugar* magazine and what to do, so if you did in class you'd know you can do it yourself, you build up a better picture.

In this example, school-based sex education and commercially produced magazines can be seen to work together in a productive way, 'building up a better picture' by providing advice that young women find helpful. Hermes (1995) suggests that the repertoire of connected knowing offers the potential for developing understandings that can give women feelings of increased strength. This is both real and imagined as women *are* preparing themselves for difficulties and entertaining fantasies of *becoming* a 'wise woman'. The critical approach of young women in school suggest that magazines and acts of readership play a part in the connections and renunciations made in relation to sexual learning. Their comments indicate that popular cultural forms are continually mediated and negotiated collectively by female friendship groups. In such moments issues of sexuality can be opened up through shared reading and discussion and closed down through derisive laughter, evasive manoeuvres and moral appeals. The actions and behaviour of young women indicate that they are discerning and self-regulating in relation to sexual matters and magazine readership. Their discriminating approach could be a valuable resource in sexuality education programmes where the use of teen magazines offers the potential for common ground between teachers and pupils' sexual cultures.

Connections and disconnections: the burden of assumed knowledge

The responses of young men, however, to areas of potential 'connected knowing' tell a different story. Here, the use of teen magazines in formal spaces such as sex education lessons produces embarrassment for boys and a reluctance to enter into the discourse of popular culture. Researchers have commented on the disruptive behaviour and non-participation of boys in school-based sex education programmes and the ways in which such programmes fail to meet the needs of young men (Lupton and Tulloch 1996; Measor *et al.* 1996; Sex Education Forum 1995). In the previous chapter I discussed a Personal and Social Education lesson involving an activity where pupils were asked to create problems and share advice for a fictitious problem page. This activity sees girls as active and willing participants while boys attempt to enact a cool detachment from the imaginative exercise of writing and discussing 'problems'. Of the seven 'letters' read aloud by pupils, six were written by girls, with girls playing a more prominent part in the discussion of all 'problems'. A follow-up discussion with a group of girls reveals their awareness of the boys' unease and discomfort. They explained it in the following terms:

Joanne: The boys were dying of embarrassment!
             (all laugh)
Ruth: Yeah, I know, maybe 'cos we read the magazines, they
             don't read them. Like for us there is a problem page in
             every magazine, girls' magazine, but they don't have
             them in the boys' magazines, like football magazines and
             that – you don't see a problem page – so that's probably
             why.

The comments of the girls indicate that they have a familiarity with problem pages which boys do not share. This gives the young women a vocabulary to articulate social/sexual problems based on collective experience and mutual recognition. The laughter of the girls suggests that they take pleasure in their shared knowledge and in the obvious embarrassment of the boys in the class. Researchers have commented on the ways in which young women actively use sexuality and an exaggerated femininity as a strategy to resist, challenge and embarrass teachers and boys (Anyon 1983; Lees 1986; Skeggs 1991; Kehily and Nayak 1996). Here, sexual knowledge developed within female friendship groups can become a way of disrupting dominant power relations when used in more formal contexts such as the classroom.

Follow-up discussion with a group of boys suggests that their lack of dialogue around certain issues may be part of a struggle to perform a coherent masculine identity (discussed further in Chapter 6) where boys' negotiation of discourse around emotions/feelings differs from that of girls:

MJK:	Have you all – among yourselves – have you spoken about things on the (Sex Education) course?
James:	Not really.
Andrew:	No, not like that.
MJK:	You don't, why not?
Blake:	'Cos we already know it.
	(all laugh)
Blake:	I do anyway.
MJK:	Well, that doesn't mean you can't talk about it does it?
Blake:	True, true.
MJK:	So why is it that you don't talk about relationships and sex?
Blake:	Not the thing boys do.
Andrew:	Not the things boys do.

Here, Blake offers two reasons for the absence of such discussion among boys; they 'know it already' and it is 'not the thing boys do'. Andrew's reiteration of this point underlines how the boys invest in a masculine identity premised on assumed knowledge and the concealment of vulnerabilities. Here, denial and effacement can be seen as necessary repetitions for the presentation of a particular version of masculinity. Julian Wood (1984) and Chris Haywood (1996) note the ways in which boys' sex talk commonly manifests itself as a loud public display of sexism and bravado. For a boy, to talk about sex in other ways, such as sharing a problem with other boys, seeking and giving advice, may risk being regarded as transgressive male behaviour. Blake's performance within the group as the lad who knows all about sex and says so receives social recognition from the other boys in the form of shared laughter; the display of sparse words and implied sexual knowledge/action, 'we already know it', is endorsed. In this exchange Blake, Andrew and James demonstrate how sexual knowledge becomes a burden to be assumed and works with a collective desire to suppress anxieties, doubts and areas of ignorance in pursuit of an imagined masculine ideal. The discussions

I conducted with girls and boys in school may suggest that sex–gender identities are played out within different cultures variously defined as 'masculine' or 'feminine' (see Thorne 1993).[5] My argument, however, is not for the establishment and maintenance of different cultures of femininity and masculinity in school. Rather, it is that cultural products have the power to tap into social and psychic investments producing gender differentiated displays, repetitions and practices. Here, it is the meanings and associations given to teen magazines by groups of boys and girls that produce *gender displays* resonant with 'doing' gender as, simultaneously, an imaginary ideal and an everyday practice. In the examples cited, acts of readership offer a sphere for the enactment of sex–gender identities that are mediated and regulated collectively by *people-like-us*. In such moments teen magazines can be embraced or repelled, believed or doubted, discussed or censored, incorporated or othered.

Concluding comments

This chapter has focused on the ways in which teen magazines provide a site for learning in relation to issues of sexuality. Ethnographic material cited here suggests that young people in school use popular cultural forms as a resource and framework to facilitate discussion, thought and action within the sexual domain. Young women, in particular, enjoy teen magazines and view them as cultural markers in an externally constructed developmental process demarcated by age and gender. For young women, collective reading of teen magazines offers an opportunity for dialogue through which femininities can be endlessly produced, defined and enhanced. The responses of young men, however, indicate that readership of teen magazines takes on a different gendered significance whereby boys express a reluctance to engage in regular readership or acts of collective readership and view such practices as emasculating. Hood-Williams' (1997) study of comics for pre-teen boys and girls suggests that comics aimed at boys such as *Beano* prepare them for readership of the tabloid press. Hood-Williams' textual analysis of comics makes a connection between the pranks found in boys' comics and forms of sociality reported in the *Sun* newspaper. Drawing upon Lacan (1977a), Hood-Williams theorises that the transition from comics to the tabloid press indicates that boys' readership practices represent a shift from symbolic resistance to the Law of the Father to one in which the Law of the Father is symbolically occupied. My analysis of teenage magazines discussed in this chapter does not suggest a close relationship between textual forms and teenage boys. This leads me to consider other ways in which young men in school may be styling their masculine identities.

The relationship between reading practices and gender difference indicates that acts of readership offer a sphere for producing and conveying sex–gender identities in school. Here, peer group relations play a part in the mediation and regulation of reading practices, where embracing magazines and repelling them can be viewed as a *gender display* intended to purvey a particular masculinity or femininity. The processes involved in the production and consolidation of school-based masculinities and femininities suggest that cultural products have the power to tap into social and psychic investments, producing gender differentiated enactments, repetitions and practices. Here, it is the meanings and associations ascribed to magazines by groups of boys and girls which produce public demonstrations of doing gender. The performative expression of these displays suggest that gendered identities operate, simultaneously, as imagined ideal and everyday practice in the lives of young women and men in school (see Walkerdine (1987) and Butler (1990) for further discussion of the ways in which gender can be seen as 'performance').

The sexual content of contemporary teen magazines can be seen as part of a 'contractual understanding' (Barker 1989) between the magazine and its readership whereby readers expect to be informed and entertained by sexual issues. In acts of collective readership, young people in school negotiate and regulate sexual discourse in ways that affirm their gender identities. In such moments sexual issues can be discussed or censored, laughed with or laughed at, incorporated or othered. The energy and agency of young people in relation to issues of sexuality suggests that the protective discourse and moralising agenda mobilised by Peter Luff MP, may appear insignificant and superfluous to the lives of many school students. Features in *More!* magazine such as 'Sex-talk' and 'real life dramas' illustrate some of the ways in which teen magazines work within the boundaries of normative discourse where prejudice and stereotyping pertaining to same-sex partnerships remain unchallenged while heterosexuality is presumed (Epstein and Johnson 1994) organised and acclaimed in pictures and text. The discourse of sexual liberation appropriated by the 'Sextalk' feature works within clearly defined, dominant sexual categories and does not extend beyond straight sex. This has implications for the use of teen magazines as resources for sexual learning, particularly in relation to sex education programmes, where different strategies may be needed to discuss certain issues and to encourage the participation of young males.

The following chapter takes up the issues of masculinities raised in this chapter. While it is clear from this chapter that young women are shaping their feminine identities in the context of the peer group and popular culture, the ways in which young men in school shape and define masculine identities is not so apparent. Chapter 6 is based upon my discussions with young men in school and aims to explore issues of masculinities as expressed by the young men I spoke with.

Understanding masculinities: young men, heterosexuality and embodiment

This chapter builds upon themes introduced in the previous chapter and explores further the relationship between heterosexuality and masculinities in educational establishments. The focus of this chapter is upon the ways in which young men in school constitute and consolidate heterosexual masculine identities. The chapter draws upon interviews with young men in an all-boys secondary school (see Introduction for details of the school and its location), many of which were conducted as group discussions. The material drawn upon in this chapter is based upon one such discussion where the ethnicity of the boys involved was mainly African Caribbean and mixed parentage; two of the boys were white British and there was one male of south Asian descent. This chapter is concerned with developing ways of understanding masculinities and suggests that school processes produce sites for the enactment of heterosexual masculinities. Furthermore, I argue that these enactments demonstrate both the normative power of hetero-sexuality and the fragility of sex–gender categories. In the lives of young men in school, heterosexuality is understood as a *practice* involving a set of social performances in relation to young women and other males. Among the young men I spoke with there was little understanding of heterosexuality as an institutional arrange-ment for the support and maintenance of a particular sex–gender order. Rather, heterosexual relations were viewed as a way of demonstrating a particular masculinity that could be utilised to command respect and confer status on some males while devaluing others. One theme of the chapter is an exploration of issues of embodiment as expressed by the young men. In these exchanges there is an emphasis on the physicality of the body, often articu-lated in terms of activity and performance, where the physical sense of maleness is constantly recuperated as 'doing' hetero-sexuality. The following section considers ways of conceptualising issues of embodiment from the perspective of different theorists in this field. In particular the work of Foucault, Guillaumin and Connell is discussed to provide an analytic framework for the empirical material that follows.

Theorising the body

As discussed in Chapter 3, the idea that the body is an important site for the exercise of power is located within a Foucaultian framework where the rise of capitalism can be seen to create a new domain of political life, referred to by Foucault as 'bio-power' (1976: 140). Here power is conceptualised as de-centralised and productive of social relations in commonplace encounters and exchanges. From this perspective the politics of the body plays an important part in disciplining individual bodies and regulating collective bodies such as populations or specific social groups. For Foucault the body is discursively constructed, realised in the play of power relations and specifically targeted in the domain of the sexual. Foucault sees sex as a political issue, crucial to the emergence and deployment of bio-power:

> It [sex] was at the pivot of the two axes along which developed the entire political technology of life. On the one hand it was tied to the disciplines of the body: the harnessing, intensifica-tion and distribution of forces, the adjustment and economy of energies. On the other hand, it was applied to the regula-tion of populations, through all the far-reaching effects of its activity.
>
> (Foucault 1976: 145)

In Foucaultian theory, disciplining the body at the level of the individual has a historical trajectory that can be traced to the Christian pastoral tradition of the seventeenth century. Christian spirituality encouraged individuals to speak their desires in order to control them. The transformation of desire in religious discourse was an attempt to purify the mind and the body by expelling worldly desire and turning the subject back to God. This spiritual experience produced for individuals 'a physical effect of feeling in one's body the pangs of temptation and the love that resists it' (1976: 23). Foucault points to the links with the sexual libertine literature of the nineteenth century such as *My Secret Garden* and the writings of de Sade where sexual activities and erotic attachments are described and documented in episodic detail. One way of understanding this 'tell all' experience is to view it in terms of internal relations or psychic structures whereby the Other is produced within the Self. From a psychoanalytic perspective this has the effect of heightening desire by producing the 'forbidden' and, simultaneously, heightening anxiety in the constant struggle to expel the Other from within. It is possible to view the homophobia of young men in school as part of this dynamic. Similarly, the desire/repulsion expressed by girls in relation to sexual activity can also be seen as an internal dynamic, variously played out in social arenas (see Chapter 5). In these examples the desire for/fear of relationship is enacted within the peer group and plays a part in the structuring of heterosexual hierarchies in school (Kehily and Nayak 1997). In peer group interactions, individuals are active in the control and regulation of their own bodies within a broader context of institutional control and regulation.

Contemporary social theory on issues of embodiment suggest that the body is the site upon which social categories and political principles can be played out (Bourdieu 1986; Frank 1991; Turner 1991). Turner (1991) suggests that social changes such as the growth of consumer culture, the development of postmodern themes and the feminist movement have brought the body into prominence in contemporary analyses. Postmodern perspectives suggest that the new-found emphasis on issues of embodiment represents a challenge to the Enlightenment tradition in Western thought that privileges the intellect over the body. Other theorists, however, appear keen to hold onto the materiality of the body and to assert its place in class–gender systems. In Bourdieu's (1986) analysis, the body remains central to contemporary ways of conceptualising the relationship between social class and aesthetic taste as 'the most indisputable materialisation of class taste' (1986: 190). Colette Guillaumin's (1993) study adopts a materialist analysis in relation to issues of gender and embodiment. Her analysis suggests that 'the body is the prime indicator of sex' (1993: 40) where external reproductive organs are ascribed a set of material and symbolic meanings elaborated in the construction of sexual difference. This separation of the sexes at the level of the body is duplicated by a material social relationship involving the socio-sexual division of labour and the distribution of power. Guillaumin indicates that the sexing of the body in society is a long-term project involving work at different levels: physical and mental labour; direct and indirect interventions; the exercise of gender-specific social practices and competences. Bodies are constructed in societal contexts where ways of being *in/with your body* have material effects:

> Restricting one's body or extending it and amplifying it are acts of rapport with the world, a felt vision of things.
> (Guillaumin 1993: 47)

For Guillaumin, the materiality of the body plays a part in the production of gender inequalities that can be seen in the different ways in which boys and girls play, use space and engage in bodily contact. Central to the construction of the sexed body is, in Guillaumin's terms the 'body-for-others', ways of relating to others in terms of physical proximity, which is learned by both sexes but experienced differently. Bodily contact among males in combat and play introduces notions of solidarity, co-operation and control of public space. However, for girls the *body-for-others* is constructed in the private domestic sphere where the female body is both closed in on itself and freely accessible. From this perspective the materiality of the body is constitutive and productive of gender inequalities in ways that are learned, experienced and lived.

Bob Connell's (1995) study of masculinities is also concerned with the ways in which gender can be understood and interpreted in relation to the body. He suggests that the physicality of the body remains central to the cultural interpretation and experience of gender. In Connell's analysis, as in Guillaumin's, the materiality of the body is important to individuals and to societal arrangements more generally and can be seen to make a difference to the ways in which gender is learned and lived. For Connell, masculinity can be defined within a system of gender relations as,

> simultaneously a place in gender relations, the practices through which men and women engage that place in gender, and the effects of these practices in bodily experience, personality and culture.
> (Connell 1995: 71)

Furthermore, Connell indicates that there is a need to assert the *agency* of bodies in social processes (1995: 60) in order to understand gender politics as an embodied social politics. Connell uses the term 'body-reflexive practice' to suggest the ways in which bodies can be seen to be located within a complex circuit as both objects and agents of social practice. In this model the body is located within a particular social order where bodily experience is productive of social relations (and socially structured bodily fantasy) which in turn can produce new bodily interactions (1995: 61–2). 'Body-reflexive practice' captures the dynamic interplay of bodily interactions working within societal and institutional constraints and also the sense of agency that suggests that experiences at the level of the body offer possibilities for transgression and change.

Bodies in school: institutions and the embodiment of masculinities

Foucault (1976) points to the ways in which schools of the eighteenth century were structured and organised to take into account the sexuality of children:

> The internal discourse of the institution – the one it employed to address itself, and which circulated among those that made it function – was largely based on the assumption that this sexuality existed, that it was precocious, active and ever present.
>
> (Foucault 1976: 27)

In particular, the sex of schoolboys, Foucault indicates, is constructed as a public problem in and through discursive strategies that encourage the deployment of a range of medical and educational interventions for the control of adolescent boys. In contemporary schooling pupils become the object of disciplinary regimes which aim to control and regulate the (sexed) body as well as the mind. Rules govern the physical use of spaces where pupils move – in classrooms, playground and corridors. These spaces, in their architectural design and layout, also prescribe, to some extent, the type of movement that is possible and desirable (see Gordon *et al.* (2000) for a full discussion of these themes). For example, the subject of 'classroom management' taught on teacher training courses suggests to student teachers that the learning environment can be shaped in particular ways by the strategic placing of tables, chairs and classroom equipment. Bodies in school can be seen in two ways; collectively as a student body, to be controlled and moved about with ease; secondly as individual bodies to be, simultaneously, trained and protected. The latter can involve complex social formations which link institutional processes with everyday practice and bodily styles. Drawing upon Bourdieu's notion of cultural capital, Shilling (1993) suggests that bodies in school are engaged in the production of 'physical capital', a form of bodily management through which individuals can exercise agency and intervene in social affairs. Sexuality, as Foucault points out, can be seen as a key feature that structures the ways in which bodies in school are organised and related to.

In secondary schools, through the social processes of schooling, there is an associative link made between the body and sexuality or, to put it another way, the body is seen as a conveyor of sex, and sexuality is seen as an embodied manifestation of the body/sex couplet. The body that emerges in relations of schooling is predominantly heterosexual. Connell (1995) uses the concept of 'hegemonic masculinities' to discuss the relationship between different kinds of masculinity and the ways in which issues of sexuality and embodiment feature in these accounts. Within the framework of hegemonic masculinities there are specific relations of dominance and subordination played out between groups of men. In these interactions heterosexuality assumes a dominant status, while homosexuality acquires a subordinate position in the sex–gender hierarchy. This chapter is concerned to explore the ways in which heterosexuality is constituted and consolidated by young men in school. The ethnographic material discussed in this chapter suggests that heterosexuality is constituted in the everyday practices of young men in school. Within the educational institution these practices have the effect of consolidating and validating a particular masculinity.

Constituting heterosexuality: sex-talk, masturbation and pornography

As pointed out above, the interactions between young men in school indicate that heterosexuality can be seen as a *practice* involving a set of social performances in relation to young women and other males. Heterosexual relations were viewed by these young men as 'natural' and as a way of demonstrating a particular masculinity that could be exercised to establish a position of privilege within the male peer group. A central theme in the demonstration of an esteemed masculinity is the notion of 'knowing it already' in matters of sexuality. In conversations with young men, I asked them how they learned about sex and was frequently met with responses such as, 'I already know about it . . . I taught myself' (Justin), 'We already know it, I do anyway' (Blake). In these exchanges certain young men seemed keen to assert, to me and the other boys in the group, that sexual knowledge was located in the self. In these declarations Justin and Blake suggest that achieving knowledge and 'knowing' in the domain of the sexual can be acquired through self-activity. Justin elaborated on his sexual learning in the following terms:

Justin: Well, my Dad, he's hinted at things, he has, yeah. He told me about, well, he never gave me much explanation like, just hints, but they came together, all things, by watching videos, magazines, listening to friends, older brother and just getting to know for myself, you know.

Here, Justin indicates that 'knowing it already' involves the active and protracted process of making sense of multiple sources. Sexual knowledge, far from being easily assumed and embodied within the masculine sense of self, is in fact learned in the piece-meal way described by young women (see Thomson and Scott 1991). However, within the male peer group, the demonstration of competence and fear of ignorance become familiar tropes in the articulation of a masculinity that is sexually knowing and heterosexually active.

In the male peer group heterosexual activity is valorised and frequently spoken about in terms of conquest and prestige (Wood 1984). As Christian, a boy in my study put it, 'All boys claim to be doing it with girls – everyone in the school'. However, while males in school may engage in the sexual boast there is evidence to suggest that the performance is not always believed:

Christian: I listen to what they say but you can't take it seriously, you can't always believe them 'cos they might just be saying that for their mates, to look strong or to make them look bigger.

Here the physical quality of looking 'strong' and 'big' in front of your mates can be seen as a symbolic attempt to display an exaggerated and inflated masculinity, capable of achieving status in the male peer group. Young men reported speaking about sex with each other by recounting details of sexual encounters with girls in terms such as, 'I did this with her last night, then I did that'. Such interactions indicate the need to maintain a masculine style premised on activity and performance. In these moments the collective structure of the male peer group offers a performative space where heterosexuality and masculinity can be fused, enacted and displayed. This space can also be seen to provide a forum for a form of secular confessional where young men disclose details of their sexual encounters with girls. Transforming desire into discourse, in this context, is turned into a *gender-specific boast* that seeks recognition rather than repentance. As other researchers have documented, sex-talk between males serves many purposes and can be seen to have a range of regulatory effects: policing the boundaries of gender-appropriate behaviour for young men and young women; providing an imaginary ideal of desirable masculinity; bolstering the reputation of particular males; concealing vulnerabilities and producing heterosexual hierarchies (Lees 1993; Wood 1984; Haywood 1996; Kehily and Nayak 1997).

The following discussion with a group of young men offers further insights into the workings of male peer groups and the links made between masculinity and heterosexual activity. In the context of a conversation in which the young men are talking about heterosexual activity as routine I ask:

MJK: So, is it uncool to be a virgin?

Christian: Nah, I wouldn't say that . . .

Justin: It depends, when you're younger, no, but when you get to Year 11 man.

Christian: But with your friends, if you tell your friends you haven't had sex, my friends anyway, they wouldn't like act up on you, I mean, they try to encourage you to have sex, but –

Justin: My friends would be going [*in low voice*] go on then, go on now then, get there now, have sex, go on then.

Christian:	Nah, that's no good.
Justin:	What's no good?
Justin:	It's nothing to be scared of.
Matthew:	But who wouldn't want to do it?
Christian:	No man, there's a difference man, there's a difference between wanting to do it and people telling you to do it. Even if you want to do it from the start man, but when people start telling you to do it, it makes you like, you want to give them a challenge, makes you want to say no.

In this discussion the young men indicate that the links between masculinities and heterosexual activity are negotiated within friendship groups. Sex with girls is presented as a general aim to be desired and expected, an eroticised 'getting there' for *all* boys. This notion of 'getting there' plays into the idea of females as territory to be conquered/penetrated, a theme which is elaborated upon below. However, the reflections of Justin and Christian suggest that heterosexual activity is differently appraised. While Justin's friends would urge 'doing it' as a display of hyper-heterosexuality, Christian's friends would offer encouragement without 'acting up on you'. Christian's comments suggest that other modes of behaviour such as acting autonomously and posing a challenge may also be incorporated into the masculine repertoire and may exist as a counterpoint to heterosexual pursuit. In such a *discursive manoeuvre* Christian is able to resist pressure to engage in heterosexual activity, while still presenting a masculine sense of self that serves to maintain his reputation in the peer group. In discussions with young men it is possible to see the male peer group as significant in negotiating meanings attached to sexual activity, where versions of heterosexuality and masculinity are produced locally. In these interactions heterosexuality is invoked as a practice; an endeavour where the 'doing' is valorised by particular styles of sex-talk. Christian counters the pressure of the male peer group by drawing upon a kind of 'outlaw' theme; the assertive male who will not be railroaded into doing what he's not ready for. This implies, of course, that he is still capable of doing it but is too much of a man to be pushed around by other men. The discourse of challenge within the masculine repertoire, therefore, gives Christian a resource that he can utilise to present an *ultra*-masculine sense of self.

So far the discussions with young men have focused on the practice of heterosexuality in sex-talk where girls become the object of desire and the subject of a contextually constructed male sex-drive. Further discussions with young men, however, suggest that heterosexuality may be constituted in other practices *before* girls are known and spoken about. In the absence of girls, in relationships or in discourse, young men may fantasise about having sex, imagining what it will be like and how they will feel. This fantasy space is usually accompanied by bodily practices such as masturbation. Peter Willmott's (1966) study of adolescent boys in East London reports that masturbation was 'common, if not universal' (1966: 54) among males between the ages of 12 and 14. His study indicates that masturbation was spoken about in terms of 'discovery' or initiation into the domain of the sexual. One of Willmott's respondents spoke of masturbation in the following terms, 'I started at 14. When I first discovered it I went really mad over it. Then after a while it turned me off a bit' (1966: 54). Connell's (1995) study also suggests that masturbation plays a part in sexual learning for young males. One of Connell's respondents spoke of enjoying masturbation 'too much'; the intensity of pleasure was such that he felt compelled to stop for fear that it would prevent him from enjoying sex with a woman (1995: 104). Through masturbation young men learn about and experience sexual pleasure, however, as Connell points out, they must then discipline their bodies to be heterosexual, where desire is specifically associated with heterosex rather that with auto-eroticism or homo-eroticism.

In the conversations I conducted with young men in school, the acknowledgement that masturbation was a common practice met with routine acceptance and denial.

Christian: People have told me you go through a phase where you start, like, wanking yourself off, stuff like that. I don't think it's true because I ain't gone through that phase yet and I don't think I'm gonna.

Matthew: You don't know though.

Adam: You don't know that.

MJK: But don't you think that's one of the ways boys learn about sex?

All: [chorusing] Yeah, yeah.

	Yeah man.
	Admit it man.
MJK:	You know, through finding sources that make them feel excited and –
Christian:	Like the computer or something. [laughs]
Matthew:	Like my mate right, he's always on the computer saying, 'Look at this' right and he gets mad excited over his computer.
Adam:	The internet.
Justin:	Consolation, that's all it is, cut all that man, how people get like – obviously they don't care about sex. I know this boy who loves porno, guy's mad about, magazines everywhere, videos. He was telling me to watch one and I says, 'No, man, I ain't watching that *dirtiness*', getting excited for no reason, it ain't worth it.

In this exchange the young men agree that masturbation forms part of their sexual learning. Furthermore, they make a link between the bodily practice of masturbating and cultural resources such as pornographic magazines, videos and internet pages. Justin appears keen to evaluate such forms of excitement for young men as dirty, worthless and second-rate. His comments draw a distinction between the 'real thing', intercourse with a woman, and any simulations of it through pornography-fuelled fantasy. Justin's dominance in this discussion indicates that some boys may feel a need to recuperate sex as heterosexual and penetrative, a move that can reclaim heterosexuality as part of a masculine identity. Rachel Thomson's (1997) analysis of young men's accounts of pornography postulates that encounters with pornographic material is 'one of the ways in which young men are brought into identification with a collective masculinity' (1997: 2). In recounting their engagement with pornographic material, Thomson documents the ways in which individual young men attempt to evade agency by asserting that the magazine/video was obtained or initiated by a friend or a group of mates, or something they just happen to stumble across. Significantly, both Justin and Matthew claim to have a mate who is into porn, while placing their own interests in and access to such material at a distance.

Thomson suggests that for young men, 'there is something potentially disempowering or emasculating about porn' (1997: 10) as it involves the practice of seeking sex without being desired. Justin's insistence that pornography is 'consolation', a poor substitute for sex with a woman, can be seen as a vindication of Thomson's point. Negotiations with pornography can be viewed as a way of policing the boundaries of acceptable masculinity where sexual pleasure is evaluated in hegemonic terms as male–female intercourse. The recourse to such a hegemonic structure can be seen to have disciplinary effects in the dynamics of masculine hierarchies.

Christian: I've never bought one, I've found one before, I've had a look, yeah, but that's all, I've never bought one.
            [background jokes about Christian and porn]
Justin: This friend of mine, right, he's got loads (of porn magazines) and I've looked at them, nasty man, horrible. All them pictures man. I say put them away, they don't teach you nothing. He might get excited, but me, not exciting or nothing. People who do that, man, they're sad.
Christian: They're sad, very sad.
MJK: (to Justin) And does he [your friend] have a girlfriend?
Justin: Yeah, he's got a girlfriend, got a nice little woman. I wish I'd seen her, I'd have liked her for myself. But them videos an' stuff are nasty, man, they should ban them videos.
Christian: Some people enjoy them though.
Justin: Yeah, but if a man watches them and they get all excited and then they turn it off and they can't get no ladies, that's why they rape.
Christian: Can't get no ladies that's why men rape.

This discussion between Justin and Christian illustrates some of the ways in which young men negotiate and evaluate masculinities in relation to issues of sexuality. Investments in pornography are viewed as a bad thing. While it is barely acceptable to engage with pornographic material, it is totally unacceptable to buy it for oneself. In Justin's terms, coveting your friend's girlfriend is acceptable; sharing his sexually stimulating literature isn't. Men who use porn are defined as 'sad' and having an attractive girlfriend, it seems, does nothing to redeem them. Justin and Christian mobilise a moral discourse to underline their view that porn is bad and *dangerous*. They suggest that there is a causal relationship between pornography and rape. Men who use porn need women as an outlet for their sexual urges and if they can't get a woman they rape. Furthermore, the young men indicate that this moralism works in tandem with the male sex drive discourse identified by Hollway (1989) which postulates that once the male urge for sex has been set in motion the sexual act must be completed. In male peer groups young men shape the parameters of acceptable and unacceptable sexual practice. Through such interactions young men implicitly produce definitions of desire and deviance that can be utilised as a technique for displaying certain versions of masculinity and deriding others.

Consolidating heterosexuality: relationships with women

Through engagements with sex-talk, masturbation and pornography, young men *constitute* a version of heterosexuality that is associated with a desirable masculinity. This heterosexual–masculine combination is negotiated collectively by young men in peer group interactions and may be reconfigured in different ways. Further discussions with this group of young men suggest that it is in relationships with women that heterosexuality is actively learned and *consolidated*. In the following discussion they were critical of the sex education they had received at school and claimed that they learned through experience:

MJK:	Would you have liked to have had a proper sex education?
Justin:	Not now, it don't make no difference to me.
MJK:	Why's that?
Justin:	Umm, because, I taught myself.
MJK:	So how did you teach yourself?
	[muted laughter]
Justin:	By getting a girlfriend.
Christian:	And you explore her.
	[mumbling from boys in the group]

Justin: Yeah, explore her and talk to her and learn about each other and you find out about each other, you teach yourself. I can hear people, I dunno man, I think they need a couple of lessons, think they need a couple of lessons.

Justin indicates that 'getting a girlfriend' makes sexual learning possible. Learning from girls in the context of heterosexual relations gives young men access to knowledge that is highly prized and based on a 'doing' that enhances masculine identities. Talking to girls and having sex with them consolidates a privileged version of heterosexual masculinity. Here, females are spoken about in terms of landscape; as strange uncharted territory that can be 'explored' and known. Seeking relationships with women in these terms turns sexual learning into a form of territorial conquest that can be incorporated into the masculine repertoire. In this configuration, sexual knowledge is acquired through 'doing' and 'doing' gives young men status that makes them *feel* powerful. This sense of male power and agency in the domain of the sexual has been conceptualised from a feminist perspective as the power to control women. In this context, however, while controlling women may be implicit, Justin uses power/knowledge as a way of controlling other young men. His response to the undercurrent of boys' whispers and laughter implies that experience gained through sexual relationships with women gives young men confidence in the male peer group and the ability to put down others.

This consolidation of heterosexual masculinities can be seen in Connell's terms as 'body-reflexive practice'; a circuit through which lived experience interacts with societal structures. The recognition accorded to masculine heterosexual activity may imply that there is a comfortable relationship between dominant masculinities and male bodily experience. Young men in school occupy physical space with ease and vie for symbolic space in competitive displays aimed at 'looking big' (see Gordon *et al.* 1996 and Gordon *et al.* 2000 for a further discussion of gender and 'space' in schools). However, as Connell points out, 'body-reflexive practice' is not necessarily coherent and may involve contradictions (1995: 61). Many of the young men I spoke with expressed ambivalence in relation to bodily experience, often characterised by expressions of disgust and abjection.

Justin:	I like my girl to give me blow jobs, from where I am right, and if I'm tired, very satisfying.
Christian:	Yeah but you wouldn't want to go with a girl after, you wouldn't want to kiss her –
Justin:	Too right! If a girl gave me a blow job there ain't **no way** her lips are going near my lips, **no way, no way**.
MJK:	You seem to find men's bodies disgusting.
Adam:	D'you know, they are really.
Justin:	Yeah man, if you touch a woman, like, you stroke her legs like [*demonstrating*] it's all smooth, she's got curves, she feel good, but men – all hairy and smelly.
Christian:	Men are nasty man! They like this (demonstrating) all square and ugh! Women are nice and rounded and [*nuzzles his nose*] you know.
Justin:	Umm, yeah, they got big bums.

In this discussion the idealisation of women's bodies is juxta-posed with the physical repugnance expressed towards male bodies. While women are constructed as 'smooth', 'rounded' and 'nice', men become 'hairy', 'smelly' and 'nasty'. The demarcation of difference in gendered bodies, activated through the senses, indicates some of the ways in which young men negotiate a path between Self and Other. In bodily encounters with young women, males create a binary that exists, literally, at the level of the skin through sight, touch and smell. Women's bodies are fetishised as comfortably curvaceous and whole; a nose-twitchingly 'nice' place to nestle. Establishing heterosexual masculinity through bodily difference can be understood as a social dynamic in which school-based peer group cultures interplay with already existing psychic dynamics (Redman 1998). In psychoanalytic terms, the fetish-isation of women's bodies by young males can be variously inter-preted as: producing masculinity through the Other of femininity; a 're-finding' of infant pleasures in maternal acts such as breast-feeding (Freud 1977); a search for recognition of phallic possession through the Other who 'lacks' the phallus (Lacan 1977).

The description of male bodies as 'smelly' and 'nasty' suggests that the invocation of olfactory experiences and metaphors is one of the ways in which young people register disgust. Anthony Synnott's (1993) study of the body in society points to the ways in which odour constructs reality and mediates social interaction:

Odour contributes not only to the moral construction of the self but also to the moral construction of the *group*. Smell is not simply an individual emission and a moral statement, it is also a social attribute, real or imagined.

(Synnott 1993: 194, italics as original)

For these young men, smelly male bodies become the object of strong rejection as well as the subject of abject preoccupation (Bubandt 1998). Male bodies are so physically disgusting that the pleasure of oral sex also carries the fear of contamination. Justin and Christian agree that after oral sex kissing must be prohibited for fear of contagion. Stevi Jackson (1982) has commented on the ways in which kissing in Western cultures assumes symbolic significance as a marker of sexual attraction and intimacy, frequently used to define boundaries in sexual encounter. In the folklore associated with prostitution, and reproduced in the movie *Pretty Woman* (dir. Garry Marshall, 1990) kissing is excluded from the sexual repertoire of prostitute–client encounters and viewed as a sign of intimacy that is 'real' and cannot be manufactured, marketed or faked. In refusing to be kissed after oral sex, young men can be seen to deny sexual intimacy while engaging in it. To explore this dynamic further I draw upon the work of Julia Kristeva and particularly her insights developed in relation to the notion of 'abjection'.

Kristeva (1982) defines the concept of 'abjection' as the process through which one expels part of one's own self as a condition for the formation of the human subject. Kristeva suggests that the infant's experiences of its body and that of its mother, often infused with bodily fluids of blood and excrement, produce an irrational sense of disgust. During the castration complex this feeling of repulsion becomes linked with the feminine and can be expressed in the conscious world as discrimination and fear of marginal groups such as Jews in Nazi Germany. In Kristeva's (1982) analysis, abjection plays a part in constructing and maintaining a coherent identity; for the human subject to remain what it is, the 'abject' has to be 'expelled' from within the self as the unspeakable other. The return of the abject, Kristeva suggests, provides for a moment of rupture in the identity of the subject. Other theorists (Burgin 1990; Modleski 1991) have pointed to the links between Kristeva's treatment of abjection and Theweleit's

(1987) study of the fantasies of German soldiers of the Freikorps whose fear of engulfment by the feminine is expressed through images of the feminine as *liquid*. Applying these ideas to the comments of the young men I spoke with it is possible to suggest that through engaging in oral sex with women, young men attempt to consolidate an identity within a dominant framework of heterosexual masculinity. The bodily experience of having oral sex involves the expulsion of part of the masculine self in sweat and ejaculatory fluid. To maintain a sense of self as heterosexual, masculine and whole, young men endeavour to prevent the return of the rejected party through kissing. Young men's treatment of their bodies in terms of the abject suggests that becoming 'proper' men involves bodily experience that is simultaneously pleasurable and risky. 'Coming', in sexual terms, gives shape to a particular version of masculine selfhood but the very act also threatens to disrupt the identity it consolidates. The analysis of sex-talk provided here suggests that through active engagement in sexual practices and bodily experience young men negotiate a perilous course between Self and Other. The social and psychic dynamics involved in the enactment of heterosexual masculinities are marked by embodied struggles that promise both the pleasure of achievement and the threat of disturbance. In these terms heterosexual masculinity can be seen as a fragile identity; endlessly sought in moments of climax but never fully *consolidated*.

Another way of reading the young men's expressions of disgust and abjection is to see them as articulations of inner struggles which find expression in homophobic rituals and practices. From this perspective kissing after oral sex can be associated with fear of the (homosexual) Other within the Self. In a previous study (Nayak and Kehily 1996) we suggested that young men engage in a range of homophobic 'performances' as a technique for handling contradictions within the Self. The everyday expressions of homophobia in male peer group cultures can be understood as a central dynamic in the struggle to produce a heterosexual masculine identity. Through homophobic enactments, young men are involved in body styling forms through which a specific masculinity is defensively performed against femininity and homosexuality. These enactments serve as 'self-convincing rituals of masculinity' (Nayak and Kehily 1996: 225) which purvey the illusion of: expelling homoeroticism/homosexuality from the Self, displaying a coherent identity for self and others; consolidating heterosexual masculinities through action. If the practice of penetrative sex with women provides a template for a desirable masculinity it defines the acceptable repertoire of heterosex as well as defining and delimiting other sexual practices. The fusion of lips and penis in oral sex can be seen, from the perspective of the young men, to be at the margins of heterosexual sex and dangerously close to practices associated with gay sex. The fear of contamination in these terms can be interpreted as a fear of being put in touch with the homosexual 'other' and liking it. For oral sex to be made safe in this reading, the expulsion of aspects of the male body must be directed at women and *remain* there.

Masculinities and homophobias

In keeping with our earlier studies (Nayak and Kehily 1996; Kehily and Nayak 1997), I found homophobias to be a routine part of school life, particularly among male peer groups. Verbal abuse such as 'batty man', 'bum-chum' and 'poufter' combined with bodily styled expressions of fear and disgust such as making crucifixes and thrusting backs against the nearest wall were common, everyday activities. Young men I spoke with agreed that 'gay' and pejorative derivations were general terms of abuse which could be used for friends 'if they get on yer nerves' (Blake) and other boys who were regarded as different. Differences, in this sense, involved a diverse array of qualities and characteristics such as 'talking funny', 'walking funny', conforming to school rules and teacher expectations, being quiet, not liking sport or lacking sporting competence, wearing the wrong trainers/clothes, demonstrating abilities in/preference for arts subjects and, in one case, having blond hair. The fear of being called 'gay' in school acted as a powerful disciplinary technique for the regulation of male behaviour and embodied social practices (cf. Epstein 1997, 1998b). In the context of male peer group cultures, the inner fear of being gay and the outer fear of being called gay involved young men in performative displays of homophobia and exaggerated forms of masculinity. In these enactments, psychic struggles and collective investments become entwined in the production of masculine identities that seek individual coherence and social recognition.

The sensitivity, for individuals and groups, surrounding issues of homosexuality was apparent in many conversations I had with young men. Young men I spoke with agreed that homosexuality was 'unnatural' and, in the school located in the south east, the phrase 'God made Adam and Eve, not Adam and Steve' was much repeated. The normalising centrality of heterosexuality demarcated homosexuality as marginal and deviant; to be dealt with in terms of displacement through humour, denial and aggression. Discussion with a group of six young men produced the following response:

MJK: I was going to ask you, you know, what about gay sex?
All: I don't think we wanna get into that.
Oh no!
No man!
I gotta go home now.
[mass laughter]

The evasion through humour, jointly articulated by the group, is suggestive of an awareness that talking about gay sex could be potentially emasculating and risks tainting those who engage in such discussions. In another discussion young men were anxious to place homosexuality beyond the bounds of their immediate environment:

MJK: What if one of your mates told you that he was gay or he thought he might be gay?
Gareth: I'd be shocked.
Ian: I would too, I'd be really shocked.
Richard: Yeah.
MJK: Why?
Ian: Well of all my friends, I couldn't imagine any of them being gay, *in the slightest.*
Gareth: I wouldn't expect him to say that when you're fifteen, I'd be worried.
MJK: Worried?
Ian: I would, yeah, you wouldn't want to be left alone with them for too long
Chris: Especially if you're sleeping round at your mate's!
[all laugh]

Here young men indicate that having a gay friend is unimaginable and would produce feelings of 'shock' and 'worry' for them.

The shock-effect is diffused in a moment of humour that draws upon the stereotype of gay men as contagious and sexually voracious. In keeping with Mac an Ghaill (1994), I found homophobias to be articulated through class–cultural formations. On occasions, after the jokes, stereotypes and denials had been proclaimed, young men may proffer a more liberal, middle-class approach to homosexuality. This could be expressed in terms of freedom of choice, 'people have a right to do what they want, it's up to them' (Christian). Or alternatively, as an enlightened tolerance based on personal contact, 'My mum knows someone who's gay, he's a good friend' (Matthew). These discussions, however, were also peppered with homophobic comments, sometimes in the same breath:

Matthew: This one guy, he's a good friend and he would never try anything because he's gay. But still in my eyes, a gay man – keep your distance – *please*, keep your distance.

Some young men I spoke with expressed the view that gay men were 'confused' about their sexuality and may have turned to men as a consequence of their lack of success with women. This resonates with the popularly held notion that homosexuality is a 'phase', an adolescent sexual experiment that most boys *grow out of* in due course.

Attempting to discuss homosexuality in dispassionate ways involved young men in elaborate verbal contortions:

Gareth: I suppose it's different if you know the person before they tell you that they're gay.
Ian: Yeah.
Gareth: 'Cos it changes your view of them.
Ian: Yeah, if you're getting to know someone and, like, meet them somewhere and it comes up in the first conversation that they're gay or lesbian then you wouldn't like, be prejudiced to them as you would to someone you've known for ages and they've kept it from you.
Gareth: 'Cos you know what they're like, the kind of person they are.
Richard: It would change the way you think about them.

Ian: Yeah, whereas if you find out first of all you just know
           and you're always going to look at them in the same way
           'cos you know what they're like.

Here, young men are involved in collective negotiations to
determine the conditions under which it is acceptable to be gay or
lesbian. Knowing from the start appears to be viewed more
favourably than the closet strategy. The comments of the young
men indicate their need to conceptualise sexuality as a fixed and
determining component of identity. This points to the double-bind
encountered by gay and lesbian youth in social structures where
there is little space to develop sexual identities and the ever present
danger that coming out will 'change' the way others think about
you (Alyson 1980; Trenchard and Warren 1984). Young men who
identified as working class, non-conformist and were disaffected
by the school environment most frequently articulated vehemently
aggressive expressions of homophobia. Physical aggression and
threats of violence such as 'If anyone called me gay I'd punch
them' (Blake) and 'No-one calls me that and gets away with it –
he'd know about it that's all' were common responses to homophobic abuse. The link between homophobia and violence can be
seen in the following discussion of a television chat-show:

Christian: There was this thing in America about that
                         gay man who had a best friend. He came
                         on a talk show and he said, 'Oh I love you,
                         I loved you all down the years'.
Adam: He got killed.
Christian: And his mate turned round and shot him.
Justin: What?
Matthew: Yeah, this man, he had a best friend, he
                         came on a talk show, you know, *Ricki
                         Lake*, and that and he said to this other
                         guy 'I love you' and that, 'I really love you'
                         and all that and 'I wanna be with you' and
                         a couple of weeks later he shot him.
Justin: The man who wasn't gay shot the other
                         man?
Christian and Adam: Yeah, yeah.

| *Justin:* | Well done, congratulations! That's took a lot of pressure off your mother, trust me, love it. |
| | [laughter] |

This discussion of the *Ricki Lake* programme[1] is illustrative of a particularly dramatic style of homophobia where the oppressive dynamics are forged through severe acts of 'queer-bashing'. Justin's reaction to the incident and the ensuing laughter suggests that, for these young men, homosexuality can be most injurious when it involves your best friend. Homosocial bonds forged in male friendship must be stringently policed to guard against erotic attachment where transgressions seemingly justify extreme measures. The young men I spoke with illustrate the ways in which expressions of homophobias in school are widespread, diverse and nuanced by class–cultural configurations. Invariably homophobic expressions involve verbal pronouncements and bodily displays that are infused with fear and denial. Homosexuality is to be *most* feared and punished when it is close to home, in the immediate environment of the school, best friend or the Self. These displays can be seen as public acts, for self and others, in the endless struggle to produce a coherent heterosexual masculinity. For many of the young men who engage in these oppressive actions, homophobias provide a fantasy of masculinity that is sustained through repetition of embodied displays. The humour, denials and aggression can be understood as styles utilised by young men to fashion an identity that can never be fully achieved. The homophobic practices of young men reveal some of the psychic struggles and social dynamics that construct the masculine ideal as both compelling and flawed.

Young men and lesbianism

While issues of homophobia aroused highly charged emotions among young males, attitudes to lesbianism could be discussed in more considered ways. As Steven expressed it, 'I don't know why but I find it easier to accept girls being lesbian than blokes being gay, I don't know why.' The apparently inexplicable acceptability of lesbianism can be seen within the context of male peer group cultures and the ways in which sexuality is invoked. The following discussion, in which the young men I spoke with make it clear that homosexuality is 'not OK', I venture to ask them about lesbianism:

MJK:　　　　What about lesbianism, is that OK then?
All:　　　　I reckon it's OK.
　　　　　　Yeah, yeah, it's OK.
　　　　　　Give it to me!
　　　　　　Love it!
Deng:　　　No lesbians is not OK. Girls is OK.
Christian:　The thing is, it seems alright to us, yeah, because we're men ain't it?
Matthew:　But think about it, would you like your mother to be lesbian or your sister?
Justin:　　I wouldn't like that, not my mum, with my sister I feel like whatever makes her happy, at the end of the day I don't wanna upset my sister, I want her to be happy so if it makes her happy, she wants to be a lesbian, fair enough, it doesn't bother me whether she's gay or not.

While there is a pervasive climate of homophobia in male peer groups, the idea of girls-doing-sex can be seen as a fantasy space in the male psyche for sexual excitement and pleasure. Lesbianism as titillating novelty, voiced in phrases such as 'give it to me', 'love it' and 'because we're men' serve to enhance displays of heterosexual masculinity in the competitive sphere of the male peer group. The limited acceptability of lesbianism can be interpreted as an assimilation of lesbian sex as erotic turn-on which unlike male same-sex encounters, does not threaten to disrupt heterosexual masculine identities. As Skeggs (1997) points out lesbianism is, of course, commodified for men's pleasure in pornographic literature and tabloid newspapers such as *Sunday Sport*. In this respect the responses of the young men I spoke with may also be mediated by popular cultural texts. However, when the conversation moves from lesbianism in the abstract to the more specific discussion of lesbians as family members there is a perceptible shift in attitude. Deng reminds the group of the collectively held homophobic framework in his assertion that 'girls is OK' not lesbians and Matthew follows up the reference point with the challenge, 'would you like your mother to be lesbian or your sister?' Like your best friend coming out as gay, Justin indicates that a lesbian mother is undesirable and too close for comfort. Attitudes to lesbianism as articulated by the young men I spoke with can be seen as a more fluid form of homophobia that creates space for sexual stimulation while simultaneously regulating erotic attachments within the family.

Fear of engulfment – fear of female sexuality

In descriptions of sexual encounters with girls, as discussed earlier, young men tended to idealise female bodies and denigrate male bodies. I was interested in exploring the implications of this for gender relations. Does the idealisation of women's bodies suggest that girls are held in high esteem in intimate personal relationships or does it offer a counter indication that females are objectified in ways that may be sexually opportunistic and exploitative? Or, maybe, sexual relationships for young men involve a complex interplay of the exemplary and other more measured feelings? At certain moments young men discuss male–female relationships in terms of disdain and fear.

Justin: I was going out with this girl, man, and I was going out with her for *tooo long*, man, and my mum like her, she used to cook dinner for her and let her sleep the night and she used to take her shopping and everything. I didn't like it at all. I wanted to get out of there man [laughs].

MJK: How come you went off her?

Justin: I dunno, I just did, things must have changed. But my mum still likes her. She keep telling me phone her. I ain't gonna phone her.

In this discussion Justin asserts that some relationships can go on for 'too long'; beyond the point where heterosexual masculinities are enhanced and enriched. The line between feeling comfortable in a relationship and wanting to 'get out' of it is difficult to identify but can be linked to certain 'changes' in everyday social practice. The female friendship that evolved between his mother and his girlfriend and their engagement in commonplace routines of shopping and cooking led Justin to feel entrapped by the doubly defining sphere of domesticity and femininity. Justin's expressed wish, 'I wanted to get out of there man' is suggestive of his felt need to escape the claustrophobic, womb-like world of domestic femininity and simultaneously his fear of engulfment by this space (Theweleit 1987). In these moments relationships with young women involve some enactment with inner dramas of the masculine psyche.

At other moments young men I spoke with discussed female sexuality as moving beyond the domestic sphere to become rampant and insatiable,

Christian: I was watching this programme right, *The Girlie Show.*
Justin: I watch that.
Christian: And there was this thing 'bout some Chinese lady, she got gang-banged by about, she got gang-banged eleven hours by a hundred and twenty men.
Justin: I saw that.
Christian: Did you see that one?
Justin: She was loving it.
Christian: She was loving it. It was dead cool, well cool!
   (all laugh)
Christian: She was going, 'Oh it's alright to get gang-banged, oh it's perfectly alright'.
Matthew: It wasn't gang-banged. She was laying there in the studio and 'nough men were just like –
Justin: I bet if you were watching it.
Matthew: No it was –
Adam: It was for the world record weren't it? Setting the world record.
Christian: It was yeah. It was about a hundred and twenty men.
Justin: I wouldn't like to bun her, no way!
Christian: And she got all these men, all these big tugga fat men with all spots and it was like, one of them – why are there so many ugly men? Everyone else can have it good then, ain't it –

Channel 4's *The Girlie Show* forms part of a contemporary genre in television programming in the UK that became known as 'Yoof TV' in a parodic acknowledgement of Janet Street-Porter's pioneering style and south London accent. Aimed specifically at the 18–25 age group, programmes such as *Network 7*, *The Word*, *Don't Forget Your Toothbrush* and *TFI Friday* can be seen as examples of the genre, characterised by the formulaic blend of young presenters and chaotic camera work providing a hectic mix of interviews, live music and features. The development of the genre, from its early 1980's inception in *Network 7* to the late 1990's incarnation *Girlie Show*, placed increasing emphasis on features which encouraged displays of excess, outrage and ritualistic humiliation. A regular feature of *The Word* was the 'I'd do anything to get on the box' challenge, where self-nominated members of the public engaged in televised tasks such as eating excrement/vomit and covering themselves in leeches/maggots/spiders. Such televisual moments can be seen as a playful inversion of traditional game-shows, re-styled to fascinate and repel a young audience on their return from the pub/club. *The Girlie Show* continued the tradition of over-the-top, 'in yer face' features popularised by *The Word*, with the additional inflection of new feminine subjectivities. Amid the high profile of 'girl power',[2] *The Girlie Show* can be seen as a moment of media-propelled mockery and subversion in which gender relations are *played with* and *played up*, rather than transgressed.

The boys' comments on *The Girlie Show* indicate that they are viewing 'new-style' television programming within the framework of 'old-style' gender relations. Rather than seeing the feature as an ironic comment on femininities and sexuality, the young men interpret it in largely 'straight' terms. Details of the sexual feat are regarded, by the young men, as remarkable, worth recalling and embellished with reference to the woman's 'Chinese' appearance and the men's bodily girth. In the discussion young men work to establish the important points: not a gang-bang but a world record; how many men over how many hours and, finally, what they think about it. For a woman to have sex with a hundred and twenty men over eleven hours is both amazing, 'well cool!', and a sexual turn-off, 'I wouldn't like to bun her, no way!' Women who 'love' sex and make it clear that they love sex with different men are admired, but their sexual availability/activity turns them into the *kind of women* who become undesirable. Female sexuality in this form becomes an object of fascination, fear and repulsion. The recourse to traditional ways of evaluating women in terms of the sexual dichotomy of virgin/whore (Griffin 1982) suggests that the media-constructed combination of new feminine subjectivities and postmodern aesthetics have made little impact on the sex-talk of this male peer group.

Heterosexual activity and reputation

Among the young men I spoke with there was an awareness of differences between males and females which were played out in the domain of the sexual. These differences involved young men in the taking up of evaluative moral positions in relation to sexual attitudes, behaviour and reputation. The asymmetrical power relations inscribed in these practices were frequently regarded as routine and natural by young men in school:

Christian: In the whole world there's a difference between men and ladies. Men are always allowed to do more than ladies.

Ali: True, true.

Here, Christian suggests that the greater freedom enjoyed by men at the expense of women is a universal principle that cannot be disputed or changed. In these terms male privilege and female containment is assumed. The sexual appraisal of young women through notions of 'reputation' has been well documented (see Chapters 4 and 5). Through the use of regulatory categories such as 'slag'/'drag' (Cowie and Lees 1987) young men are active in defining and policing the sexual behaviour of young women while denying agency in claims of a gender-specific world order. In the following discussion young men speculate on the different approaches to sexual activity and reputation taken up by males and females:

Christian: You know miss, like, if you have sex and that, a boy will admit to it but a girl will never admit to something.

MJK: Umm, Why is that?

Christian: I dunno.

Justin: Some girls think sex is nasty.

Christian: You know the thing is, yeah, men can never be called slushers can they?

Justin: Why can't they be called slushers? I've been called a slusher.

Christian: But if a woman goes with two men she gets called it.

Justin: There's a difference between, right, a woman who loves sex and a woman who goes with every man. See a woman can love sex and have sex with one man a hundred times in a day and that woman's no slusher but if she has sex with a hundred men then she's a slusher. Think about it.

Christian: I know but a woman gets called a slusher if she goes off with a man and has sex after an hour, but if you think about it –

Justin: An hour's quite long!
(laughs)

Christian: I know, if you think about it, you're letting her have sex with you after an hour, there's no difference, d'you know what I'm saying?

Justin: I know what you're saying but I been called a slusher as well.

Christian: And what did you say 'bout that?

Justin: I'm quite happy. I'm quite proud of it.

In this exchange Justin and Christian consider the implications of sexual activity for males and females. The reluctance of young women to 'admit' to sexual encounters is noted by Christian and directly linked with notions of reputation, particularly the acquisition of the label 'slusher'. In the schools where I conducted research casual sex was viewed negatively as something to be avoided by males and females alike. I observed intra-gender conversations where boys' sexual behaviour was subject to evaluative endorsements in similar terms to girls, often using the same words and phrases. In both schools where I carried out fieldwork there were certain young men who had acquired a reputation among peers for sexual 'looseness'. The dispute between Justin and Christian over whether males can be called 'slusher' or not is illustrative of this tendency. However, whereas Justin is 'happy' and 'proud' to be called a 'slusher', I did not encounter any girls who were pleased to be associated with the term. This suggests that the notion of sexual reputation, though more generally applied, may still take on a potentially damaging quality for young women while remaining more fluid and potentially positive for young men (Holland *et al.* 1990b, 1998; see Bland 1995 and Mort 1987 for a historical treatment of these themes).

Justin makes a further, closely worked distinction in the use of the term 'slusher'; between 'a woman who loves sex and a woman who goes with every man'. Young women make a similar distinction between girls who are romantically involved and committed to a man and those who 'sleep around' (Griffin 1985; Lees 1986, 1993). This indicates that it is not sexual activity *in itself* that carries the stigma of indecent and inappropriate behaviour but the social context of the actions. 'Slusher', 'slag', 'slapper' and other such terms can be seen as socially ascribed categories, taking their cues from culturally coded approaches to gender and sexuality. However, as Christian astutely observes, the difference between personal sexual practices and those of so-called slushers may be negligible. This suggests that the continual negotiations of the male peer group are not only about regulating young women but also serve to create boundaries and distinctions *between* men. The competitive culture of male peer groups, seen in moments of humour and hostility, is played out in the domain of sexuality. In these encounters, individual fears and anxieties relating to female sexuality are interwoven with the need to perform and maintain status within the male peer group.

Masculinities and ethnicity

So far we have observed the ways in which sexuality provides a sphere for the negotiation and demonstration of heterosexual masculinities. In the everyday social interactions of male peer groups, young men *constitute* a desirable identity through embodied styles of sex-talk and homophobic display. Sexual activity with women and the subsequent male boast can be seen as an attempt to *consolidate* a particular version of heterosexual masculinity that seeks personal affirmation and social recognition. In male peer group encounters, young men negotiate and establish heterosexual hierarchies by defining themselves *as against* women, gays and other subordinate identities. Viewing the sex–gender hierarchy in terms of ethnicity suggests further ways in which relations of dominance and subordination can be produced. Ethnographic accounts point to the ways in which black males in school in the UK acquire a reputation for toughness, hyper-heterosexual posturing and resistance to the disciplining processes of schooling (Mac an Ghaill 1988; Sewell 1997). Mac an Ghaill's (1988) study identified a group of African-Caribbean males, the Rasta Heads, whose bodily style displayed a visible form of resistance to school routines and academic achievement which they associated with emasculating modes of femininity and homosexuality. Mac an Ghaill suggests that the high profile anti-school culture of the Rasta Heads should be read within the context of their class-cultural position as second generation migrants experiencing the effects of institutional racism and the collapse of the youth labour market. Sewell (1997) similarly identifies a group of African-Caribbean males, the Hedonists, characterised by their enjoyment of bodily pleasures and the rejection of mental labour. Sewell's discussion of the Hedonists indicates that from their perspective the process of schooling assaults, 'the thing that was most precious to them – their "manhood"' (1997: 122) by making them look small. The Hedonists' behaviour can be understood as a response to the ritual humiliation of schooling, couched in terms of exaggerated displays of phallocentrism. Sewell's comments echo Julien and Mercer's (1988) analysis of black masculinity as a response to oppression:

> Black men have incorporated a code of 'macho' behaviour in order to be able to recuperate some degree of power over the condition of powerlessness and dependency in relation to the white slave master.
>
> (Mercer and Julien 1988: 136)

The invocation of ethnicity and racial categories in discussions of sexuality can be seen as a way of creating further intra-gender distinctions within male peer group cultures. In the following discussion Ali, a Muslim male, is cross-examined about the sexual practices of Asians:

Christian: You can't have sex until you're married can you?
Ali: Why's that?
Christian: You, your religion, can't have sex can you?
Ali: If it's not allowed I wouldn't be here would I?
Christian: No, **before** you're married. D'you have to be married before you can have sex with her?
Ali: You can have sex with anyone, just like, it doesn't come into it what's allowed, whether you're supposed to or not, people do.
Matthew: But you get, like, arranged marriage?
Ali: No, some people do, it just depends.
Christian: If you think about it Ali yeah, just saying, you might not but just saying you had an arranged marriage,

yeah, how d'you feel, how d'you feel having sex with your new wife to be without knowing her.

Ali: I wouldn't do it.

Christian: You wouldn't do it at all?

Ali: I wouldn't marry her.

Christian: No, I'm just saying, what about if?

Ali: I just wouldn't alright.

Justin: Exactly, right, you wouldn't go through with it, it's just like she's been put there to make children right.

The interrogative style adopted to question Ali suggests that his masculinity is being appraised as well as his racial identity. Other researchers (Mac an Ghaill 1994; Nayak 1997; Sewell 1997) have commented on the ways in which Asian males are feminised as weak and ineffectual by other young males and placed in a subordinate relation to the perceived strength and dynamism ascribed to African Caribbean masculinity. In the exchange involving Ali, young men operate with an *already constructed* notion of Asian culture as Other, marked by restriction for men and oppression for women. The persistent questions concerning sex before marriage and arranged marriage indicate some of the ways in which received notions of difference can be projected onto ethnic subjects. The collectively held view that Asian males are deprived of agency in the sexual domain produces a style of questioning which positions Ali as 'victim' of strange sexual customs. For these young men the racial identity of 'Asian' is intimately bound up with the imposition of alien and unfathomable cultural practices. The race/culture couplet drawn upon in this encounter serves to ground racial stereotypes in fictions of Otherness that can be located and fixed within 'imagined communities' (Anderson 1983). For Christian, the most unfamiliar aspect of Asian culture becomes the projected encounter of finding yourself in bed on your wedding night, having sex with a woman you do not know. In other circumstances having sex with a woman you do not know is regarded as sexually enterprising, an achievement of masculine drive and endeavour referred to by young men as 'pulling power'. However, viewed through the lens of cultural Otherness, Asian masculinity is seen as sexually disempowering and, ultimately, emasculating.

At a later point in the discussion Ali attempts to explain that there is diversity and difference within Asian communities, reflected in marital practices. His comments are poorly received and frequently curtailed by others in the group in an exchange which further illustrates the links between sexuality and ethnicity:

Deng: Would you go out with an Indian?
               [. . . muted laughter]
Christian: I'm not being racist or nothing. Listen, listen, there's a reason why I wouldn't, the reason why I wouldn't is, yeah, 'cos mostly they're Muslim and first of all that couldn't really happen.
Justin: True, true.
Ali: How's that? My uncle got married to a Catholic girl.
Christian: But what I'm saying is yeah, you're trying to tell me that our aunt is white yeah, but if an English man wanted to marry your other aunt, right, would your family be having it, and he wasn't Muslim, would they be having it?
Ali: It depends, right, they wouldn't –
Christian: Exactly, exactly, see what I mean, if she was that nice.
Ali: But like there are some in our family and they're Kenyans right, you know they're Asians in Kenyan right, well, every person in the family was married to a white person or a black person and not a Muslim.
Christian: But I'm not talking 'bout that, what I'm saying is yeah, the reason why I wouldn't, if she was that nice and she wasn't allowed, she didn't have to wear that thing round her head and she didn't have to go to the mosque five times a day, then, yeah, I probably would.
Matthew: Is that how many times you have to go to the mosque?
Ali: No.
Christian: It is, it's five times a day.
Ali: The only time I go to the mosque is when –
Christian: [to Ali] Not you, not you man, properly, if you're a proper Muslim, proper like the leader of the mosque, five times a day.
Ali: Yeah the leader of the mosque.

In this discussion issues of 'race' are spoken through sexuality and couched in the leading question, 'Would you go out with an Indian?' Going out with someone involves acting upon sexual attraction that bespeaks desire for inter-personal intimacy that is both bodily and emotional. Who you would go out with, in these terms, says something about *you*; what kind of person you are and where you draw the line in matters of sexual desire and bodily boundaries. Christian is keen to point out that his reluctance to go out with an Indian girl is not racism but a form of cultural commonsense, based on notions of difference and compatibility. As Barker (1981) points out, this configuration can be seen as an example of 'new racism'; a contemporary style which elides charges of discrimination by placing emphasis on similarities/ differences between cultural groups. In this case the deployment of new racism involves a particularly repressive image of Islam and the practices of 'proper' Muslims. For Christian to go out with a Muslim girl she would have to dispense with all the signifying practices of Islamic culture: family restrictions, wearing a veil, going to the mosque. In the following discussion young men elaborate upon the subject of mixed relationships:

Deng:	Would it matter what nationality your wife would be when you're older?
Christian:	No why? United nations ain't it? [laughs]
Justin:	When you get home what d'you like? [laughter]
Deng:	No, Matthew, what d'you say about mixed relation-ships? Matthew though, serious now, what d'you think? I swear I ask you before and you said you don't encourage it.
Matthew:	No, that was Sulliman, that was Sulliman man.
Deng:	No, listen yeah, would you like to get married or have a relationship with your own kind as it was? D'you prefer, yeah, black girls or white girls Matthew?
Matthew:	Both.
Deng:	Nah, tell the truth.
Matthew:	Both man.
Justin:	He tell the truth, he say both ain't it.
Deng:	[to Christian] What about you?
Christian:	I like half caste girls.
Justin:	I don't mind, I'm half black and I'm half white so it don't matter to me.

In this discussion imaginary others are brought home in reflec-tions on sexual partners. The initial idea, posed by Christian and

Justin is of sexual relationships as a site of racial fusion, a 'united nations' melting pot where sexual desire is not constrained by ethnic boundaries ('When you get home what d'you like'). However, this is followed by verbal jousting that fragments the myth that anything goes. While the discourse of multiculturalism assumes that mixed relationships are fine, the commonsense culturalism drawn upon by the young men suggests otherwise. Deng's questioning of Matthew indicates that the notion of ethnic matching in sexual relationships is a powerful dynamic that deserves 'serious' consideration. The encounter is marked by the tension of two competing discourses which cannot be fully elaborated; a compelling mode of multiculturalism which endorses mixed relationships and the logic of cultural heritage which says have relationships with 'your own kind'. In such interactions issues of 'race' are articulated through sexuality and become a testing ground for racially located masculine identities.

In the following conversation the concept of sexual attraction is utilised to create *further* distinctions between males and females:

Justin: I know this Asian girl, she's **niceee**, I'd go out with her but I'm not into all that religion stuff . . . I'm not fussy, I'm not racist or prejudiced. Go out with a girl you like. Don't matter if she purple, green or pink.

Matthew: But would you go out with a girl who was homeless, or from a children's home?

Christian: There ain't nothing wrong with it.

Matthew: What about a girl from a football team? I'm not being funny but would you?

Christian: I would go out with a girl who's homeless but from the time yous lot knew about it, yeah, I'd never hear the end of it.

Matthew: But if you're going out with a girl who's homeless yeah, don't you think somehow she'd be going, 'Can I stay at your house tonight?'
[laughter]

In this discussion the focus shifts from sexuality and ethnicity to defining difference in other terms. In a further consideration of who you could/would go out with, young men negotiate boundaries for themself and others. Here the bounds of acceptability extend those of 'race' and ethnicity to include girls who may be too physical, too scruffy, new-age-y, linked to movements or life-styles outside of the mainstream. As in other moments, humour is used to regulate the real and imagined behaviour of young males. Frosh *et al.* (2002: 258) in their study of young masculinities in the UK point to 'the impossibility of understanding masculinities in isolation from other constituting features of boys' lives'. Their study concludes that masculinities are shaped by a complex network of identity factors including ethnicity, social class and sexuality. The young men in my study also demonstrate the many ways in which these identity factors are interrelated and can be drawn upon in the complex interweaving of ideas and categories.

Concluding comments

In this chapter I have attempted to point out the links between heterosexuality and masculinity in the lives of young men in school. My analysis suggests that these links, however, are not 'natural' and remain a troubling aspect of young men's talk and behaviour in the sphere of social and sexual practices. In the sex-talk of young men in school, heterosexuality and masculinity have to be naturalised through practices that incorporate them into a particular version of masculine identity. This version which is invoked in talk and reified in action, views heterosexuality as central to a masculine sense of self that is premised on 'doing' and dis-playing. Bringing heterosexuality and masculinity together in this way involved bodily practices and performances that have the effect of *constituting* a heterosexual masculine identity. The young men I spoke with suggest that heterosexuality and masculinity can be *consolidated* in bodily experience through sexual encounters with young women. Psychoanalytic insights, however, indicate that the consolidation of heterosexuality is ever partial and incom-plete, a fragile structure involving psychic and social dynamics. In this respect the concept of abjection provides a useful theory to understand the expulsion of elements of the Self onto the Other in relation to both homophobic fears and fears relating to engulf-ment by women. Finally, I want to pose, once again, the Labov (1972) question which asks, 'So what?' in order to evaluate both whether a tale is worth telling and the performance of the teller. Why is it important to document the links between heterosexuality and masculinity? What do they tell us? My tentative conclusions at this point indicate that there may be a need for young men to shore up a dominant heterosexual masculinity beyond potentially emasculating experiences such as not knowing, incompetence, not being wanted/desired, name-calling, losing, and exposure to engulfment in the form of domestic femininity or sexually voracious women.

So far this study has been concerned to explore issues of gender and sexuality amongst the student population in the school. The focus of critical attention has been upon the informal culture of students in order to develop an understanding of *their perspectives* in relation to the domain of the sexual. However, I feel it is important to recognise that the student sexual cultures identified in this chapter and in previous chapters are shaped in relation to other cultures in the school. This chapter indicates that women and other boys provide categories of sexual otherness for the young men with whom I conducted research. However, as Chapters 3, 4 and 5 illustrate, the collective negotiation of student sexual cultures is frequently shaped in relation to teachers in the school. Teachers can provide a focal point for student cultures, the structuring presence/absence through which students define themselves as learners and as sexual subjects within the school. In some contexts teachers provide a point of identification for students who view the teacher as 'like me' or 'like I want to be'. In other contexts students draw upon oppositional strategies to define their identities *as against* teachers. It is for these reasons that the following chapter shifts the focus from students to teachers. The aim of the next chapter is to develop an account of the ways in which teachers think about and relate to issues of sexuality and to look at the implications of this for teaching and learning, especially in the area of Personal, Social and Health Education.

Chapter 7

Sexing the subject: teachers, pedagogies and sex education

This chapter is concerned with the experiences of teachers and the ways in which pedagogic strategies and school processes are productive of sexual identities in educational arenas. A central theme of the chapter is an exploration of the relationship between the 'micro politics of schooling' (Ball 1987) and expressions of sexuality among teachers and pupils in the school. A life-history approach is used in interviews with teachers as a way of gaining access to auto/biographical accounts of individuals as (formerly) pupils and (presently) pedagogues. The chapter suggests that teachers' biographies and personal experiences play a significant part in shaping and giving meaning to the pedagogic styles they adopt. Approaches to sexualities in school and, particularly, the teaching of sex education is informed by this dynamic. The chapter outlines three ways of looking at and studying teachers' work and culture: teachers and the labour process; life history approaches; relations of desire. These three ways of looking represent different and divergent routes to developing an understanding of who teachers are and what they do. They are cited here in order to place the teaching of sex education within a broader context of educational research into teachers and teaching before considering emerging features and issues involved in the practice of sex education.

Teachers and the labour process

The conceptualisation of teaching as work has been the subject of much academic research (e.g. Miller 1996; Nias 1984; Ozga 1988).

As Lawn and Grace (1987) point out, early educational analyses of teachers as workers placed them in relations of constraint as more or less well controlled agents working within the ideological state apparatus of schooling (Althusser 1971; Sharp and Green 1975; Bowles and Gintis 1976). Subsequent work in the sociology of education tended to view teachers as central to structural and cultural relations that are constitutive of the labour process in schools (see Hargreaves and Woods 1984). Studying teachers from this perspective offers an insight into salient features of teachers' lives in school such as the sexual division of labour in teaching, notions of career and professionalism and the changing nature of teachers' work. In contemporary studies of teachers and teaching it is recognised that teachers have an occupational culture of their own which 'gives meaning, support and identity to teachers and their work' (Hargreaves 1994: 165). Andy Hargreaves (1994) suggests that the culture of teachers can be defined as a set of shared values and beliefs; an assumed way of doing things among communities of teachers. Significant to an understanding of teacher cultures is the acknowledgement that the relationship between teachers and their colleagues has an effect upon practice. As David Hargreaves (1980) indicates, the occupational culture can be viewed as:

> a medium through which many innovations and reforms must pass; yet in that passage they frequently become shaped, transformed or resisted in many ways that were unintended or unanticipated.
>
> (Hargreaves, D. 1980: 126)

In this respect teachers' culture can be seen to mediate educational policy and implementation of the curriculum of the school. However, the culture of teachers is by no means coherent. In his (1980) study David Hargreaves suggests that the occupational culture of teachers is ordered around three themes: status, competence and social relationships. Teachers in the late 1970s, according to Hargreaves, were commonly concerned with broad issues such as their standing in society and matters of respect and renumeration, as well as everyday issues such as coping with pupils and their reputation among colleagues. Since the completion of Hargreaves' study the field of education in the UK has been marked by a series of educational reforms which have introduced, amongst other things, a national curriculum, local management of schools (LMS) and appraisal schemes for teachers (see Introduction for a further discussion of these issues). An overarching feature of these legislative changes is the increase in centralised control and state intervention accompanied by a decrease in autonomy at the level of the local. Such changes are not particular to the UK; parallel developments can be seen in North America, Canada, Australia and other European countries. This shift in relations of power in the domain of education has had many consequences, some of which have been discussed by researchers in terms of 'marketisation' (see Ball 1990; Epstein and Kenway 1996; Menter *et al.* 1997). The effects of marketisation on education can be seen in terms of the emergence of new structures and processes in the workplace. In the local context of the school, extended forms of managerialism and a decrease in the professional autonomy of classroom teachers can be seen to produce significant shifts in the nature of teachers' work and identities. The rapidly changing nature and structure of teachers' work has led Mac an Ghaill (1992) to comment on the occupational culture of teachers as being in a state of crisis. Mac an Ghaill's (1992) UK-based study postulates that teacher cultures can be located within three main ideologies: Old Collectivists, New Entrepreneurs and the Professionals. In Mac an Ghaill's study teachers' identifications with or against trade unionism, new managerial practices and traditional educational values is utilised as a heuristic device to position individual teachers within analytic categories. Such typologies indicate the presence of different and competing approaches to the practice of teaching that can be seen to reflect a diverse range of political investments and personal identities.

Andy Hargreaves' (1994) study of teachers' work and culture in Canada suggests that the changes facing teachers and schools can be located within the context of the transition from modernity to postmodernity. Hargreaves argues that schools can be seen to represent outmoded modernist institutions, failing to keep pace with the contemporary world of flexible economies, globalisation and new patterns of production and consumption. Hargreaves identifies four broad forms of teacher culture in the contemporary era: individualism, collaboration, contrived collegiality, balkanisation. Balkanisation, in Hargreaves' analysis, refers to the process whereby teachers work in small sub-groups around a specific curriculum project. These forms of occupational culture among teachers can be seen as individual and collective responses to educational change and uncertainty as experienced in particular schools. Studies of teachers' occupational cultures such as those discussed above indicate that the nature of teachers' work and the ways they relate to it is dynamic and changes over time.

Life history approaches

A generative approach to the study of teachers' work and culture has been the use of life history and auto/biographical methods in educational research (e.g. Ball and Goodson 1985; Connell 1989; Goodson and Walker 1991; Sikes and Troyna 1991). This body of literature has focused on the narrative accounts of individual teachers as a way of understanding their relationship to the labour process, pedagogic styles and issues of identity. In these studies teachers' biographies can be conceptualised as a link between the individual and social structures, capable of providing insights into the interplay between subjectivities and institutional arrangements. As illustrated in Chapter 2, auto/biographical methods offer productive possibilities for an analysis of the ways in which individuals construct and reconstruct themselves and are *constructed into* existing social relations (Stanley 1992). Personal narratives also elicit particular accounts of individuals' lives which frequently have the effect of producing a coherent identity seeking to reconcile the past within the context of the present. In Chapter 2 I used auto/biographical methods to produce an account of myself as an English teacher with an emergent interest in issues of sexuality. In this chapter I build upon and develop this approach through a recognition of the importance of biography and identity to the teachers I interviewed. Furthermore, I suggest that teachers' personal experiences have implications for the ways in which issues of sexuality are approached in the practice of sex education and in pupil–teacher relations more generally.

Maggie MacLure's (1993a, b) studies of teachers' jobs and lives in the UK suggest that the notion of identity becomes an *organising principle* in the complex profile of teachers' biographies. Through identity claims teachers develop a narrative which constructs the self in relation to others. Such claims frequently involve disclaimers and moral positionings; an articulation of *what kind of teacher you are* also defines and demarcates *what you are not*. In autobiographical accounts teachers 'draw together a wide range of disparate concerns within a single argumentative structure' (MacLure 1993b: 317). In this way the identity of teacher becomes *an argument* which asserts a coherent personal stance in relation to changing or fluid issues such as the curriculum, pedagogic styles, professionalism and life-style. MacLure identified two discernible versions of identity among the teachers she interviewed: 'spoiled' identities and 'subversive' identities. Spoiled identities refer to accounts where respondents contrasted the present very unfavourably with a 'golden age' of teaching and learning in the past. In subversive accounts individuals construct the identity of teacher as dull and unadventurous and suggest that they have distanced themselves from such an identity by pursuing other (out of school) activities which bespeak the kind of person they want to be. Research into teachers' lives and work indicates that teachers play an active part in mediating, negotiating and shaping school processes. The culture of teachers provides a forum for the construction of teacher identities and pedagogic styles. Moreover, the agency of teachers in relation to their work has a bearing on the ways in which the curriculum is conceptualised and taught as I go on to demonstrate in the following sections.

Teaching and relations of desire

The context in which teachers' work and the way biographies and experiences of individual teachers become intertwined in the sphere of pedagogic practice can be seen particularly in approaches to education which consider issues of emotional and erotic attachment. Sikes and Troyna's (1991) study of student teachers and newly qualified teachers in the UK suggest that teachers enter the profession with an imaginatively realised 'ideal model' of the kind of teacher they would like to be, based on their experiences and aspirations. I would add that the 'ideal model' can also be seen as a psychic location which, in terms of identity, can be construed as a process of *becoming*; an internalised version of self projected onto existing social relations. From this perspective, teaching is intimately bound up with desire and involves an interplay between the internal and external world of emotional investments, subjectivities and processes of social recognition (hooks 1994; Miller 1996; Robertson 1996). Here, there is an acknowledgement that teachers' desire to be liked, if not loved and adored by their students, can have a powerful effect on pedagogic practices. Jane

Miller's (1996) historical study of women's relationship to the schooling process extends the teaching as desire metaphor to a discussion of pedagogy in terms of seduction. Miller's analysis considers the ways in which a beguilingly attractive sexuality inflects women's lives in the social arena of work and relationships. The work of Robertson, hooks and Miller suggests that there is a relationship between teaching and the erotic which can be seen in pedagogic approaches which are structured, in part, through unconscious dynamics and relations of desire. These relations of desire, however, are rarely recognised by the official culture of the school. Rather, in the official context the concern is with a rational desexualisation of social encounters where the domain of the sexual, and particularly sexual knowledge, is constructed as dangerous (Britzman 1995; Epstein and Johnson 1998). However, if we were to utilise some of the psychoanalytic insights used elsewhere in the book (see particularly Chapters 4 and 6) it is possible to see the teacher in Lacanian theory as the 'subject presumed to know' (Lacan 1977a). Like the analyst or therapist, the teacher is also subject to mechanisms of desire such as projection and transference. Transference can be defined in the context of therapy as a process of emotional intensity whereby feelings are transferred unconsciously from the patient to the analyst. Lacan (1977) recognises this dynamic as one of desire in which transference can be viewed as love which is addressed to, or directed to, knowledge. It is possible to see teacher–pupil relationships from this perspective as a site for the playing out of unconscious desires.

Teaching sex education

The teaching of sex education is a complex and contested political issue, forming the backdrop to pedagogic practice in this area of the curriculum (see Chapter 3). Sue Lees' (1993) UK study of gender and schooling identifies three political stances in relation to the teaching of sex education: conservative, liberal and feminist.[1] The conservative framework is concerned with morality and imagined ideals of family life and can be seen to present an unchanging and naturalised social–gender order. The liberal model is premised on the notion of providing young people with appropriate information to make informed, socially responsible choices. For Lees this model fails to recognise the hegemonic aspects of dominant power relations seen in 'information' which is often limited and 'takes little account of the context of sexual relationships' (1993: 217). The feminist stance is regarded by Lees as potentially the most progressive as it seeks to question social norms and commonsense assumptions particularly in matters of sex–gender inequality. Within the feminist framework it is possible to address issues of gender relations, personal perspectives and sexual diversity. However, in the schools in which I conducted research, models for sex education invariably broke down at the level of individual practice. Teachers I observed and interviewed adopted aspects of different political stances and rarely identified with one model. Moreover, focusing on frameworks as outlined by Lees highlights the *delivery* of sex education at the expense of considering the ways in which these knowledges are *received*. Although some teachers I interviewed applied aspects of feminist practice to the teaching of sex education, often in the form of biographical detail and open discussion, this was not always met warmly by pupils. Comments such as, 'She's always doing that', 'So bloody what?' and 'I bet she knows the Queen!' capture the feelings of resentment, tedium and derision characteristic of many responses voiced to me by pupils. Wolpe (1988: 154–5) notes that a feminist teacher in her study who had attempted to establish a sisterly bond with young women in her class was regarded as 'plain nosy' by these girls. This suggests that power relations between teachers and pupils shape the context for sex education and mediate classroom interactions in specific ways.

A central dynamic structuring the teaching and learning of sex education is the teacher/pupil binary. The social relations of schooling which structures the ways in which power operates suggests that teachers cannot approach issues of sexuality in a decontextualised manner (Kehily and Nayak 1996; Lupton and Tulloch 1996). In interactions with pupils in relation to issues of sexuality, teachers carry with them a set of associations that are not easily divorced from their other teaching initiatives. The identity of 'teacher' and the hierarchical structure of institutional arrangements inform the learning agenda in significant ways. The positionality of teachers as instructors/professional educators encourages the deployment of formal teaching methods based on a view of the teacher as holder-of-knowledge and *in control* in the classroom. In terms of sex education, however, formal methods may not be so appropriate to teaching and learning in this field. Many researchers have commented on the need for more informal approaches to sexuality education which recognise pupil sexual cultures as a starting point for teaching and learning (Redman 1994; Thomson 1994; Epstein and Johnson 1998; Lupton and Tulloch 1996; Holland *et al.* 1990a; Measor 1989). As part of such informal techniques, teachers often expect pupils to confide in them, open up areas for discussion and talk frankly. Such strategies can be viewed by working-class pupils as a particular middle-class mode to be resisted. As I indicated earlier, in one school where I conducted research, attempts to teach sex education using informal methods was not necessarily regarded as successful or welcome from a pupil perspective. Many pupils I spoke with at Oakwood School found informal approaches totally unacceptable and were quick to point out the discontinuities with other areas of the curriculum where they were explicitly told what to do and discussion was not encouraged.

In their study of young women and sexual identities in the UK, Thomson and Scott (1991) claim that the subversive potential of sexual knowledge in the classroom context characterised a number of accounts. Their interviews with young women that had left school identifies the ways in which the binary oppositions of teacher/pupil relations are worked through in the sexual domain:

> The sex education class then, becomes a forum within which the two worlds of adolescent sexuality and the authority of school culture come into open confrontation, and it is this juxtaposition that most clearly marks these young women's memories of the classes. It is clear from our data that young people used their own culture of sexuality in order to challenge and embarrass the teacher.
>
> (Thomson and Scott 1991: 12)

Thomson and Scott's use of the terms 'two worlds' and 'open confrontation' indicate that the teaching and learning of sex education can be a struggle between the different cultures of teachers and pupils which are defined in relation to each other. Their analysis offers a consideration of the *cultural* ways in which sexuality is experienced within schools. Thomson and Scott suggest that sex education lessons can become 'social events' (1991: 10–15) where the contrast between the sexual knowledge of pupils and sex education messages may produce laughter and disruption.

At the level of individual practice, teachers of sex education balance the demands of the classroom with organisational constraints and policy statements. Bonnie Trudell's (1992) study of sex education in the US suggests that this balancing act produces 'defensive teaching'; forms of pedagogy where teachers make splits between ideals and practice in order to control potentially uncomfortable moments. This strategy is reminiscent of my own experiences as a newly qualified teacher, described in Chapter 2, where I constantly reshape my practice in an attempt to achieve and maintain control in the classroom. It is also possible to detect 'defensive teaching' at work in Mrs Evans' management of the 'agony aunt' lesson discussed in Chapter 4. The recourse to 'defensive teaching' can be understood as an attempt to seek safety and avoid controversy in an area where 'risk' can be seen to engender personal vulnerability, parental complaint and adverse media interest. The difficulties of teaching sex education in the contemporary context are outlined by Epstein and Johnson:

> There has been a determined minority attempt to narrow the terms of sexual recognition while at the everyday level and in entertainment and youth related media sexual categories have become more diverse and more fluid. In schools, this distance is expressed as an alignment of pupil cultures with the forms of commercial popular culture in opposition to the sexual culture in school.
>
> (Epstein and Johnson 1998: 30–1)

As noted in More Sugar? (Chapter 5), there is often a disjuncture between the domain of the school and the world of popular culture which exists in and around the school. As Richard Johnson (1996: 167) points out, sex education, 'has become a central stake in the struggle over sexual and gender identities'. A key feature of this struggle outlined by Epstein and Johnson's (1998) UK-based study is the social and political conditions which 'attempt to impose very narrow terms of sexual recognition upon a sexually diverse society' (1998: 31).

Five teachers and a school nurse

The following section explores and analyses the experiences of five teachers (one of whom is a student teacher) and a school nurse as articulated in individual interviews carried out during the course of my research. All of them worked in or were attached to schools where I carried out research for this study. In the discussion below they are referred to by their preferred mode of address used in interactions with students in the classroom. I am particularly interested in the respondents' approaches to issues of sexuality, both in terms of their own sexual identity/biography and the teaching of sex education in school. The relationship between personal biographies and pedagogic practice is also of interest to me in accounts where the interview provided a space for reflections on these themes. I want to stress that the intention is not to evaluate the pedagogic practice of individual teachers but rather to focus upon the interplay between identities, experiences and approaches to teaching and learning, particularly in the domain of sexuality. My analysis of the material generated by interviews with education professionals draws upon and is informed by the literatures outlined above. In the following sections I argue that pedagogic practice can be seen in relation to, and as a product of, the contingencies of auto/biography, desire and the labour process. A close reading of the transcripts indicated that there were four themes which appeared to be important to an understanding of respondents' approaches to sexuality: becoming/being a teacher; sexual biography; approaches to sexual diversity; and approaches to students. Within the scope of these themes respondents spoke of themselves and the relationship between subjectivity, sexuality and pedagogy. I have used these themes as organising categories for this chapter.

Becoming/being a teacher

Miss Green had been in teaching for twenty-one years and is head of Religious Studies and Personal and Social Education at Oakwood School. She described her motives for becoming a teacher as 'idealistic', wanting to help young people through pastoral care in the school context, rather than through exam success and academic achievement. She said, 'For me the youngsters who sit in front of me are not just brains, not just sort of heads-on-bodies, they are people'. Miss Green made a direct link between the kind of pupil she was and the kind of pupil she wants to help in the course of her career:

Miss Green: Yeah I failed at school, I was terrible, but I had a lot of problems from my own background, a lot of emotional problems so I had a lot of emotional garbage which you couldn't get rid of but it had to be dealt with but there was not room for learning because I was such a mess in other respects. Like so many of our kids who come to school, they bring an awful lot of emotional garbage, they bring all the problems and there we are saying, 'Now you must learn this'. It's unrealistic, it's of no – it doesn't mean anything to them so I know what they feel like to some extent.

Miss Green's empathy with pupils like her former self supported her perception that curriculum-based learning seems irrelevant and inappropriate at times. Her use of the term 'emotional garbage' indicates the power of the emotional realm and the felt need to find ways of dealing with pain and hurt in order to move on. The language in which Miss Green compared herself as a pupil with the pupils she teaches now utilised a therapy/counselling discourse which is humanistic and person-centred. Miss Green's teacher identity was interwoven with a pedagogic style that valued pupil centredness, confidence building and relating to pupils as individuals. The 'pressures' of teaching, however, means that her 'idealism' is compromised on an everyday basis by, 'making wrong decisions, upsetting kids who don't deserve to be upset because you're under stress'. Miss Green's somewhat stark assessment of herself as a teacher was the hope that, in the long term, she has done more good than harm to pupils as individuals.

Mr Carlton, a Craft, Design and Technology (CDT) teacher with many years experience at Oakwood, expressed his position in school in terms of a strong working-class regional identity:

Mr Carlton: I'm from here, right, from this part of the world. I grew up in this part of the world, went away and came back and taught here ever since and I've never been to another school – which could be a mistake, but the kids here I've always managed to relate to and I treat them probably the way their parents treat them and I think that's what it comes down to. They know that if I tell them something then I tell them from the heart, not from what other people are telling them. I try to always tell them the truth, even if it hurts, you know, tell them the truth.

Mr Carlton's identification with the pupils he teaches is based upon his commitment to common bonds of community, class and location. He suggests that this shared experience forges an emotional connection between himself and the pupils which enables him to speak to pupils as a parent would, from 'the heart'. Mr Carlton's pedagogic style was passionately pupil-centred, 'In my book the kids come first all the time, every time and it's up to me to see that they get the best out of every situation'. Mr Carlton talked about teaching his subject and getting the best out of young people as part of the same process:

Mr Carlton: If you can't be bothered, you're not going to get anywhere, they're [the kids] the most important thing, they're the raw material that we've got to work with and you've got to work with that raw material and it's something that I've always done, taken a material and made something out of it whether it be a piece of wood or a piece of metal or a piece of a person, you've got to get the kids to work and enjoy the work that they do.

Here, the terms used by Mr Carlton indicated that he locates his teaching activity within the context of industrial processes and manual labour. The analogy with the workplace resists contemporary notions of professionalism and the language of new managerialism pervasive in discussions of teaching as a practice in the contemporary period. Rather, Mr Carlton's conceptualisation of teaching forms a point of continuity with his working-class identity and regional affiliations to an area renowned for its industrial heritage and large manufacturing base. Mr Carlton further suggests that because CDT is about 'making things' it is possible to break down barriers between teacher and pupils to some extent. In his classroom, he explains, there is no desk providing a symbolic divide between the two groups; teachers and pupils are involved in the same process of productivity, developing and 'making things' out of 'raw material'. Miss Green and Mr Carlton offer accounts of themselves as teachers that make direct links between their background and experiences and their activities as a teacher. The gendered nature of their experience as teachers illustrate the differences between 'making things' and *being made* in the encounter between gendered subjectivity and educational experience as I will demonstrate more clearly below. However, for both teachers there is an emotional connection between their identity (sense of self) and the pedagogic practices they favour. In the context of the interview, Mr Carlton and Miss Green offer a version of themselves as teachers that reads *what you do* through the lens of *who you are*. From this perspective teacher identity becomes a subjective appropriation of personal narratives and pedagogic styles that become fused in moments of self-definition as, 'this is me, this is what I am about'.

Sexual biographies, teaching and learning

Approaches to sex education in school are intimately bound up with issues of identity and experience. Beth Marshall, the nurse attached to Clarke School, indicated that her experiences as a teenager shaped her ideas on the importance of sex education:

Beth Marshall: I felt that I had quite a good sex education myself at school. We had a very open science teacher which was good but I was aware that there were other people of a similar sort of age to me that had ended up pregnant at fourteen and with two or three children by the time they were eighteen and you think well, you know, there should be some way of stopping it really or giving people the information so they don't necessarily end up trapped into a life that they're not going to enjoy. So I think that was what – there was a need there – and that's what made me become more involved.

Beth's own experience of sex education as 'open' and 'good' has influenced her approach to sexuality and serves as a counter narrative to that of her peers who became pregnant. Beth regarded giving young people information on sexual matters as important; having far-reaching effects on sexual behaviour, lifestyle and quality of life. The link made by Beth between sex education and teenage pregnancy is illustrative of the public health pragmatism that forms a constitutive element of contemporary sex education and health promotion programmes aimed at young people (Thomson 1994). As a school nurse, Beth gave sex education lessons on methods of contraception and was also available at lunchtime for advice sessions with individual students. Beth suggested that pupils confide in her and sought advice because she was 'independent' of parents and the school and 'because I think they know I'm not going to get embarrassed'. In her position as a health practitioner, Beth attempted to retain and recreate the kind of 'openness' she valued as a teenager. Beth offered the following example of her practice:

Beth Marshall: There was a child I saw regularly who was desperate to have a baby of her own and, er, . . . I mean we talked about it and I suggested to her that she go and see friends that have had babies and talked to them about how they coped with their life and what a change it had made and, . . . she's no longer at school, she's left some time now and she still hasn't got a child and I think because, I don't know whether it was because of talking to me or whether it just made her appreciate that it's not just a case of having a little pink bundle, you know, there's a lot of, a lot more responsibility that goes into it. I don't know whether it made her more aware or not or maybe she just sort of grew through that.

In this account Beth is able to give practical advice that engages with the young woman's concerns and takes her seriously. The moralism of health promotion work of this kind is couched in terms of awareness and 'responsibility' and can be seen to be implicit and rooted in 'commonsense'. Beth's approach contrasts sharply with the overtly regulatory strategies found in New Right policy documents such as *Health of the Nation* (Department of Health 1992) where reducing teenage pregnancy is seen as a 'goal' driven by medical, economic and moral imperatives. At other points, however, Beth indicates that, for some young women, having a baby can be a positive experience:

Beth Marshall: Some of the girls that I know that have been to
see me at school and have now got, had either
left early or have had babies at sixteen and I've
seen them and they all seem very happy. I mean,
I haven't seen anybody sort of drudging along
looking really miserable. They've all got new
pushchairs and they're all out together.

The seemingly contradictory view that teenage pregnancy is
generally not a good thing but girls who become pregnant and
have babies appear 'really happy' makes sense at the level of the
individual. Beth outlines a way of looking that is responsive to
personal circumstances and pragmatic; through the support, information and guidance provided by school nurses and sex education
programmes, young women can make choices appropriate to their
needs. Beth's observations support the view that, for some young
women, motherhood may offer a way of resolving some of the
pressures of everyday life by propelling them into the 'adult' role
of 'parent', a role that confers status and gives them a position
and a sense of purpose within their local community (Thomson
2000).

The public health pragmatism outlined by Beth was incorporated into many teachers' accounts of teaching personal and social
education. However, this discourse of personal choice and 'safe'
health can be seen to compete with other discourses which also
shaped the PSE curriculum. Miss Green drew upon the notion of
childhood innocence in reminiscences of her own sexual learning
and in her approach to sexuality as a teacher. She talked about
her adolescence in the following terms:

Miss Green: As far as sexuality was concerned we all did a lot of
pretending, we all pretended we all knew all about it
and nobody ever knew who knew what. I certainly
didn't know any more than anybody else and we all
just went on pretending. It was all very silly really . . .
it wasn't so much what we knew, it all revolved
round who did what and what experience you'd
actually had and there was quite a lot of, 'Oh she's
got a boyfriend', 'have you done this?', 'do you do
that?' And the very one who didn't claim to have
a boyfriend was the one who ended up getting

> pregnant . . . It's always the way, the ones who claimed to have done the most and be the most sexually experienced were the very ones who probably weren't.

Miss Green's memory of adolescent sexuality was articulated as an elaborate pretence of knowledge and experience where nothing was what it seemed. Her account indicates the assumed importance, among the female peer group, of (hetero)sexual knowledge gained through a boyfriend and sustained through rumour and gossip. Ultimately, teenage pregnancy becomes the irrefutable evidence of who knows what, existing as both a marker of sexual knowledge/experience and the stigma of knowing and doing. Miss Green's reflections on her sexual coming-of age in the supposedly 'liberated' period of the late 1960s/early 1970s inferred that most girls feigned a knowledge of the sexual while one or two girls quietly attained it. Her approach to the sexuality of young people in the 1990s suggests a certain continuity in her thinking:

Miss Green: I go on a health course and they tell me that a certain percentage of young people under the age of sixteen are sexually active and I stand in front of a class teaching them something about the life of Jesus or something and I look at them and I stop and think, is this really true? Can *you*, this percentage of *you* really be, 'cos to me they look like children and I'm finding this difficult to handle, to take on board. I do believe it and I look at some youngsters and I can well believe it, but if you take the statistics and you look at them across [the classroom], you think, well really.

The reluctant recognition that young people are sexually active produced feelings of belief and disbelief because they 'look like children'. Here Miss Green draws upon a widely held assumption in the West that sexuality remains central to definitions of childhood and adulthood and can be defined as a preserve of adulthood. 'Looking like children' invokes a discourse of childhood innocence which positions children as sexually inactive and in need of protection from the potentially corrupting 'adult' world of sex (Higonnet 1998; Jackson 1982; Kitzinger 1988). Miss Green's juxtaposition of 'the life of Jesus' with the 'facts' of young people's sexual behaviour indicates the ways in which different discourses can be drawn upon to produce moments of subjective realisation. From Miss Green's perspective, most young people *look* innocent and if they're not then they should be. The exception in this schema is the small number of sexually precocious 'children' who bear the testament of sexual experience on their bodies.

At a later point in the interview Miss Green returned to the theme of teenage pregnancy and suggested that there has been a change in attitude to young single mothers which has produced further social problems:

Miss Green: Well teenage pregnancy is increasing and that seems to be very depressing. I don't know, I think that's almost out of our sphere of influence because it seems to be socially acceptable now. We've swung from a time when awful things happened to young-sters who got pregnant and they were expected to give up their babies, there was no question of them keeping them and no support and no sympathy, to almost an attitude we seem to have, I mean this became a parliamentary debate didn't it – about youngsters who are getting pregnant to get a flat? In my last school, I know because I had three in my Religious Studies group who did it. I mean, I know for a fact it has been happening and they were quite open why they've done it, they'll get accommoda-tion, they'll get this, that and everything else. We seem to have swung and that seems to be something I don't think our influence as teachers is going to say much about that. I think it's society's attitude really. I might be wrong, it's just how I feel about it at the moment.

Here, Miss Green outlines the key features of a recurrent moral panic: teenage pregnancy is out of control and is exacerbated by a climate of social acceptability and state provision of council accommodation, benefits and services for young single mothers. Miss Green is clearly disturbed by these events and feels that teachers and schools have little impact upon such phenomena. Miss Green's comments are infused with a moral tone and a sense of resignation which implies that sexual standards and sexual behaviours are shaped by the world beyond the school gates. As a teacher, Miss Green can observe the changes and chart the moral decline but feels powerless to intervene. Whereas Beth has an implicit moral agenda that is incorporated into the PSE curriculum in discussions with students, Miss Green has an explicit moral agenda which exists as a personal stance and is not overtly referred to in her teaching of sex education. For both Beth and Miss Green there is a complex configuration between what-you-think and what-you-teach which is never directly translated into forms of pedagogy. Miss Green is responsible for sex education at Oakwood but feels that the 'real' sexual learning happens outside school. Beth, however, is not a member of the school staff but recognises the school as an important site for sexual learning.

A sense of what is possible and appropriate for schools to achieve within the domain of the sexual is an important starting point for some teachers. Miss Woods was a senior teacher and Head of House at Oakwood School. She had been teaching for twelve years and had gained experience in four different secondary schools in the region. Miss Woods expressed her concerns in the following way:

Miss Woods: Problems today start with schools being expected to deliver things which the family unit could effectively deliver, er, in a different way because there is constant contact there, they [the pupils] can go back with questions . . . a science lesson can do the basics and PSE can answer questions about things they might see, like the HIV billboards. But I would like to see the family being able to do that. I could never have done it with my parents, I'll be perfectly honest, so here's me setting standards and goals and asking parents to take on the role knowing full well my parents wouldn't have handled it. I hope if I was a parent I would.

Miss Woods uses the language of managerialism in which terms such as 'expectation', 'delivery' and 'effectiveness' become important signifiers in outlining a social order of who should do what and why. Miss Woods realises, from her own experience, that the family cannot always take on responsibility for sex education but her wish for this to happen can be seen as a powerfully imagined ideal. Miss Woods talks about her own sexual learning in the early 1970s as a difficult and 'painful' time in her life. At her all-girls secondary school, Miss Woods explained, there was very little formal sex education but there was a well developed pupil sexual culture with plenty of informal learning. Miss Woods describes two hierarchies: the 'in-crowd' of attractive, street-wise girls who gained credibility through sexual experience and the 'other group' of quiet, immature girls who were naive and inexperienced.

Miss Woods: I was very much **not** a part of the in-crowd, very left out, you did feel left out because to be part of it you had to **at least** have experienced deep French kissing and it had to be with a certain member of the local sixth form, so the quality of who you were kissing, all these sorts of things . . . the drug scene was very prolific and the 'you can sleep with anybody' thing was certainly very loudly spoken. People like me would think there was something wrong with me – 'My God, what's going on?'

Feeling left out and being out-of-step with the times draws upon the contrast between personal experience and external social relations; the sexual revolution is turning everybody round but some of us are in the same place. Miss Woods' reminiscences indicate the importance of sexual practice to peer group status and suggests that girls may codify and rank sexual encounters in similar ways to boys, as discussed in Chapter 6. Like Beth and Miss Green, Miss Woods dwells upon issues of teenage pregnancy and compares her experiences as a pupil with her experiences as a teacher:

Miss Woods: I remember having one film all about the risk of getting pregnant and it was all about this girl who got caught and it was a terribly messy experience for everyone, it was awful. She was running through a field, running away from the situation. I can still remember it . . . and that was the only sex education we received . . . it was very bad to get pregnant if you weren't married, that was it.

I mean today, for example, last night some girls came to the Christmas concert and they brought their babies with them, now that would never have happened in my day. If a girl was [pregnant], she was expelled from school fullstop, she didn't have any ties with the school afterwards and the school wouldn't have anything to do with her.

In interviews with Beth, Miss Green and Miss Woods, it is clear that they place issues of contraception and pregnancy at the centre of the sex education curriculum. Their own experience of sexual learning underlined the message that teenage pregnancy was a central concern for young women and continues to be so despite changes in social attitudes. As sex education practitioners each of the respondents outline a sexual biography that positions themselves as *the ones that didn't get pregnant*. From their narratives it is clear that a feature of girls' sexual maturation in their lifetime is to observe the stigma of pregnancy in female peer groups and internalise the message. Another significant aspect of their sexual biographies appears to be the sexual climate in which they grew up. Although related to in different ways, the popular notion of the 1960s and 1970s as an era which resisted repression and forged new sexual agendas, shaped the ways in which respondents viewed issues of sexuality and their place within the sex-gender order. Beth's experiences lead to investments in openness and individual responsibility, while Miss Green and Miss Woods indicate that it may be important for girls to go against the grain by resisting pressure to become sexually active/experienced. The experiences related by Miss Woods and Miss Green resonate with issues raised in Chapter 5 where girls discuss issues of sexuality in relation to teenage magazines. The accounts of teachers and of students point to the abiding notion of reputation for girls as an important structuring feature in their lives and their identities. This has implications for the practice of sex education, suggesting that it may be important to address issues of gender and social experience specifically in such contexts.

The gendered significance of transitions to adulthood is further outlined by Mr Carlton's account of his experiences. Unlike the three female respondents, Mr Carlton talked about his youth in strikingly different terms:

Mr Carlton: Not to put too fine a point on it, I was, er, completely and utterly a bastard when I was younger and no female meant anything to me. Now please don't take offence at that (laughs) but I was one of the boys, rugby player, drinking quite a lot, playing the field. And then I met the person I wanted to spend the rest of my life with and her attitudes have rubbed off a lot on me. She made me see that things I was talking about then were not quite right.

MJK: What sort of things?

Mr Carlton: How deep d'you want to go? (laughs) . . . My attitude to women was appalling . . . she [my partner] always thinks about how what she does affects other people and that's rubbed off on me because before I couldn't give a damn.

Mr Carlton's construction of himself as the rugby-playing, hard-drinking, philandering lad illustrates the ways in which the cultural transition into adulthood is a specifically gendered project. Mr Carlton's masculine identity is publicly played out and privately appraised in the intimacy of sexual partnership. In his account, 'falling in love' produces a dramatic shift in perspective that encourages reflexivity, especially in the sphere of gender relations. Mr Carlton suggests that his experiences provide a point of identification with the boys in the school:

MJK: What would you do if you came across lads who were like you when you were young?

Mr Carlton: I dread it (laughs). No I don't dread it, no, no, um, I think most lads are like what I was when I was young, or I was like them. It's just a stage of growing up and all I try telling them is there's nothing new, I've done all this. You're not going to shock me by the things that you do because I've done it all and worse 'cos I've got fifteen, twenty years more experience of doing it than you've got. Don't try and pull a fast one . . . and once they see that – I bet most of the people you've spoken to who say they can relate to me are boys.

Indeed, many boys I spoke with during my time at Oakwood did speak warmly of Mr Carlton as 'someone you can have a laff with' and 'the best teacher in the school'. The dynamics of this relationship can be seen as a style of camaraderie, structured through power relations and marked by moments of sexism and the privileging of hegemonic forms of masculinity. Certainly the idea that 'laddishness' is a developmental phase for young males would support this view. However, many girls in the school also held Mr Carlton in high esteem and sought him out as someone to confide in moments of crisis. Mr Carlton did have considerable experience of talking with girls who became pregnant and, in these circumstances, he saw his role as supporting their decision in relation to the pregnancy and talking through the implications with them. It is a measure of his success as a teacher that he was still in touch with many former pupils, girls and boys, whom he had counselled over the years.

Teachers and sexual diversity

The normative presence of heterosexuality is as much a part of teachers' cultures as it is an integral part of pupil sexual cultures. Staff-room talk of partners, children and erotic attachment assumed that *everyone* was heterosexual and sexual banter among teachers served to sustain and regulate this view. In this environment, sexual diversity frequently presents itself as an issue that teachers are fearful of and find difficult to incorporate into the sex education curriculum. Miss Green talked about this fear in terms of external constraint:

Miss Green: Homosexuality, we don't really touch, um, in the sense that the law says we must not promote homosexuality and, in fact, that is a very difficult one because the government's definition of promoting has almost been to the extent of even discussing it. If you have local authorities who are refusing to put on certain plays because they have some reference or homosexual content and that is considered promoting it, then that puts teachers in a very difficult position. It would mean that talking about it, raising issues even, can be construed as promoting.

Here Miss Green is referring to Section 28 of the Local Government Act (1988) which states that local authorities should not 'promote homosexuality'. As schools in England and Wales are no longer managed by local authorities, this Act does not strictly apply to the teaching of sex education. However, Miss Green's concerns should be taken seriously as an illustration of the symbolic power of the law. Though she points to the contradictions posed by the elision between discussion and promotion, it is clear that this legislative measure can have a powerful silencing effect on individuals and institutions. In this case Miss Green's 'difficult position' can be understood as a concern to avoid the controversy and media attention which may ensue if homosexuality was directly addressed in school. The conservatism of schools in the domain of the sexual can be seen as a response to the traditionalist campaigning of the New Right which combines a moralism in sexual politics with an agenda of accountability and choice for public service institutions. In this climate schools may be encouraged to regard sexual progressivism as risky, potentially damaging and counterproductive to survival in the commodified sphere of educational markets. In other respects, however, Section 28 may play into already existing feelings of discomfort and homophobia on the part of teachers, where recourse to 'the law' may be a way of displacing issues of sexual diversity (see Moran (2001) for a full discussion of Section 28 and its impact on education). Significantly, in other sites where sexual diversity was more readily embraced, Clause 28 provided the impetus for campaigns for gay and lesbian rights (see Stacey 1991; Cooper 1994; Smith 1994) which can be seen as a powerful template for radical activism (Epstein and Johnson 1998).

The appearance of homosexuality as biologically inherent was a feature of many accounts offered to me by pupils in school. Many young men, in particular, spoke of being gay as 'wrong' and 'unnatural' since it violates 'traditional' masculinity. This acted as a rationale for a range of homophobias in pupil cultures, as noted and discussed in Chapter 6. The view that being gay is, in some way, unnatural was also shared by some teachers I spoke with, suggesting that versions of biological determinism can be frequently worked and reworked in school. Miss Green spoke of gay pupils in the following way:

Miss Green: You look at some youngsters and you can be, you know there are one or two, perhaps more so with boys. I mean I can think of lads I have taught and you've thought, yes, you know, you appear to have the makings of, not you are *going to become*, but you *are gay*. Perhaps sometimes when they are eleven or twelve you are, it's unfortunate for them, but you can sort of spot them and then you meet them much later on and you know definitely you were right but you wonder what's happened to them in the intervening years, who was there for them, who was there to help them, who dared say anything to them?

In phrases such as 'you can sort of spot them', Miss Green suggests that gay is identified and defined against the appearance of a normative version of heterosexuality. From this perspective gay pupils can be seen as 'victims' of their genetic make-up, marked as different by their physical appearance and biological destiny. The heterosexist discourse used by Miss Green focuses on the sexual difference of gay pupils rather than the homophobic practices of students in school.

Miss Green: There are boys whose behaviour is sometimes – I can only use, you see, I can only use the word camp and they sometimes have mannerisms . . .
MJK: And their progress through school, what happens to them?
Miss Green: Yes, they are usually victims of one sort or another, teased, not perhaps bullied but sometimes bullied, teased, isolated.

Here the discourse of heterosexism can be seen as an 'explanation' for the repertoire of discriminatory behaviour constitutive of homophobias in school. Being 'camp' and having mannerisms turns certain pupils into targets for abuse, or, viewed another way, the pathologising of sexual minorities by sexual majorities produces inequalities which can be located and played out on the body of gay males.

It is clear from Miss Green's account that gay students in school experience pain and isolation which has been described as the 'burden of aloneness' (KOLA 1994). The lack of support available to gay pupils suggests that the domain of the school, in the contemporary climate, does not view heterosexism as difficult or problematic. The homophobic practices to be found in pupil cultures are rarely challenged by teachers and schools remain hostile places for gay pupils. Indeed, as Miss Green's account indicates, the 'heterosexual presumption' (Epstein and Johnson 1994) of pupils may be shared by many teachers. The interplay between homophobic practices and the discourse of heterosexism produces sexual inequalities that become structural, integrated into institutional arrangements which normalise and privilege heterosexual relations.

In the three schools where I conducted research I did not encounter any students who claimed a gay identity. Young men who were called gay in school suggested to me that it was factors other than sexual orientation that provided the impetus for homophobic name-calling. These factors could include a positive approach to teachers and schoolwork, lack of interest in sport, a penchant for 'arty/feminine' subjects and a preference for close female, rather than male, friendships or, as I noted in an earlier chapter, even having blond hair. The seemingly arbitrary range of characteristics that could be codified as 'gay' is suggestive of the links between gender and sexuality and the ways in which the school provides resources for the fashioning of sex–gender identities.

Alison, a student teacher in the first year of a teacher education degree, identified as lesbian and came out to friends during Year 11 of secondary school. In an interview she reflected on her school experiences as a period marked by the pain and pleasure of discovering difference:

Alison: Well going back to when I was at school, my friendship was mainly people who worked hard and got good exam results and I didn't work hard and sometimes got good exam results and they were all straight and I wasn't and I used to have major arguments with them about it.

MJK: What sort of things?

Alison: Well one of my school friends stopped speaking to me when I came out, never spoke to me again and that was someone I'd been close to for about seven years. And I had a lot of other friends who were less wanting to work hard at school and got less good exam results but some of them could if they wanted and one of them was open to talking about things and other friends who were just going through difficult times and we just kind of hung together but didn't really talk much.

MJK: So was there a sense at school where you saw yourself as different?

Alison: Oh yeah, yeah. My last year at school was the year of the general election and we had a mock election in the school and as well as the usual political parties people could make up their own political parties and I actually got told at one point, 'We don't want you in our party, don't want you voting for us, we're the Shoot Homosexuals Party'. I mean I was personally sought out and told this so I mean, you know. It wasn't a secret even though I hadn't actually decided or come to a knowledge of being gay. It wasn't a secret in the school. I did have 'sing if you're glad to be gay' written on my school bag, for reasons unknown to myself, it just felt right to write it. And I also felt because two of my closest friends were gay men that I couldn't say 'no, I'm not gay' because that would be denying them but I don't know whether, I mean that was how it consciously felt but maybe it was actually because it would be denying myself, I don't know.

Alison describes her burgeoning sexual identity against the backdrop of widespread school-based homophobias that damage friendship and, at times, take the form of personal threat and physical violence. Alison describes an approach to school and schoolwork which involved moving from one friendship group to another in order to find a space where her sexual politics were tolerated, if not recognised and accepted. Her account confirms the view that sexuality is an integral feature of pupil peer group cultures and plays a part in establishing hierarchies and divisions among the student population. Alison's sense of sexual difference is marked by feelings of confusion and ambiguity. Embracing sexual difference in the Tom Robinson anthem of the late 1970s existed alongside feelings of bewilderment and indecision which suggests that the process of *becoming* can be troubled and troubling. The feelings of ambivalence described by young people in relation to sexual identity is noted by Mac an Ghaill (1991) in his study on young gay males:

> The students described the formation of their sexual identity as part of a wider process of adolescent development, with all its fluidity, experiments, displacements, and confusions. For them sexuality could not be reduced to a conventional perception of a heterosexual–homosexual (straight–gay) continuum, on which each group's erotic and emotional attachments are demarcated clearly and unambiguously. They spoke of contradictions . . . the complexity and confusion of young males' sexual coming of age.
>
> (Mac an Ghaill 1991: 297)

Alison's reflections on her sexual identity from late adolescence into adulthood would support Mac an Ghaill's observations:

Alison: I think I avoided the issue of sexuality and whether I was heterosexual or not . . . I used to say things to myself like, 'Well the next relationship I have will be with a woman' but I also thought, when I was having a relationship with a man, like the first man, 'I want this relationship to go on for the rest of my life'. That would have been a terrible idea, but part of me did think that, but another part of me thought, 'Well, I want to be with a woman'. . . At one point, quite early on, I attached the label bisexual to myself, then I was with a woman and I attached the label gay to myself, then I had a bit of an encounter and I reacquired the bisexual label some years later and then I ditched it again.

Alison's account of the twists and turns involved in internally voiced thoughts and external labels indicate that her sense of sexual identity is far from secure and unproblematic. The identity labels of gay–bisexual–straight were appropriated by Alison at different points in her life as a response to the sexual relationship she was in at the time. However, the labels do not seem to capture the feelings of emotional attachment and erotic desire expressed by Alison. The intensely powerful feelings involved in sexual relationships seem to suggest to Alison that her identity should be shaped and 'explained' by them. The attempt to consolidate sexual identity in and through sexual relationships is also a characteristic feature of young men in this study. In these examples young men seek to fashion a version of heterosexual masculinity based on sexual interactions with young women. These accounts indicate that the subject repeatedly attempts to consolidate sexual identity in relationships but the consolidation is never fully achieved. For young males in school, the peer group acts as a sphere for the display and regulation of sex-gender identities, a place where young men define themselves and others. For Alison, however, there is no place in school where she can achieve a sense of belonging, no place of identification with people-like-me (see Halberstam (1998) for a discussion of the constraints and limitations for gender expression encountered by young women who do not readily embrace femininity). So where does Alison look to for her ideas on sex–gender identity?

During the course of the interview Alison indicated that she had to be particularly resourceful in finding material which spoke to her of sexual diversity. In this respect media sources, popular culture and community based initiatives become important to her sense of self from the age of fifteen onwards and can be seen to provide her with coping strategies in the absence of more tangible forms of support from teachers, friends and family:

Alison: I read a book when I was about fifteen called *All That False Instruction* which was purple and had in pink letter on the cover *A novel of lesbian love*. I got six books out of the library that I didn't want so I could hide it and I hid it under the bed for a month and read that. That was quite dramatic, not 'cos of its, because it was a perfectly ordinary novel, but it was – this is a lesbian novel and there is actually one in [name of town] library and I have personally read it sort of thing. It wasn't 'cos of the text, it was just 'cos it was there and it was such a palava getting it out and hiding it under the bed.

The elaborate process of discovery and concealment involved in finding the book and hiding it can be seen to have symbolic significance for pupils developing a gay/lesbian identity in school. Being gay or being associated with anything gay must be kept secret from the normative realm of school, library and family. The need for secrecy creates the confined space of the closet and, from the closet, individuals like Alison embark on the search for different forms of recognition. Alison describes another activity she engaged in at the age of fifteen in the following way:

Alison: I used to read the *Guardian* and I used to cut articles about gay politics out of the *Guardian* and stick them on my bedroom wall for no apparent reason. I mean it wasn't apparent to myself, never mind anybody else.

After leaving school at sixteen, Alison took a job in an office and, again, found that she was pursuing her own public/private agenda that involves concealment in one sphere and discovery in another.

Alison: There was a radical bookshop just down the road and I used to sneak out at lunchtime and go and read *The Joy of Lesbian Sex* to cheer myself up at lunchtime, not because I was obsessed with sex but because it was some sort of a window onto something I thought that I wanted that I didn't really know much about.

The 'novel of lesbian love', the self-made collage from the *Guardian* and *The Joy of Lesbian Sex* were cited by Alison as significant to her developing sense of identity and difference. It is interesting to contrast Alison's experiences with those of the young women I studied in Chapter 5. Girls claiming a heterosexual identity brought cultural resources (e.g. teen magazines) into school and assimilated them into friendship groups and school arrangements where they provided a sphere for sexual learning. For Alison, cultural resources were also important for her sexual learning, however, she describes her relationship to them as solitary acts, pursued privately out of school without reference to friends or school structures. Alison's account is illustrative of the ways in which heterosexist discourses produce compelling modes of sex–gender conformity in school where other forms of desire are not recognised or spoken.

Mr Carlton, however, suggested that it was possible to challenge the homophobia of pupil cultures in interactions with students:

MJK: Do you find the students have got quite conservative attitudes to, say, homosexuality, for example?

Mr Carlton:	It's a taboo area for a lot of them and it's parental attitudes. Yes, I suppose conservative is probably a good word, I don't like the word but that's the one that describes it best and I would not want to say things that go directly against parental opinions except they're not my opinions, so I'm giving my opinion. If the parents disagree with it then I want to talk to them as well. Now I can't do that, so I tend to put things in a way that, 'Well that's my view, that's your parents, you make your own mind up'.
MJK:	So would you say, 'Well this is my view, you may hear others?'
Mr Carlton:	Oh every time and I try to show a variety of opinions through other sources. One of my closest friends is gay, I'm not, but he don't mind that so why should I mind him being gay, you know.

Here Mr Carlton suggests that the homophobia of pupils can be traced to parental attitudes and teachers have to be mindful of parental sensibilities in areas where there may be a potential source of disagreement between them and the school. To overcome this difficulty, Mr Carlton has developed teaching strategies that pose alternatives in terms of personal opinion and individual choice. The 'one-of-my-best-friends-is' argument is often regarded as the articulation of a liberal position that favours tolerance rather than diversity. In the school context, however, Mr Carlton's approach can be seen as a significant challenge to dominant sexual categories, introducing students to ideas and perspectives that they may not have considered previously. Mr Carlton's interventionist approach can be seen to be effective in situations where the teacher–pupil relationship is positive and mutually affirming: in this context it is possible to stimulate discussion, challenge normative assumptions and provide other ways of looking.

Approaches to students

In this section I focus upon the ways in which teachers view their relationship with students and the different approaches they adopt to informal processes of schooling such as peer group cultures and the 'hidden curriculum' of sexual learning outside of Personal,

Social and Health Education. Drawing upon the analysis developed in Chapter 3, my argument here is that teacher–pupil relations shape the informal sphere of school and provide us with insights into the everyday cultures of teachers and students. The ways in which teacher–pupil relations are played out at the informal level has an impact on the official curriculum and school policy which is mediated through the informal cultures of teachers and pupils. Kenway and Willis' (1998) study of gender and feminism in Australian schools suggests that teachers tend to adopt two overlapping orientations to the emotional world of students: the 'therapeutic'; and the 'authoritarian'. The authors indicate that the therapeutic approach recognises the importance of the experiential realm, while the authoritarian approach places more emphasis on students as cognitive and rational learners. Aspects of these approaches can be identified in teacher's practice of PSHE.

Miss Green, in keeping with Thomson and Scott (1991) indicate that teachers and pupils move in separate spheres:

Miss Green: There's a big gulf between us, they've got a whole world which we are not part of . . . to maintain order you have to have a distance. There are two different worlds and maybe that's how it's got to be.

For Miss Green the world of teachers and the world of pupils cannot be bridged because of the inherent structure of school relations. The discipline and order which teachers must maintain is premised on 'distance' from pupil cultures. The notion of 'two cultures' supports the concept of the 'hidden curriculum' that suggests that much of what pupils learn in school can be seen as social learning and takes place in informal spaces outside the official curriculum. Miss Green agrees that there is a hidden curriculum in relation to sexual learning but holds out the hope that Personal and Social Education will also have a voice:

MJK: Do you think that the hidden curriculum might be more effective for students learning about sex than the official curriculum?

Miss Green: Oh I suspect that's the way they get the misinformation or real information, a bit of both I suspect, yes, I'm sure it always will be. It was when I was at school . . . I can only say I hope a lot of the accurate information we are able to give them through PSE will filter through to the hidden curriculum and I'm sure it will. It will be made use of in the same way as some of the messages they get from the media will be made use of. Some are going to be conflicting . . . but I just hope that the message, the correct information that we're giving them in school is going to be sufficiently helpful to them to make sense of all the other things.

Here Miss Green suggests that PSE is able to provide accurate information that can be assimilated into pupil perspectives. There is a certain appeal to rationality outlined by Kenway and Willis (1998) in Miss Green's support of PSE, promoting the notion that the 'accurate' and 'correct' will triumph over misinformation and will ultimately enable students to make sense of competing messages. In certain moments Miss Green indicated that it is possible to gain access to the pupil world:

MJK: Do you ever catch glimpses of how the students may be thinking and feeling about sex? Do you ever hear tales or gather pieces of information?

Miss Green: Not unless I actually sit down and talk to a group of youngsters. I was on cover one day and it was girls PE and they couldn't do the lesson so I'd watched a programme about young people and sex and thought 'was this really the case?' So I started talking to these girls and they were very open and quite willing to talk and, yes, only if I do that sort of thing because obviously we don't intrude.

In this example Miss Green discovered that a different set of teacher–pupil relationships become possible when the normal school timetable was disrupted. The openness of pupils in this instance challenged, albeit temporarily, the idea of two closely bounded school cultures.

Whereas Miss Green was accepting of school structures and the ways in which they impact upon pupil–teacher relations, Mr Carlton suggested that personal relationships between teachers and pupils can transgress school structures. His pedagogic style and personal biography insisted that, in his case, teacher and students occupy the same world through their shared identifications of class and locality. This mutual recognition between Mr Carlton and the young people he taught created the conditions for an affirmative approach to PSE. In this area of the curriculum, as in CDT, Mr Carlton has developed his own pedagogic style:

Mr Carlton: Six years ago it started and it (PSE) was awful. It was all bits of paper and it was worksheet, worksheet, worksheet and I was getting brassed off with handing these worksheets out so I thought, 'What's PSE? Who can say what PSE is?' PSE is you and me sitting down talking to each other, getting their ideas out of them and that's what I did.

Mr Carlton described his approach to PSE as a highly individualised pedagogy, based on his experiences, which incorporated strategies such as: responding to local events, being provocative, winding people up and using humour. His ability to communicate with pupils was enhanced by his use of colloquial terms and regional dialect.

Mr Carlton: Accent is an automatic turn off. You get someone who's talking in a southern accent and they [the pupils] don't wanna know. Where, if you call a spade a spade . . . The way I talk to kids sometimes is the way they talk to each other and if that involves using four letter words I use them. If it makes it understood and used in context then, to me, that's not wrong . . . Some teachers here might disapprove of the language but if you've got to explain something and you're talking 'a penis', well to the kids, 'a dick' you know. You make people understand through the language.

It is interesting to note that controversy over use of language acquires significance in debates where different political perspectives are at stake. Historically, in struggles around gender, ethnicity and class, language becomes a locus of concern; the promotion of certain terms and the prohibition of others become important signifiers carrying associative meanings and identities in moments of political change and social awareness (see Volosinov 1973; Fairclough 1989). Mr Carlton illustrates the ways in which language can be seen as a site of struggle at the level of the local. His approach to language forms an integral part of his pedagogic repertoire, providing a further point of identification between himself and the students he teaches. His willingness to use the language of pupil cultures, particularly in relation to sexuality, risks disapproval from other teachers but offers a compelling mode of engagement for students. Mr Carlton's championing of the vernacular contrasts with the views and practices of other sex educators I observed and spoke with. Beth, the school nurse at Clarke School, used the accepted commonplace terms for contraceptives and sexual practices when addressing a class, though she did acknowledge slang terms that may be in use among young people:

Beth: This is a condom or sheath. You may have other words for this, like johnny, rubber, French letter, nodder, but it's the same thing.

Mrs Evans, however, actively discouraged the use of colloquial terms in discussions of sexual matters and often prefaced student responses with comments such as, 'Now you can say whatever you feel here, as long as you use the proper names for things' (fieldnotes 22.1.96). Though both teachers claimed student-centred pedagogies, Mr Carlton and Mrs Evans clearly differed in approaches to language. The divergent styles of the two teachers illustrate the diversity within student-centred approaches and the ways in which pedagogies become personal. In this respect the use of particular words and ways of speaking highlights the links between language and identity and the ways in which language can be used by individuals to create and demarcate boundaries. Through the endorsement of particular language registers and vocabulary, teachers establish the terrain of comfort/discomfort, acceptability/unacceptability, recognition/non-recognition upon which sexual issues can be broached.

Concluding comments

In this chapter I have focused on the experiences of five teachers
and a school nurse. My analysis of their experiences traces the
connections between their auto/biographies and subjective investments to suggest that the personal plays a part in the development
of pedagogic practice. The glimpse into the life histories of the
practitioners I interviewed illustrate that their approaches to
teaching and learning have been shaped by their past experiences
as pupils and as gendered sexual subjects. In many cases respondents provided an account of what kind of school student they
were and how they learned about sex which was insightful and
instructive in terms of an analysis of pedagogic practice in the field
of sexuality education. The interviews I conducted indicate that
experience is translated into pedagogic practice in complex and
unexpected ways. The realisation that the sex educators I interviewed were, in their different contexts, the 'good girls' who didn't
disrupt their education by unplanned pregnancy becomes significant to an understanding of contemporary practice and will be
explored more fully in Chapter 8.

The analysis of interview material in this chapter also suggests
that teacher–pupil relationships provide the context for the practice of sex education and can influence the success of initiatives in
this field. Policy approaches to sex education (see Sex Education
Forum 1995) emphasise the importance of curriculum documents
which strike the 'right' note, encourage certain pedagogic
approaches over others and specify criteria for teaching and learning. My argument, however, is that the success of sex education
depends on a contingency of local factors that cannot necessarily
be accounted for at the level of policy. Mr Carlton, for example, is
unlikely to match the selection criteria drawn up in a person speci-
fication for the post of sex educator. Rather, his profile as rugby-
playing, heavy-drinking lad would place him beyond the bounds
of desirability for the teaching of a subject that requires sensitivity
and understanding, especially in relation to issues of gender politics.
However, the success of Mr Carlton's approach to sex education
and PSE generally indicates that other factors may be in play in
the development of 'good practice'. His identifications as local,
working-class, speaker of the regional dialect and part of the community give him a grounding in the school which facilitates the
development of positive and mutually affirming student–teacher

relations. In other words, the qualities, characteristics and identities valued by the student population become important to the success of pedagogic practice as a whole. At Oakwood School there is an engagement between the local culture of the school and Mr Carlton's organic approach to teaching and learning that makes him popular with students and successful as a teacher. This observation points to the importance of context to policy initiatives and pedagogic strategies and the difficulties involved in specifying a formula for 'success'.

Chapter 8

Sexuality, gender and schooling reconsidered: notes towards a conclusion

In this final chapter I summarise and conclude my ethnographic account of sexuality, gender and school relations. The summary will be organised into three sections: firstly, a discussion of the main research findings; secondly, the implications of these findings for teaching and learning in the field of sex education; and finally, the implications of my findings for future research and praxis in relation to issues of sexuality, gender and schooling.

Summary of the research findings

In this section I aim to summarise the key points and main research findings as developed in previous chapters. While the findings gleaned from the research are discussed throughout the book here I profile the main findings that have emerged from the study as a whole.

Chapter 1 'Fragments from a fading career', presented a set of biographical moments that elaborated upon my personal invest-ments in ideas and issues informing this study. Using the concept of 'memory-work' (Haug *et al.* 1987) as a research method and a mode of analysis, the chapter indicated the ways in which my early experiences as a teacher shaped my approach to school rela-tions and the sphere of the sexual within the school. The personal narratives presented in this chapter illustrated some of my invest-ments in ideas of radical pedagogy that I both internalised and continually struggled over. The chapter pointed to the complex relationship between unconscious dynamics at the level of the indi-vidual and their engagement with external social structures – a recurrent theme of the study. In 'Fragments from a fading career' the object of analysis is the personal, the development of my pedagogic practice and the shaping of my research agenda. The reflexive account developed in this chapter makes explicit the ways in which personal experience remains an integral part of research activity and teaching style. Chapter 1, therefore, aims to offer an insight into both how I came to be personally invested in the research and how the research can be seen as the product of these investments. In Chapter 7 I returned to the theme of biography and the personal: firstly, to look at teachers and their pedagogic practice; and secondly, to consider these themes in relation to the methodological issues informing the study. Aspects of life history method are used to study teaching as an activity that is intimately connected with personal experience in conscious and unconscious ways.

Chapter 2 introduced my intention to bring together different bodies of literature in my analysis of sexuality and schooling to provide a context for the empirical work. These bodies of literature draw upon theorists working within socio-historical approaches and psychoanalytic approaches to understanding human sexuality. Chapter 2 provides an overview of this work and, importantly, sets out my aim to combine poststructuralist insights on discourse and power relations with psychoanalytic theories on the formation of subjectivity and psychic processes in my analysis of sexual cultures in school. As noted in the chapter, I develop this approach in order to suggest that an understanding of psychic dynamics at the level of the subject may also help us to understand social relationships within the school. My approach to the relationship between the world of the unconscious and the world of the social, demonstrated throughout the study, builds upon the work of contemporary theorists and particularly that of Valerie Walkerdine. The chapter discusses Walkerdine's work in detail and points to the generative impact of her writing on my thinking and, in turn, the shaping of this study. In this chapter I also signalled my interest in heterosexuality as a focus for study and analysis. I noted that the concern with heterosexuality as a dominant sexual category has been inspired by recent debates in the field of sexuality and particularly my engagement with queer theory. Finally, the chapter highlighted my intention that the study will contribute to academic debate and practitioner knowledge in the field of sexuality, gender and schooling. It outlined an emergent body of work in this area that the study is both connected to and in dialogue with.

In Chapter 3, 'Producing heterosexualities: the school as a site of discursive practices' I introduce Foucaultian theories and apply them to the study of education through an analysis which argues that schools can be viewed as sites of discursive practice in relation to sexuality. 'Producing heterosexualities' provided an interpretive frame for looking at the field of sexuality, gender and schooling and, additionally, as a way of reading this and subsequent chapters. Specifically, the chapter develops the focus on heterosexuality to point to the ways in which the school produces heterosexualities through the everyday activities of school-based practice in different discursive spaces. 'Producing heterosexualities' identifies and discusses three sites of discursive practice where versions of heterosexuality can be invoked and naturalised: the official curriculum; pedagogic practice; and informal pupil cultures. The approach developed in this chapter involved making the notion of heterosexuality plural (heterosexualities) and understanding and addressing them as discursive formations defined in relation to each other. The later part of the chapter focusing on informal school relations drew upon ethnographic material from the fieldwork I conducted as part of this study. Issues of pedagogy were discussed with reference to a teacher of Personal and Social Education whom I observed and interviewed and with whom I built up a relationship during my time in the school. Similarly, informal student cultures are approached through ethnographic accounts gathered in the same school. Ethnographic material discussed at this point indicates that the production of heterosexualities in school can be seen as a gendered project in which young women and young men are positioned in particular ways. The chapter pointed out the ways in which asymmetrical power relations involved in issues of gender have the effect of positioning young women as objects of male sexual power and as carriers of a potentially dangerous and disruptive feminine sexuality. The discussion of female sexuality in relation to one student, Naomi, introduces the theme of embodiment as an important feature of sex–gender enactments and one that is returned to in Chapter 6. The three sites of discursive practice discussed in Chapter 3 highlight a key feature of the study, that of students as active subjects who produce sex–gender identities through specific discursive strategies. The chapter pointed to the ways in which pupil agency in the domain of the sexual operates as a counterpoint to discourses of sexuality in the official curriculum and in classroom practice.

Chapter 4, 'Agony aunts and absences: an analysis of a sex education class', developed and extended the approach to student cultures introduced in the previous chapter. Through an analysis of one sex education lesson, the chapter identified and discussed issues that were raised by pupils during the course of the lesson. Furthermore, the chapter explores the difficulties of sex education as a practice. The analysis developed in this chapter provides an example of the approach outlined above in which I bring together the use of discourse analysis with psychoanalytic theories. In 'Agony aunts' I argued that the classroom task, the act of writing a fictitious letter to a fictitious problem page can, in itself, open up a space for the projection of fears and desires. My treatment of the themes raised by students in this context used discursive explanations alongside psychoanalytic interpretations to explore the ways in which sexuality can be seen as an expression of psychic and social processes. This approach develops our understanding of sexuality as viewed and experienced by young people in school, rather than from the adult-centred perspectives of reproduction and restraint discussed in Chapter 3. An emergent theme in Chapter 4 is young women's use of popular culture as a resource in the articulation of sexual matters. I point out that the language of teenage magazines in particular provides young women with a discourse that they can appropriate in creative ways as a form of *expertise* which links verbal competence with femininity. This way of looking at popular culture – as a cultural resource for thinking and speaking the sexual – is further explored in the following chapter.

Accordingly, Chapter 5 develops an analysis of teenage magazines based upon ethnographic material and a closely worked textual analysis of the magazines themselves. This chapter, 'More Sugar? Teenage magazines, gender displays and sexual learning' argues that students' engagement with teenage magazines produced *gender displays*, spaces through which versions of masculinities and femininities can be constituted and publicly performed. The chapter identifies the importance of the same-sex peer group in the negotiation and enactment of sex–gender identities. Based upon observations of and interviews with friendship groups the chapter points to clear gender differences in the way students relate to, use and speak of the magazines. I argue that, for young women, there exists a relationship between magazine readership and the enactment of feminine identities. Young men, however,

204 Notes towards a conclusion

did not share the same relationship with teenage magazines and, in discussions, actively resist the discursive skills and sexual information provided by sustained engagement with the magazine format. This leads me to ask questions about how young men in school fashioned and performed their masculine identities – in what contexts and using which resources? These issues are addressed and explored in Chapter 6.

Issues of masculinity become the focus for Chapter 6 based upon my discussions with groups of young men in school. This chapter 'Understanding masculinities: young men, heterosexuality and embodiment' demonstrates the ways in which young men constitute and consolidate their sex–gender identities. The chapter argues that young men incorporate heterosexuality into the masculine repertoire through notions of activity and performance that directly involve the male body. Practices that young men engaged in such as sex-talk, masturbation and pornography are discussed in order to develop an analysis of young men's investments in versions of heterosexuality and masculinity. I suggest that these practices can be fused in ways that display competence and confer status within the male peer group. 'Understanding masculinities' further argues that young men attempt to *consolidate* their particular heterosexual masculine identities in another realm of activity, that of sexual relationships with women. In the many discussions I conducted with young people during the course of the study, the most surprising feature of these exchanges for me was the way that these young men referred to their bodies as objects of disgust and loathing. Educational research has routinely commented on the ways in which boys and young men occupy positions of dominance in school and take up space with ease either through rituals of disruption in the classroom or out-of-class activities such as sport. This version of normative masculinity as centred, dominant and at-large could also be applied to the young men I observed and spent time with. However, over time I came to understand their position of dominance as fragile and uncertain. I was surprised to find that young men I spoke with appeared less than comfortable with their bodies. The chapter develops an analysis of these expressions through the use of Kristeva's theory of 'abjection'. The chapter draws upon this analysis to discuss other ways in which young men attempt to define their identities in relations to a range of Others. Firstly, the Others of homophobic discourse, real and imagined, are discussed in ways that point to the psychic dynamics involved in this encounter. Secondly, the chapter discusses young men's relationship to the domain of the feminine, and particularly female sexuality, in terms of fear and desire. The discussion, which draws upon young men's engagement with popular cultural forms, argues that female sexuality can become the object of fascination, fear and repulsion at different moments. Finally, Chapter 6 discusses issues of sexual reputation and ethnicity to further explore the relationship between masculinity and other social categories. The chapter concludes that young men appear concerned to perform and maintain a dominant heterosexual masculinity in order to protect themselves from potentially emasculating experiences they routinely encountered in the social sphere.

In Chapter 7 I turn the research gaze away from the realm of informal student cultures and towards the culture of teachers and sex education practitioners. The chapter 'Sexing the subject: teachers, pedagogies and sex education' notes the way that student cultures may be shaped and played out *in relation* to the culture of teachers and the dominant values of the school. The focus on teachers, moreover, aims to consider the ways in which they think about and relate to issues of sexuality and the implications of this for their pedagogic practice. The chapter outlines and discusses different literatures on teacher cultures that offer diverse perspectives on teaching and teacher identities. Auto/biographical and life history methods are used once again in order to document and study the personal narratives of individual teachers as they presented an account of themselves as pedagogues and former pupils. The accounts generated in interviews with teachers indicate that it is possible to identify connections between personal experience and pedagogic practice, especially in approaches to sex education. The analysis of this material, however, suggests that these points of connection may be haphazard and may manifest themselves in ways that cannot always be anticipated. The main argument developed in 'Sexing the subject' pointed to the limitations of policy in the field of sex education and the difficulties of outlining a model for teaching and learning in this area of the curriculum. The chapter concludes by placing emphasis on the need for 'good practice' to emerge organically from a contingency of local factors which cannot necessarily be identified at the level of policy.

The above summary profiles the research findings as developed throughout the study and points to a key finding of the project:

the importance of the same-sex peer group in the production of sex–gender identities. Overall, the chapters highlight the significance of peer group interactions to the collective enactment of masculinities, femininities and their relationship to the sexual. The key argument of the study remains the importance of the activity and agency of student cultures in the regulation and performance of gendered heterosexualities. Through exchanges in friendship groups in school, young men and young women engage in elaborate forms of social learning whereby they learn about sex and *do* gender. This way of looking illustrates the ways in which sexuality, as produced and experienced by students in school, is discursively tied to gender in the enactment of masculinities and femininities. The acquisition of sexual knowledge and the enactment of gender is in dialogue with popular cultural forms such as teenage magazines, television programmes and pornographic representations. Furthermore, the analysis of student peer groups stresses the inter-relationship of psychic and social processes to collectively generated versions of sex–gender identities that valorise forms of heterosexuality while deprecating forms of homosexuality.

The main findings of the study provide many points of continuity with earlier ethnographic studies that have focused upon issues of sexuality, gender and schooling. The pervasive presence of homophobia, the concern with notions of 'reputation' and the naturalisation of heterosexuality within the school site echo many of the themes of earlier work. This continuity may lead us to ask questions about the nature and scope of change that can be affected within educational arenas. In the larger societal context where public representations and individual practice suggest the possibility of more fluidity in sex–gender categories and identities why is this possibility rarely reflected in school? In the public sphere of representations sexual diversity has become more visible while shifts in the economic and the domestic sphere offer the possibility of change in gender relations and family forms. Yet many young people in school, like the respondents in this study, remain preoccupied with the less radical and often more reactionary aspects of sexuality and gender and utilise them to style their own forms of social learning that can be both agentic and regulatory. My work with young people in school suggests that the key to this apparent contradiction lies in the sexual cultures of young people themselves. Within the context of student sexual cultures, issues of gender and sexuality take on a logic and a momentum that makes sense to the young people involved. My observations point to the abiding significance of gender and sexuality for young people as important sites for the exercise of autonomy and agency within the confined spaces of the school. From the perspective of young people themselves, their informal peer group cultures remain one of the few sites within school that is not shaped by the demands of teachers, parents, politicians and policy makers. The educational experience of students in the UK and elsewhere is increasingly marked by policies and practices which position students as receptacles for formal learning. The National Curriculum is to be delivered *to them*, targets are set *for them* and their 'progress' is monitored and recorded in league tables and national tests. Within this seemingly disempowering environment of educational imperative and external control, student sexual cultures become imbued with significance as adult-free and education-free zones where students can collectively negotiate what is acceptable/ desirable and what is 'too much'. The collective activity of young people exists in tension with the individualising culture of contemporary education practice. By placing emphasis on the importance of the group over the individual and the power of the group to negotiate and re-work commonly held assumptions, young people in school work against the grain of contemporary educative processes that individualise students and prioritise personal endeavour. They also work against the commonly held adult assumption that sexuality remains a feature of adult life that children and young people should be protected from. In the sphere of student sexual cultures young people relate to issues of gender and sexuality by drawing upon the cultural resources available to them. My research indicates that such resources, though diverse and varied, frequently present dominant versions of sex–gender categories that can be utilised by young people to fashion their own versions of dominant sex–gender identities. Thus the trying on of dominant forms is played out within student cultures and exists at the expense of marginal sex–gender identities.

Research findings in brief

- Students are active subjects engaged in producing sex–gender identities within informal peer group cultures.

- The agency and activity of young people in relation to sexual issues exists as a counterpoint to the official curriculum.
- Same-sex friendship groups, referred to in the study as *student sexual cultures*, play an important part in the negotiation and enactment of sex–gender categories.
- Within student sexual cultures young people engage in important forms of social learning.
- The pervasive presence of homophobias, a concern with notions of sexual reputation and the naturalisation of heterosexuality remain well-worked themes within student sexual cultures.
- Popular culture is appropriated by young people in creative ways and is used as a way of thinking about and speaking about sexual themes and issues, particularly by young women.
- Engagements with popular culture provide young people with a space through which versions of masculinity and femininity can be constituted and publicly performed as *gender displays*.
- The enactment of heterosexual masculinity may offer young men some protection from potentially emasculating experiences.
- Issues of sexuality and gender become imbued with significance in student sexual cultures because young people regard them as an area of their lives in which they have control and autonomy.
- Good practice in the sphere of sexuality education emerges organically from a contingency of local factors where the values of the student population cohere with teaching strategies and pedagogic approaches.

Implications for the practice of sex education

Research in the field of gender and education has been instrumental in proposing strategies for gender reform and intervention in schools. Kenway and Willis's (1998) Australian study on the effects of gender reform on schools indicates that the remaking of gender can have positive outcomes for the school as a whole. Their study concludes that schools where gender reform was successful were: open and refreshed by new ideas; encouraged and celebrated difference; recognised the importance of changing their practice and themselves. Applying the success of gender reform initiatives to the area of sexuality is not an easy project, however, the main findings of the study relating to student peer groups and their engagement with sex–gender categories and identities have many implications for teaching and learning in the field of sex education. Some of these implications have been discussed in the main body of the study. In this section I aim to bring together issues and ideas that suggest routes for the development of sex education as a pedagogic practice. Chapter 4 pointed to the gender differentiated ways in which students utilised popular culture in the articulation of sexual themes. The chapter indicated that the style and language of teenage magazines could provide a popular and productive resource for teaching sex education. Young women enjoyed the magazine format and appropriated the discourse of these magazines in positive ways. Young men, however, were not so comfortable with the use of teen magazines and did not participate in the sex education lesson as readily and enthusiastically as girls. This indicates that teachers may have to devise other strategies to encourage the participation of boys. Chapter 5 further explored the resistance of young males to teenage magazines and pointed to the potentially emasculating effect of sustained engagement with a form that they considered to be 'feminine'. Issues of emasculation for young men involved a rejection and disavowal of the feminine that was connected with their fears of being gay or being perceived as gay. This point calls for strategies within sex education and social learning more generally to address issues of gender and sexual diversity. The development of such strategies could explore issues of sex–gender identity and gender-appropriate behaviour in critical ways that engage with young people's insecurities and anxieties in this area.

The study illustrates the ways in which engagement with popular cultural forms in educational spheres is not necessarily progressive. Chapter 5, 'More Sugar? Teenage magazines, gender displays and sexual learning' pointed to the ways in which young women used teenage magazines to regulate discussion within the female peer group. The chapter also indicated that the treatment of gay themes and issues of sexual diversity within the magazines tended to rely on dominant ways of looking and did not challenge stereotypes or discriminatory practices in this area. 'Understanding masculinities' (Chapter 6) discussed young men's engagement with popular cultural forms and suggested that pornography could be used to establish differences *between* males and shape desirable versions of heterosexual masculinity. The chapter also discussed young men's views on gender relations based on their readership of contemporary television programmes that drew upon and played with new feminine subjectivities. Analysis of these practices indicated that young men used popular culture to recuperate traditional heterosexual masculinities. The social practices of young men and women in relation to popular cultural forms indicates that using popular culture in sex education is not, in itself, automatically desirable or productive. While popular culture has the power to engage young people, the forms of engagement may not necessarily enhance sexual learning. It is in this area that researchers and practitioners could collaborate to develop models and approaches to popular culture as a resource for learning that could be used in the classroom.

In Chapter 6 the theme of embodiment examined in the analysis of young men's responses has further implications for pedagogic practice. Chapter 6 indicated that sex–gender identities are lived in and through the body. Within the context of the official school, bodily expressions tend to be confined to sport, dress and the occupation of physical space. Interviews with young men suggested that their concerns with the body were a little different. While grounded in the experience of physicality, the comments of those young men suggest that bodily experiences extend into the realm of the senses. Young men indicated that the sensory experiences of touch and smell become significant in relation to their own bodies and the bodies of the women with whom they have sexual relationships. This adds an additional dimension to the 'missing discourse of desire' in sex education identified by Michelle Fine (1988). The theme of embodiment analysed in this chapter points to the difficult yet important task of addressing issues of pleasure, desire and disgust in discussions of sexuality with young people.

Another consideration in relation to the above arises from my treatment of pupils as collectivities engaged in the production of sex–gender identities. My analysis indicates that salient versions of masculinity and femininity are negotiated and promoted within same-sex peer groups. However, this process can have the effect of perpetuating some of the features I aim to critique. In relation to masculinity, my concerns are summarised by Pattman *et al.* (1998):

> The danger is that research becomes so preoccupied with the ways boys aggressively and competitively assert themselves that it fails to acknowledge the possibilities of 'softer', less polarized and more 'transgressive' masculine identities, except

as subordinate masculinities in opposition to which hegemonic masculinities are always enacted.

(Pattman *et al.* 1998: 140)

In defining collective investments in sex and gender within the peer group I may have overlooked individuals who are not circumscribed by the regulatory boundaries of dominant groups within the school and who may, in their own ways, be creatively shaping sex–gender identities in positive terms.

The main findings relating to practice noted in Chapter 7 concerned the role of teachers in the implementation of sex education programmes. The chapter argues that teachers who achieved some measure of success in this area of the curriculum were secure in their identity as 'teacher', were well liked by pupils, had an understanding of the local community and saw themselves as part of the local culture of the school and its community. The chapter also drew attention to the insight that female teachers of sex education were the former 'good girls' who had survived schooling with their reputations untarnished and their femininity enhanced by *not becoming pregnant*. This has implications for the practice of sex education and the messages of caution contained therein, specifically aimed at young women. It is possible that models of peer education, such as those used in drugs education, could broaden the message in this respect by incorporating moral as well as practical issues into discussions which focus on the experiential with people of a similar age-group.

Implications for pedagogic practice in brief

The following points for the development of sexuality education arise from discussions I have had with teachers in in-service sessions as well as from the research and related reading in this field:

- Recognise the importance of local values, identities and understandings in the development of sensitive and culturally specific sexuality education.
- A recognition of pupil cultures may offer a starting point for teachers.
- It may not be helpful to presume that pupils are 'innocent' in the domain of the sexual; some may be sexually active and all

pupils will be aware of the significance of sexual cultures to their lives and identities.

- Student-centred approaches may be helpful for teachers and pupils to develop their own moral/political positions.
- Popular culture can be seen as a resource for sexual learning and can be utilised by teachers for discussion.
- Young people do not absorb ideas passively but are active in constructing beliefs from a range of sources.
- Teachers may wish to establish ground-rules with students to provide parameters for discussion and behaviour.
- Respect differences and be aware of power relations.
- Work with colleagues, governors and parents to create a progressive policy supportive to practitioners.

Implications for further research

In this final section of the chapter I make some suggestions with regard to further research into sexuality and schooling. The theme of reputation discussed in the book may suggest the emergence of a new moral order or indeed the return to an old one in matters of sexual behaviour and sexual activity. While many of the gender inequalities identified by earlier studies persist, it is possible that young people may be changing their attitude and behaviour to sex in the light of HIV/AIDS and a changing sexual climate. Derogatory terms usually reserved for young women with a reputation for sexual 'looseness' are now also being applied to young men who boasted about and engaged in casual sex. Most young people I spoke with, male and female, viewed sexual promiscuity in negative terms as risky, potentially damaging and anti-liberatory. One-night stands were regarded as extraordinary rather than routine and there was some hint that the moralism implied in these positions was taking on a new form, as distinct from pre-1960s notions of propriety. Although I do not want to make any claims on the basis of these comments I was struck by the difference between their expressions and my own early experiences of sexual activity in the 1970s. Further research in this field could build upon the insights of existing studies to explore the sexual behaviour of young people and the social meanings they ascribe to sexual encounters and relations of intimacy.

The theme of embodiment discussed in the light of interviews with young men also indicates that further research in this area could be productive in developing our understanding of young people and sexuality. Young men's expressions of disgust in relation to their own bodies was an unexpected dimension that I stumbled upon, almost by accident, quite late into the fieldwork period. Recent social theory has explored issues of embodiment in terms of the symbolic significance of the body in contemporary thought (see Featherstone *et al.* 1991). Further research in this field could apply these ideas to a study of young people in school, as yet unexplored in this literature. Another fruitful area of enquiry in relation to themes of embodiment and sexuality could be the extended use of psychoanalytic insights. I found Kristeva's theory of abjection particularly generative in developing an analysis of young men's expressions of bodily disgust. More widespread use of psychoanalytic theories in this field could produce interesting accounts of psychosocial processes. This method could also be pursued in relation to issues of femininity and embodiment. Susan Bordo's (1993) cultural analysis of feminism and the body suggests that women in contemporary Western societies learn the rules for the construction of femininity directly through bodily discourse:

> through images that tell us what clothes, body shape, facial expressions, movements and behaviour are required . . . women must develop a totally other-oriented emotional economy.
>
> (Bordo 1993: 170–1)

My research has not incorporated this aspect of contemporary femininity which I regard as a complementary approach to the one developed in this study, and one which could be explored in further school-based work. My discussions with young people in school also point to the potential for further work in the field of ethnicity and sexuality that could draw upon emergent work on new ethnicities (Nayak 1997; 2001), which includes seeing the responses of white respondents as racially informed accounts.

Finally, I would suggest that there is a need to translate research findings and insights in relation to sexuality, gender and schooling into practitioner-orientated accounts that could be used as resources for teaching and learning as part of the Personal, Social

Notes

1 Fragments from a fading career: personal narratives and emotional investments

1 An earlier version of this chapter appeared in the *Nordic Journal of Women's Studies* (1997) 5(1): 34–47.
2 I am indebted to Richard Johnson, course tutor for M.Soc.Sci. Cultural Studies at the University of Birmingham and leader of the course *Cultural Formations and Social Identities* in which this memory-work took shape. His teaching remains a source of support and inspiration.
3 Banding is a classificatory system used in UK secondary schools to place students in classes according to their academic ability. There were three bands in the school where I worked – upper, middle and lower.

3 Producing heterosexualities: the school as a site of discursive practices

1 This consists of a video and teaching materials available from CARE (Christian Association for Religious Education) London SW1 3YP. The video is directed by Norman Stone and Sonia Palmer. The sleeve notes of the video read, 'aimed at 14–15 year old PSHE students, *Make Love Last* presents the case for waiting for sex'.
2 In this much-publicised case of 1985, Victoria Gillick successfully brought a legal action against the Department of Health and Social Security to prevent under 16-year-olds from receiving contraceptive services without the knowledge and consent of their parents.

4 Agony aunts and absences: an analysis of a sex education class

1 An earlier version of this chapter was published in *Melbourne Studies in Education*, 40(2): 127–48.
2 For a further discussion of these issues see Johnson (1996).
3 See Hollway (1989) for a discussion of discourses of male sexuality, especially the 'male sex-drive'.
4 I am indebted to Kate Corr for a consideration of these themes.

5 More Sugar? Teenage magazines, gender displays and sexual learning

1 An earlier version of this chapter appeared in the *European Journal of Cultural Studies*, 4(1): 211–27.
2 *Newsnight* report, BBC 2, 5.2.96. Peter Luff, MP tabled a private member's bill in the House of Commons which called for a party political consensus on parental duties and responsibilities re adolescents and the censorship of teenage magazines as suitable for specific age ranges. Teen magazines were also the subject of a Radio 4 phone-in programme, *Call Nick Ross*, 6.2.96.
3 See Thorne (1993) for a discussion of gender appropriate categories and the possibilities and constraints for 'gender crossing' among boys and girls.
4 See also McRobbie and Garber 1982; Griffin 1982; Lees 1986, 1993, Cowie and Lees 1987 for a discussion of the ways in which young men draw upon patriarchal discourse where misogynist labelling and a concern with female sexual reputations become key markers for the construction of young women's identities.
5 Thorne's (1993) analysis points to the limitations of viewing boys and girls as occupying different cultures. This approach, she suggests, exaggerates gender differences, overlooks intra-gender variation and raises questions about whose experiences are represented in educational research.

6 Understanding masculinities: young men, heterosexuality and embodiment

1 I am grateful to Debbie Epstein for pointing out that this incident in fact occurred on the *Jenny Jones* programme, not *Ricki Lake* as stated by Matthew.
2 Epitomised by the success of the *Spice Girls* and other all-girl bands such as *All Saints* and *Cleopatra*.

7 Sexing the subject: teachers, pedagogies and sex education

1 There are many other models for sex education outlined by researchers, including: Aggleton *et al.* (1989) scientific, obfuscatory, romantic; Carson (1992) traditionalist, progressive, radical and libertarian; Johnson (1996) neo-conservative, neo-liberal, social liberal and emergent.

Appendix

Transcription code

. . .   refers to short pause
–   refers to change in direction, break or interruption
[. . .]   refers to a section of the data which is omitted
[laughs]   refers to verbal expressions which are connected with speech
[*demonstrating*]   refers to non-verbal actions and body language connected with speech
(to Naomi)   provides clarification of words and actions
[unclear]   refers to word or passage which is inaudible
with emphasis   refers to that which is said with emphasis

Bibliography

Adam, B.D. (1998) 'Theorising homophobia', *Sexualities* 1(4): 387–404.

Acker, K. (1995) *Pussycat Fever*, Edinburgh/San Francisco: AK Press.

Aggleton, P., Homans, H. and Warwick, I. (1989) 'Health education, sexuality and aids', in S. Walker and L. Walker (eds) *Politics and the Processes of Schooling*, Milton Keynes: Open University Press.

Alderson, C. (1968) *Magazines Teenagers Read*, London: Pergamon Press.

Alloway, N. and Gilbert, P. (1997) 'Boys and literacy: lessons from Australia', *Gender and Education* 9(1): 49–59.

Althusser, L. (1971) 'Ideology and ideological state apparatuses', *Lenin and Philosophy and Other Essays*, London: New Left Books.

Altman, M. (1984) 'Everything they always wanted you to know: the ideology of popular sex', in C. Vance (ed.) *Pleasure and Danger, Exploring Female Sexuality*, London: Pandora.

Alyson, S. (ed.) (1980) *Young, Gay and Proud*, Boston, MA: Alyson Publications.

Anderson, B. (1983) *Imagined Communities, Reflections on the Origins and Spread of Nationalism*, London: Verso.

Anyon, J. (1981) 'Social class and school knowledge', *Curriculum Inquiry* 11(1).

Anyon, J. (1983) 'Intersections of gender and class: accommodation and resistance by working class and affluent females to contradictory sex-role ideologies', in S. Walker and L. Barton (eds) *Gender, Class and Education*, Lewes: Falmer Press.

Apple, M. (1979) *Ideology and Curriculum*, London: Routledge & Kegan Paul.

Apple, M. (1982) *Education and Power*, Boston: Routledge & Kegan Paul.

Arnot, M. and Weiler, K. (eds) (1993) *Feminism and Social Justice in Education: International Perspectives*, London: Falmer.

Atkinson, P. (1990) *The Ethnographic Imagination, Textual Constructions of Reality*, London: Routledge.

Atkinson, P. (1992) *Understanding Ethnographic Texts*, London: Sage.

Atkinson, P., Delamont, S. and Hammersley, M. (1993) 'Qualitative research traditions', in M. Hammersley (ed.) *Educational Research, Current Issues*, London: Paul Chapman.

Ball, S.J. (1981) *Beachside Comprehensive*, Cambridge: Cambridge University Press.

Ball, S.J. (1987) *The Micro-Politics of the School*, London: Methuen.

Ball, S.J. (1990) *Politics and Policy Making in Education, Explorations in Policy Sociology*, London: Routledge.

Ball, S.J. (1993) 'Self-doubt and soft data: social and technical trajectories in ethnographic fieldwork', in M. Hammersley (ed.) *Educational Research: Current Issues*, London: Paul Chapman.

Ball, S.J. and Goodson, I. (1985) *Teachers' Lives and Careers*, London: Falmer.

Barker, M. (1981) *The New Racism, Conservativism and the Ideology of the Tribe*, London: Junction Books.

Barker, M. (1989) *Comics, Ideology, Power and the Critics*, Manchester: Manchester University Press.

Barrs, M. (ed.) (1973) *Identity*, Harmondsworth: Penguin.

Benton, M. and Benton, P. (eds) (1971) *Touchstones 5, a Teaching Anthology*, Sevenoaks: Hodder & Stoughton.

Bland, L. (1995) *Banishing the Beast, English Feminism and Sexual Morality 1885–1915*, London: Penguin.

Bordo, S. (1993) *Unbearable Weight, Feminism, Western Culture and the Body*, Berkeley: University of California Press.

Bourdieu, P. (1986) *Distinction: a Social Critique of the Judgement of Taste*, London: Routledge.

Bowles, S. and Gintis, H. (1976) *Schooling in Capitalist America*, London: Routledge & Kegan Paul.

Bristow, J. (1997) *Sexuality*, London: Routledge.

Britzman, D. (1995) 'What is this thing called love?' *Taboo, Journal of Culture and Education* 1: 65–93.

Brooks, A. (1997) *Postfeminisms: Feminism, Cultural Theory and Cultural Forms*, London: Routledge.

Bubandt, N. (1998) 'The odour of things: smell and the cultural elaboration of disgust in Eastern Indonesia', *Ethnos, Journal of Anthropology* 63(1): 48–80.

Burgess, R.G. (ed.) (1991) *Field Research: a Sourcebook and Field Manual*, London: Routledge.

Burgin, V. (1990) 'Geometry and abjection', in J. Fletcher and A. Benjamin (eds) *Abjection, Melancholia and Love: the Work of Julia Kristeva*, London: Routledge.

Butler, J. (1990) *Gender Trouble, Feminism and the Subversion of Identity*, London: Routledge.

Butler, J. (1993) *Bodies that Matter: on the Discursive Limits of 'Sex'*, London: Routledge.

Byrne, E. (1978) *Women and Education*, London: Tavistock.

Cameron, D. and Frazer, E. (1996) 'The murderer as misogynist?' in S. Jackson and S. Scott (eds) *Feminism and Sexuality, a Reader*, Edinburgh: Edinburgh University Press.

Canaan, J. (1986) 'Why a "slut" is a "slut": cautionary tales of middle class teenage girls' morality', in H. Varenne (ed.) *Symbolising America*, Lincoln: University of Nabraska Press.

Carson, D.L. (1992) 'Ideological conflict and change in the sexuality curriculum', in J. Sears (ed.) *Sexuality and the Curriculum, the Politics and Practice of Sexuality Education*, New York: Teachers' College Press.

Centre for Contemporary Cultural Studies (1982) *Making Histories*, London: Hutchinson.

Cesara, M. (1982) *Reflections of a Woman Anthropologist: No Hiding Place*, London: Academic Press.

Clifford, J. and Marcus, G. (eds) (1986) *Writing Culture: the Poetics and Politics of Ethnography*, Berkeley: University of California Press.

Cohen, A.K. (1955) *Delinquent Boys: the Culture of the Gang*, Chicago: Free Press.

Comfort, A. (ed.) (1974) *The Joy of Sex, a Gourmet Guide to Lovemaking*, London: Quartet.

Connell, R.W. (1985) *Teachers' Work*, Sydney: George Allen & Unwin.

Connell, R.W. (1987) *Gender and Power, Society, the Person and Sexual Politics*, Cambridge: Polity.

Connell, R.W. (1989) 'Cool guys, swots and wimps: the interplay of masculinity and education', *Oxford Review of Education* 13: 291–303.

Connell, R.W. (1995) *Masculinities*, London: Polity.

Connelly, F.M. and Clandinin, D.J. (1988) *Teachers as Curriculum Planners: Narratives of Experience*, New York: Teachers' College Press.

Cooper, D. (1994) *Sexing the City: Lesbian and Gay Politics within the Activist State*, London: Rivers Oram Press.

Cortazzi, M. (1993) *Narrative Analysis*, London: Falmer Press.

Coward, R. (1984) *Female Desire*, London: Paladin.

Cowie, C. and Lees, S. (1987) 'Slags or drags?' in *Feminist Review* (ed.) *Sexuality: a Reader*, London: Virago.

Curry, M.J. (2001) 'Preparing to be privatized, the hidden curriculum of a community college ESL writing class', in E. Margolis (ed.) *The Hidden Curriculum in Higher Education*, New York: Routledge.

Davies, B. (1983) 'The role pupils play in the social construction of classroom order', *British Journal of Sociology of Education* 4(1): 55–69.

Davies, B. (1997) 'Constructing and deconstructing masculinities through critical literacy', *Gender and Education* 9(1): 9–30.

Denzin, N.K. (1970) *The Research Act*, Chicago: Aldine.

Department of Health (1992) *Health of the Nation: a Strategy for Health in England*, London: HMSO.

de Sade, D.A.F. (1993) *The Passionate Philosopher, A Marquis de Sade Reader*, M. Crossland (ed.), trans. M. Crossland, London: Minerva.

Donald, J. (1985) 'Beacons of the future: schooling, subjection and subjectification', in Veronica Beechey and James Donald (eds) *Subjectivity and Social Relations*, Milton Keynes: Open University Press.

Dollimore, J. (1991) *Sexual Dissidence: Augustine to Wilde, Freud to Foucault*, Oxford: Clarendon Press.

Dreyfus, H.L. and Rabinow, P. (1982) *Michel Foucault, Beyond Structuralism and Hermeneutics*, Brighton: Harvester Press.

Dworkin, A. (1981) *Our Blood: Prophecies and Discourses on Sexual Politics*, New York: G.P. Putnam.

Dwyer, K. (1982) *Moroccan Dialogues: Anthropology in Question*, Baltimore, MD: Johns Hopkins University Press.

Dyer, R. (1993) *The Matter of Images: Essays on Representation*, London: Routledge.

Easthope, A. (1990) *What a Man's Gotta Do, the Masculine Myth in Popular Culture*, Boston: Unwin Hyman.

Edwards, T. (1998) 'Queer fears: against the cultural turn', *Sexualities* 1(4): 471–83.

Ellsworth, E. (1994) 'Why doesn't this feel empowering? Working through the oppressive myths of critical pedagogy', in Lynda Stone (ed.) *The Education Feminism Reader*, London: Routledge.

Epstein, D. (ed.) (1994) *Challenging Gay and Lesbian Inequalities in Education*, Buckingham: Open University Press.

Epstein, D. (1996) 'Keeping them in their place: hetero/sexist harassment, gender and the enforcement of heterosexuality', in L. Adkins and J. Holland (eds) *Sexualising the Social*, Basingstoke: Macmillan.

Epstein, D. (1997) 'Boyz' Own Stories: masculinities and sexualities in schools', *Gender and Education* 9(1): 105–15.

Epstein, D. (1998a) '"Are you a girl or are you a teacher?" The "least adult" role in research about gender and sexuality in the primary school', in G. Walford (ed.) *Doing Research about Education*, London: Falmer.

Epstein, D. (1998b) 'Real boys don't work: underachievement, masculinity and the harassment of "sissies"', in D. Epstein, J. Elwood, V. Hey and J. Maw (eds) *Failing Boys? Issues in Gender and Achievement*, Buckingham: Open University Press.

Epstein, D. and Johnson, R. (1994) 'On the straight and the narrow: the heterosexual presumption, homophobias and schools', in D. Epstein (ed.) *Challenging Gay and Lesbian Inequalities in Education*, Buckingham: Open University Press.

Epstein, D. and Johnson, R. (1998) *Schooling Sexualities*, Buckingham: Open University Press.

Epstein, D. and Kenway, J. (eds) (1996) *Discourse* 17(3).

Epstein, D., Elwood, V. and Maw, J. (eds) (1998) *Failing Boys? Issues in Gender and Achievement*, Buckingham: Open University Press.

Enslin, E. (1994) 'Beyond Writing: Feminist practice and the limits of ethnography', *Cultural Anthropology* 9(4): 537–8.

Erben, M. (1996) 'The purposes and processes of biographical method', in D. Scott and R. Usher (eds) *Understanding Educational Research*, London: Routledge.

Esland, G. (1971) 'Teaching and learning as the organisation of knowledge', in Michael Young (ed.) *Knowledge and Control*, London: Collier-Macmillan.

Fairclough, N. (1989) *Language and Power*, London: Longman.

Fanon, F. (1967) *Black Skin, White Masks*, New York: Grove Press.

Featherstone, M., Hepworth, M. and Turner, B. (eds) (1991) *The Body, Social Processes and Cultural Theory*, London: Sage.

Finch, J. (1984) '"It's great to have someone to talk to": the ethics and politics of interviewing women', in C. Bell and H. Roberts (eds) *Social Researching*, London: Routledge & Kegan Paul.

Fine, M. (1988) 'Sexuality, schooling and adolescent females: the missing discourse of desire', *Harvard Educational Review* 58(1): 29–53.

Firestone, S. (1972) *The Dialectic of Sex, the Case for Feminist Revolution*, London: Paladin.

Foucault, M. (1973) *The Archeology of Knowledge*, London: Tavistock.

Foucault, M. (1976) *The History of Sexuality, Volume 1*, trans. R. Hurley, Harmondsworth: Penguin.

Foucault, M. (1977) *Discipline and Punish, the Birth of the Prison*, Harmondsworth: Penguin.

Foucault, M. (1980) *Power/Knowledge: Selected Interviews and other Writing 1972–1977*, C. Gordon (ed.), London: Harvester Wheatsheaf.

Foucault, M. (1988a) 'Technologies of the Self', in L. Martin, H. Gutman and P.H. Hutton, (eds) *Technologies of the Self, a Seminar with Michel Foucault*, London: Tavistock.

Foucault, M. (1988b) 'The political technology of individuals', in L. Martin, H. Gutman and P.H. Hutton, (eds) *Technologies of the Self, a Seminar with Michel Foucault*, London: Tavistock.

Frank, A. (1991) 'For a sociology of the body', in M. Featherstone, M. Hepworth and B.S. Turner (eds) *The Body, Social Process and Cultural Theory*, London: Sage.

Freire, P. (1972) *Pedagogy of the Oppressed*, Harmondsworth: Penguin.

Freud, S. (1905) [edition 1977] *Three Essays on the Theory of Sexuality*, in Pelican Freud, Vol. 7, trans. J. Strachey, Harmondsworth: Penguin.

Freud, S. (1931) [edition 1977] *Female Sexuality*, in Pelican Freud, Vol. 7, trans. J. Strachey, Harmondsworth: Penguin.

Friedan, B. (1974) *The Feminine Mistique*, New York: Dell.

Frosh, S., Phoenix, A. and Pattman, R. (2002) *Young Masculinities*, Basingstoke: Palgrave.

Fuller, M. (1984) 'Black girls in a London comprehensive', in M. Hammersley and P. Woods (eds) *Life in School, the Sociology of Pupil Culture*, Milton Keynes: Open University Press.

Furlong, V. (1976) 'Interaction sets in the classroom: towards a study of pupil knowledge', in M. Hammersley and P. Woods (eds) *The Process of Schooling, a Sociological Reader*, London: Routledge & Kegan Paul.

Gilbert, R. and Gilbert, P. (1998) *Masculinity Goes to School*, London: Routledge.

Giroux, H. (1988) 'Literacy and the pedagogy of voice and political empowerment', in *Educational Theory* 38: 61–75.

Goodson, I. (1991) 'Teachers' lives and educational research', in I. Goodson and R. Walker (eds) *Biography, Identity and Schooling: Episodes in Educational Research*, London: Falmer Press.

Goodson, I.F. (1992) Studying teachers' lives, an emergent field of inquiry, in I.F. Goodson (ed.) *Studying Teachers' Lives*, London: Routledge.

Goodson, I.F. and Walker, R. (eds) (1991) *Biography, Identity and Schooling: Episodes in Educational Research*, London: Falmer.

Gorbutt, D. (1972) 'The new sociology of education', *Education for Teaching*, 89.

Gordon, L. (1988) 'The politics of child sexual abuse: notes from American history', *Feminist Review*, 28.

Gordon, T., Holland, J. and Lahelma, E. (1996) 'Nation space: the construction of citizenship and difference in schools', paper presented at British Sociological Association annual conference, University of Reading.

Gordon, T., Holland, J. and Lahelma, E. (1998) 'Friends or foes? Interpreting relations between girls in school', paper presented at Ethnography and Education conference, University of Oxford.

Gordon, T., Holland, J. and Lahelma, E. (2000) *Making Spaces: Citizenship and Difference in Schools*, London: Macmillan.

Griffin, C. (1982) *The good, the bad and the ugly: images of young women in the labour market*, Centre for Contemporary Cultural Studies Stencilled Paper, no. 40, University of Birmingham.

Griffin, C. (1985) *Typical Girls? Young Women from School to the Job Market*, London: Routledge.

Guillaumin, C. (1993) 'The constructed body', in C.B. Burroughs and J.D. Ehrenreich (eds) *Reading the Social Body*, Iowa: University of Iowa Press.

Halberstam, J. (1998) *Female Masculinity*, Durham and London: Duke University Press.

Hall, S. and Jefferson, T. (eds) (1976) *Resistance through Rituals, Youth Subcultures in Post-war Britain*, London: Hutchinson.

Hammersley, M. and Woods, P. (eds) (1976) *The Process of Schooling, a Sociological Reader*, London: Routledge & Kegan Paul.

Harding, S. (ed.) (1987) *Feminism and Methodology*, Bloomington: Indiana University Press.

Hargreaves, A. (1994) *Changing Teachers, Changing Times, Teachers' Work and Culture in the Postmodern Age*, New York: Teachers' College Press.

Hargreaves, D. (1967) *Social Relations in the Secondary School*, London: Routledge & Kegan Paul.

Hargreaves, D. (1980) 'The occupational culture of teachers', in P. Woods (ed.) *Teacher Strategies, Explorations in the Sociology of the School*, London: Croom Helm.

Hargreaves, D. and Woods, P. (eds) (1984) *Classrooms and Staffrooms: the Sociology of Teachers and Teaching*, Milton Keynes: Open University Press.

Haug, F. *et al.* (eds) (1987) *Female Sexualisation, a Collective Work of Memory*, trans. E. Carter, London: Verso.

Hawkes, G. (1996) *A Sociology of Sex and Sexuality*, Buckingham: Open University Press.

Haywood, C. (1996) 'Out of the curriculum: sex talking, talking sex', *Curriculum Studies* 4(2): 229–49.

Henriques, J., Hollway, W., Urwin, C., Venn, C. and Walkerdine, V. (1984) *Changing the Subject, Psychology, Social Regulation and Subjectivity*, London: Methuen.

Herek, G. (1987) 'On heterosexual masculinity: some psychological consequences of the social construction of gender and sexuality', *American Behavioural Scientist* 29: 563–77.

Hermes, J. (1995) *Reading Women's Magazines*, Cambridge: Polity.

Hewitt, M. (1991) 'Bio-politics and social policy: Foucault's account of welfare', in M. Featherstone, M. Hepworth and B. Turner (eds) *The Body, Social Process and Cultural Theory*, London: Sage.

Hey, V. (1997) *The Company She Keeps, an Ethnography of Girls' Friendships*, Buckingham: Open University Press.

Higonnet, A. (1998) *Pictures of Innocence: the History and Crisis of Ideal Childhood*, London: Thames & Hudson.

Hill Collins, P. (1990) *Black Feminist Thought: Knowledge, Consciousness and the Politics of Empowerment*, London: Routledge.

Hird, M. (2000) 'Gender's nature, intersexuality, transsexualism and the "sex"/"gender" binary', *Feminist Theory* 1(3): 347–64.

Holland, J. (1993) *Sexuality and Ethnicity: Variations in Young Women's Sexual Knowledge and Practice*, London: Tufnell Press.

Holland, J. and Ramazanoglu, C. (1994) 'Coming to conclusions: power and interpretation in researching young women's sexuality', in J. Purvis and M. Maynard (eds) *Researching Women's Lives from a Feminist Perspective*, London: Falmer.

Holland, J., Ramazanoglu, S. and Scott, S. (1990a) *Sex, Risk and Danger: AIDS Education Policy and Young Women's Sexuality*, London: Tufnell Press.

Holland, J., Ramazanoglu, S., Scott, S., Sharpe, S. and Thomson, R. (1990b) *'Don't Die of Ignorance', I Nearly Died of Embarrassment, Condoms in Context*, London: Tufnell Press.

Holland, J., Ramazanoglu, C., Scott, S., Sharpe, S. and Thomson, R. (1991) *Pressure, Resistance and Empowerment: Young Women and the Negotiation of Safer Sex*, London: Tufnell Press.

Holland, J., Ramazanoglu, C., Sharpe, S. and Thomson, R. (1998) *The Male in the Head, Heterosexuality, Gender and Power*, London: Tufnell Press.

Hollway, W. (1984) 'Gender difference and the production of subjectivity', in J. Henriques *et al. Changing the Subject, Psychology, Social Regulation and Subjectivity*, London: Methuen.

Hollway, W. (1988) 'Heterosexual sex: power and desire for the other', in S. Cartledge and J. Ryan (eds) *Sex and Love and other Contradictions*, London: Women's Press.

Hollway, W. (1989) *Subjectivity and Method in Psychology, Gender, Meaning and Science*, London: Sage.

Hollway, W. (1995) 'Feminist discourses and women's heterosexual desire', in S. Wilkinson and C. Kitzinger (eds) *Feminism and Discourse*, London: Sage.

Holt, J. (1964) *How Children Fail*, London: Pitman.

Hood-Williams, J. (1996) 'Goodbye to sex and gender', *The Sociological Review* 44(1): 1–16.

Hood-Williams, J. (1997) 'Stories for sexual difference', *British Journal of Sociology of Education* 18(1): 81–9.

hooks, b. (1994) *Teaching to Transgress: Education and the Practice of Freedom*, London: Routledge.

Hutton, P.H. (1988) 'Foucault, Freud and the technologies of the self', in L. Martin, H. Gutman and P.H. Hutton (eds) *Technologies of the Self, a Seminar with Michel Foucault*, London: Tavistock.

Illich, I. (1971) *Deschooling Society*, London: Calder & Boyars.

Jackson, S. (1980) 'Girls and sexual knowledge', in D. Spender and E. Sarah (eds) *Learning to Lose, Sexism in Education*, London: The Women's Press.

Jackson, S. (1982) *Childhood and Sexuality*, Oxford: Basil Blackwell.

Jackson, S. (1996) 'Heterosexuality as a problem for feminist theory', in L Adkins and V. Merchant (eds) *Sexualising the Social, Power and the Organisation of Sexuality*, New York: St Martin's Press.

Johnson, R. (1996) 'Sexual dissonances: or the "impossibility" of sexuality education', *Curriculum Studies*, special issue on the *Sexual Politics of Schooling* 4(2): 163–89.

Johnson, R. (1997) 'Contested borders, contingent lives: an introduction', in D.L. Steinberg, D. Epstein and R. Johnson (eds) *Border Patrols, Policing the Boundaries of Heterosexuality*, London: Cassell.

Jones, A. (1993) 'Becoming a "girl": poststructuralist suggestions for educational research', *Gender and Education* 5(2): 157–66.

Jones, C. and Mahony, P. (eds) (1989) *Learning Our Lines: Sexuality and Social Control in Education*, London: Women's Press.

Kehily, M.J. (1993) 'Tales we heard in school': sexuality and symbolic boundaries', unpublished M.Soc. Sci dissertation, Department of Cultural Studies, University of Birmingham.

Kehily, M.J. (1995) 'Self-narration, autobiography and identity construction', *Gender and Education* 7(1): 23–31.

Kehily, M.J. and Nayak, A. (1996) 'The Christmas Kiss: sexuality, storytelling and schooling', *Curriculum Studies* 4(2): 211–27.

Kehily, M.J. and Nayak, A. (1997) 'Lads and laughter: humour and the production of heterosexual hierarchies', *Gender and Education* 9(1): 69–87.

Kelly, L. (1988) *Surviving Sexual Violence*, London: Polity.

Kenway, J. and Willis, S. with J. Blackmore and L. Rennie (1998) *Answering Back, Gender and Feminism, in School*, London: Routledge.

Kitzinger, J. (1988) 'Defending innocence: ideologies of childhood', *Feminist Review* 28: 77–87.

KOLA (1994) 'A burden of aloneness', in D. Epstein (ed.) *Challenging Gay and Lesbian Inequalities in Education*, Buckingham: Open University Press.

Kristeva, J. (1982) *Powers of Horror*, trans. L. Roudiez, New York: Columbia University Press.

Kuhn, A. (1995) *Family Secrets, Acts of Memory and Imagination*, London: Verso.

Labov, W. (1972) *Language in the Inner City*, Philadelphia: University of Pennsylvania Press.

Lacan, J. (1977a) *Ecrits, a Selection*, trans. A. Sheridan, London: Tavistock.

Lacan, J. (1977b) *The Four Fundamental Concepts of Psychoanalysis*, J.A. Miller (ed.), trans. A. Sheridan, London: Tavistock.

Lacan, J. (1982) *Feminine Sexuality: Jacques Lacan and the Ecole Freudienne*, J. Mitchell and J. Rose (eds), London: Macmillan.

Lacey, C. (1970) *Hightown Grammar*, Manchester: Manchester University Press.

Lather, P. (1991) *Getting Smart, Feminist Research and Pedagogy With/in the Postmodern*, London: Routledge.

Lather, P. and Smithies, C. (1997) *Troubling the Angels: Women Living with HIV/AIDS*, Boulder, CO: Westview Press.

Lawn, M. and Grace, G. (eds) (1987) *Teachers: the Culture and Politics of Work*, Lewes: Falmer Press.

Lawrence, D.H. (1949) *The Rainbow*, Harmondsworth: Penguin.

Lee, C. (1983) *The Ostrich Position, Sex, Schooling and Mystification*, London: Unwin.

Lees, S. (1986) *Losing Out: Sexuality and Adolescent Girls*, London: Hutchinson.

Lees, S. (1993) *Sugar and Spice, Sexuality and Adolescent Girls*, Harmondsworth: Penguin.

Lees, S. (1994) 'Talking about sex in sex education', *Gender and Education* 6(3): 281–92.

Levi-Strauss, C. (1966) *The Savage Mind*, London: Weidenfeld & Nicolson.

Levi-Strauss, C. (1969) *Totemism*, Harmondsworth: Penguin.

Lingard, B. and Douglas, P. (1999) *Men Engaging Feminisms: Profeminism, Backlashes and Schooling*, Buckingham: Open University Press.

Lobban, G. (1975) 'Sex roles in reading schemes', *Educational Review* 27(3).

Lupton, D. and Tulloch, J. (1996) '"All red in the face": students views on school-based HIV/AIDS and sexuality education', *Sociological Review* 44(2): 252–71.

Mac an Ghaill, M. (1988) *Young, Gifted and Black, Student–Teacher Relations in the Schooling of Black Youth*, Milton Keynes: Open University Press.

Mac an Ghaill, M. (1991) 'Schooling, sexuality and male power: towards an emancipatory curriculum', *Gender and Education* 3(3): 291–309.

Mac an Ghaill, M. (1992) 'Teachers' Work: curriculum restructuring, culture, power and comprehensive schooling', *British Journal of Sociology of Education* 13(2): 177–99.

Mac an Ghaill, M. (1994) *The Making of Men*, Buckingham: Open University Press.

Mac an Ghaill, M. (1996) 'Deconstructing heterosexualities within school arenas', *Curriculum Studies* 4(2): 191–209.

MacKinnon, C.A. (1983) 'Feminism, Marxist, method and the state: toward feminist jurisprudence', *Signs, Journal of Women in Culture and Society* 8(4): 635–58.

MacLure, M. (1993a) 'Mundane autobiography: some thoughts on self-talk in research contexts', *British Journal of Sociology of Education* 14(4): 373–84.

MacLure, M. (1993b) 'Arguing for your self: identity as an organising principle in teachers' jobs and lives', *British Educational Research Journal* 19(4): 311–22.

Martin, R. (1988) 'Truth, power, self, an interview with Michel Foucault', in L. Martin, H. Gutman and P.H. Hutton, (eds) *Technologies of the Self, a Seminar with Michel Foucault*, London: Tavistock.

Martino, W. and Meyenn, B. (ed.) (2001) *What About the Boys, Issues of Masculinity in Schools*, Buckingham: Open University Press.

McCourt, F. (1999) *'Tis, A Memoir*, London: Flamingo.

McRobbie, A. (1978a) *'Jackie*: and ideology of adolescent femininity', occasional paper, Centre for Contemporary Cultural Studies, University of Birmingham.

McRobbie, A. (1978b) 'Working class girls and the culture of femininity', in Centre for Contemporary Cultural Studies, *Women Take Issue*, London: Hutchinson.

McRobbie, A. (1981) 'Just like a Jackie story', in A. McRobbie and T. McCabe (eds) *Feminism for Girls: an Adventure Story*, London: Routledge & Kegan Paul.

McRobbie, A. (1991) *'Jackie* magazine: romantic individualism and the teenage girl', in *Feminism and Youth Culture: from 'Jackie' to 'Just Seventeen'*, London: Macmillan.

McRobbie, A. (1996) 'More!: New sexualities in girls' and women's magazines', in J. Curran, D. Morley and V. Walkerdine (eds) *Cultural Studies and Communications*, London: Arnold.

McRobbie, A. and Garber, G. (1982) 'Girls and subcultures', in S. Hall and T. Jefferson (eds) *Resistance through Rituals: Youth Subcultures in Post-war Britain*, London: Hutchinson.

Measor, L. (1989) '"Are you coming to see some dirty films today Miss?" Sex education and adolescent sexuality', in L. Holly (ed.) *Girls and Sexuality, Teaching and Learning*, Milton Keynes: Open University Press.

Measor, L., Tiffin, C., and Fry, K. (1996) 'Gender and sex eduation: a study of adolescent responses', *Gender and Education* 8(3): 275–88.

Mercer, K. and Julien, I. (1988) '"Race", sexual and politics and black masculinity: a dossier', in R. Chapman and J. Rutherford (eds) *Male Order: Unwrapping Masculinity*, London: Lawrence & Wishart.

Menter, I. Muschamp, Y. Nicholls, P. and Ozga, J. with Pollard A. (1997) *Work and Identity in the Primary School, a post-Fordist Analysis*, Buckingham: Open University Press.

Millard, E. (1997) 'Differently literate: gender and the construction of the developing reader', *Gender and Education* 9(1): 31–48.

Miller, J. (1990) *Seductions: Studies in Reading and Culture*, London: Virago.

Miller, J. (1995). 'Trick or Treat? The Autobiography of the Question', *English Quarterly* 27(3).

Miller, J. (1996) *School for Women*, London: Virago.

Millett, K. (1970) *Sexual Politics*, New York: Doubleday,

Mitchell, J. (1974) *Psychoanalysis and Feminism*, London: Allen Lane.

Mitchell, J. and Rose, J. (eds) (1982) *Feminine Sexuality, Jacques Lacan and the Ecole Freudienne*, trans. J. Rose, Basingstoke: Macmillan.

Modleski, T. (1991) *Feminism Without Women, Culture and Criticism in a 'Postfeminist' Age*, London: Routledge.

Moran, J. (2001) 'Childhood sexuality and education: the case of Section 28', *Sexualities* 4(1): 73–89.

Mort, F. (1987) *Dangerous Sexualities: Medico-moral Politics in England since 1930*, London: Routledge & Kegan Paul.

Nava, M. (1984) 'Youth service provision, social order and the question of girls', in A. McRobbie and M. Nava (eds) *Gender and Generation*, London: Macmillan.

Nayak, A. (1997) 'Tales from the darkside: negotiating whiteness in school arenas', *International Studies in Sociology of Education* 7(1): 57–79.

Nayak, A. (2001) '"Ice white and ordinary": new perspectives on ethnicity, gender and youth cultural identities', in B. Francis and C. Skelton (eds) *Investigating Gender, Contemporary perspectives in education*, Buckingham: Open University Press.

Nayak, A. and Kehily, M.J. (1996) 'Playing it straight: masculinities, homophobias and schooling', *Journal of Gender Studies* 5(2): 211–30.

Nias, J. (1984) 'The definition and maintenance of self in primary teaching', *British Journal of Sociology of Education* 5(3): 167–80.

Nias, J. (1989) *Primary Teachers Talking: a Study of Teaching as Work*, London: Routledge.

Ozga, J. (ed.) (1988) *Schoolwork: Approaches to the Labour Process of Teaching*, Milton Keynes: Open University Press.

Pattman, R., Frosh, S. and Phoenix, A. (1998) 'Lads, machos and others: developing "boy-centred" research', *Journal of Youth Studies* 1(2): 125–42.

Patton, C. (1993) 'Tremble, Hetero Swine!', in M. Warner (ed.) *Fear of a Queer Planet, Queer Politics and Social Theory*, Minneapolis: University of Minnesota Press.

Perlstein, R. (1995) '"Funny doctor, I don't feel antidisciplined": Cultural Studies as disciplinary habitus (or reading Cultural Studies)', *Parallax* 1: 131–41.

Personal Narratives Group (eds) (1989) *Interpreting Women's Lives*, Bloomington: Indiana University Press.

Plummer, K. (1995) *Telling Sexual Stories, Power, Change and Sexual Worlds*, London: Routledge.

Pratt, M.L. (1992) *Imperial Eyes: Travel Writing and Transculturation*, London: Routledge.

Radway, J. (1984) *Reading the Romance: Women, Patriarchy and Popular Literature*, Chapel Hill, NC: University of North Carolina Press.

Redman, P. (1994) 'Shifting ground: rethinking sexuality education', in D. Epstein (ed.) *Challenging Lesbian and Gay Inequalities in Education*, Buckingham: Open University Press.

Redman, P. (1998) 'Investing in romance: making up heterosexual masculinities', unpublished PhD thesis, University of Birmingham.

Reissman, C.K. (1993) *Narrative Analysis*, London: Sage.

Rich, A. (1980) 'Compulsory heterosexuality and lesbian existence', *Signs* 5(4): 631–60.

Richardson, D. (ed.) (1996) *Theorising Heterosexuality, Telling it Straight*, Buckingham: Open University Press.

Robertson, J. (1996) 'Fantasy's confines: popular culture and the education of the female primary school teacher', paper presented at Crossroads in Cultural Studies conference, Tampere, Finland.

Rofes, E. (1995) 'Making our schools safe for sissies', in G. Unks (ed.) *The Gay Teen, Educational Theory for Lesbian, Gay and Bisexual Adolescents*, London: Routledge.

Rose, J. (1986) *Sexuality in the Field of Vision*, London: Verso.

Rosser, E. and Harre, R. (1976) 'The meaning of trouble', in M. Hammersley and P. Woods (eds) *The Process of Schooling, a Sociological Reader*, London: Routledge & Kegan Paul.

Rubin, G. (1975) 'The traffic in women: notes on the "political economy" of sex', in R. Reiter (ed.) *Toward an Anthropology of Women*, New York: Monthly Review Press.

Rubin, G. (1984) 'Thinking sex: notes for a radical theory of the politics of sexuality', in C. Vance (ed.) *Pleasure and Danger, Exploring Female Sexuality*, London: Pandora.

Saxby, H. (1973) quoted in Myra Barrs (ed.) *Identity*, Harmondsworth: Penguin.

Scott, D. (1996) 'Ethnography and education', in D. Scott and R. Usher (ed.) *Understanding Educational Research*, London: Routledge.

Searle, C. (1974) *Mainland*, London: Calder & Boyars.

Sears, J. (ed.) (1992) *Sexuality and the Curriculum, the Politics and Practices of Sexuality Education*, New York: Teachers' College Press.

Sedgwick, E.K. (1990) *Epistemology of the Closet*, Berkeley, University of California Press.

Sedgwick, E.K. (1993) 'How to bring your kids up gay', in M. Warner (ed.) *Fear of a Queer Planet, Queer Politics and Social Theory*, Minneapolis: University of Minnesota Press.

Sedgwick, E.K. (1994) *Tendencies*, London: Routledge.

Segal, L. (1990) *Slow Motion, Changing Masculinities, Changing Men*, London: Virago.

Seidman, S. (1998) 'The Brits are coming . . . again: sex studies in the UK', *Sexualities* 1(1): 107–12.

Sewell, T. (1997) *Black Masculinities and Schooling: How Black Boys Survive in Modern Schooling*, Stoke-on-Trent: Trentham Books.

Sex Education Forum (1995) *The Effectiveness of Sex Education*, Sex Education Forum Occasional Parliamentary Briefing Paper, No. 1, London: National Children's Bureau.

Sex Education Forum (1997) *Supporting the Needs of Boys and Young Men in Sex and Relationships Education*, London: National Children's Bureau.

Sharp, R. and Green, A. (1975) *Education and Social Control*, London: Routledge & Kegan Paul.

Sharpe, S. (1976) *Just Like a Girl*, Harmondsworth: Penguin.

Shilling, C. (1991) 'Body talk and body image: schooling and the production of physical capital', paper presented to the British Sociological Association annual conference, University of Manchester, March 1991.

Shilling, C. (1993) *The Body and Social Theory*, London: Sage.

Shor, I. and Freire, P. (1988) 'What is dialogic method?' *Educational Theory* 38.

Sikes, P., Measor, L. and Woods, P. (1985) *Teacher Careers, Crises and Continuity*, Lewes: Falmer.

Sikes, P. and Troyna, B. (1991) 'True stories: a case study in the use of life history in initial teacher education', *Educational Review* 43: 3–15.

Skeggs, B. (1991) 'Challenging masculinity and using sexuality', *British Journal of Sociology of Education* 11(4): 127–38.

Skeggs, B. (1995) 'Theorising ethics and representation in feminist ethnography', in B. Skeggs (ed.) *Feminist Cultural Theory: Production and Process*, Manchester: Manchester University Press.

Skeggs, B. (1997) *Formations of Class and Gender, Becoming Respectable*, London: Sage.

Skelton, C. (2001) *Schooling the Boys, Masculinities and Primary Education*, Buckingham: Open University Press.

Smith, A.M. (1994) *New Right Discourses on Race and Sexuality: Britain 1968–1990*, Oxford: Blackwell.

Spender, D. and Sarah, E. (1980) *Learning to Lose*, London: The Women's Press.

Stacey, Jackie (1991) 'Promoting normality: Section 28 and the regulation of sexuality', in S. Franklin, C. Lury and J. Stacey (eds) *Off-Centre: Feminism and Cultural Studies*, London: HarperCollins.

Stacey, Judith (1988) 'Can there be a feminist ethnography?' *Women's Studies International Forum* 11(1): pp. 1–27.

Stanley, L. (1987) 'Biography as microscope or kaleidoscope? The case of "power" in Hannah Cullwick's relationship with Arthur Munby', *Women's Studies International Forum* 10(1).

Stanley, L. (1990) 'Moments of writing: is there a feminist auto/biography?' *Gender and History* 2(1).

Stanley, L. (1992) *The Auto/biographical I: the Theory and Practice of Feminist Auto/biography*, Manchester: Manchester University Press.

Stanley, L. and Wise, S. (1983) *Breaking Out: Feminist Consciousness and Feminist Research*, London: Routledge & Kegan Paul.

Stanley, L. and Wise, S. (1993) *Breaking Out Again: Feminist Ontology and Epistemology*, London: Routledge.

Steedman, C. (1985) '"The mother made conscious": the historical development of a primary school pedagogy', *History Workshop Journal*, No. 20.

Synnott, A. (1993) *The Body Social, Symbolism, Self and Society*, London: Routledge.

Tagg, J. (1980) 'A means of surveillance: the photograph as evidence in law', *Screen Education*, No. 36.

Theweleit, K. (1987) *Male Fantasies, Vol. 1: Women, Floods, Bodies, History*, Cambridge: Polity.

Thomson, R. (1994) 'Moral rhetoric and public health pragmatism: the recent politics of sex education', *Feminist Review* 48: 40–60.

Thomson, R. (1997) '"It was the way we were watching it": young men's accounts of pornography', paper presented at British Sociological Association conference, University of York.

Thomson, R. (2000) 'Legal, protected and timely: young people's perspectives on the heterosexual age of consent', in J. Bridgeman and D. Monk (eds) *Feminist Perspectives on Child Law*, London: Cavendish.

Thomson, R. and Scott, S. (1990) *Researching Sexuality in the Light of AIDS; Historical and Methodological Issues*, London: Tufnell Press.

Thomson, R. and Scott, S. (1991) *Learning about Sex: Young Women and the Social Construction of Sexual Identity*, London: Tufnell Press.

Thorne, B. (1993) *Gender Play, Girls and Boys in School*, New Brunswick, NJ: Rutgers University Press.

Thorogood, N. (2000) 'Sex education as disciplinary technique: policy and practice in England and Wales', *Sexualities* 3(4): 425–38.

Tinkler, P. (1995) *Constructing Girlhood, Popular Magazines for Girls Growing up in England 1920–1950*, London: Taylor and Francis.

Tolson, A. (1990) 'Social surveillance and subjectification: the emergence of "subculture" in the work of Henry Mayhew', *Cultural Studies* 4(2).

Tong, R. (1989) *Feminist Thought, a Comprehensive Introduction*, Boulder, CO: Westview Press.

Trenchard, L. and Warren, H. (1984) *Something to Tell You: the Experiences and Needs of Young Lesbians and Gay Men in London*, London: Gay Teenage Group.

Trudell, B. (1992) 'Inside a ninth grade sexuality classroom, the process of knowledge construction,' in J. Sears (ed.) *Sexuality and the Curriculum*, New York: Teachers' College Press.

Trudell, B. (1993) *Doing Sex Education: Gender, Politics and Schooling*, London: Routledge.

Turner, B.S. (1991) 'Recent developments in the theory of the body', in M. Featherstone, M. Hepworth and B.S. Turner (eds) *The Body, Social Process and Cultural Theory*, London: Sage.

Unks, G. (ed.) (1995) *The Gay Teen: Educational Practice and Theory for Lesbian, Gay and Bisexual Adolescents*, London: Routledge.

Vance, C. (ed.) (1984) *Pleasure and Danger, Exploring Female Sexuality*, London: Pandora.

Vance, C. (1995) 'Social construction theory and sexuality', in M. Berger, B. Wallis and S. Watson (eds) *Constructing Masculinity*, New York: Routledge.

Visweswaran, K. (1994) *Fictions of Feminist Ethnography*, Minneapolis: University of Minnesota Press.

Volosinov, V.N. (1973) *Marxism and the Philosophy of Language*, trans. L. Matejka and I. Turner, London: Seminar Press.

Walkerdine, V. (1981) 'Sex, power and pedagogy', *Screen Education* 38: 14–24.

Walkerdine, V. (1984) 'Some day my prince will come: young girls and the preparation for adolescent sexuality', in A. McRobbie and M. Nava (eds) *Gender and Generation*, London: Macmillan.

Walkerdine, V. (1985) 'On the regulation of speaking and silence', in C. Steedman, C. Urwin and V. Walkerdine (eds) *Language, Gender and Childhood*, London: Routledge & Kegan Paul.

Walkerdine, V. (1986a) 'Post-structructuralist theory and everyday social practices: the family and the school', in S. Wilkinson (ed.) *Feminist Social Psychology, Developing Theory and Practice*, Milton Keynes: Open University Press.

Walkerdine, V. (1986b) 'Video replay: families, films and fantasy', in V. Burgin, J. Donald and C. Kaplan (eds) *Formations of Fantasy*, London: Methuen.

Walkerdine, V. (1987) 'Femininity as performance', *Oxford Review of Education* 15(3): 267–79.

Walkerdine, V. (1990) *Schoolgirl Fictions*, London: Verso.

Walkerdine, V. (1997) *Daddy's Girl, Young Girls and Popular Culture*, Basingstoke: Macmillan.

Walkerdine, V. and Lucey, H. (1989) *Democracy in the Kitchen: Regulating Mothers and Socialising Daughters*, London: Virago.

Weedon, C. (1987) *Feminist Practice and Poststructuralist Theory*, Oxford: Basil Blackwell.

Weeks, J (1977) *Coming Out: Homosexual Politics in Britain from the Nineteenth Century to the Present*, London: Quartet.

Weeks, J. (1981) *Sex, Politics and Society: the Regulation of Sexuality Since 1880*, Harlow: Longman.

Weeks, J. (1985) *Sexuality and its Discontents*, London: Routledge.

Weeks, J. (1986) *Sexuality*, London: Tavistock.

Weeks, J. (1998) 'The "homosexual role" after 30 years: an appreciation of the work of Mary McIntosh', *Sexualities* 1(2): 131–52.

Weiner, G. and Arnot, M. (eds) (1987) *Gender under Scrutiny: New Inquiries in Education*, London: Hutchinson.

Weiss, L. and Carbonnell-Medina, D. (2000) 'Learning to speak out in an abstinence based sex education group: gender and race work in an urban magnet school', *Teachers College Record* 102(3): 620–51.

Whatley, M. (1991) 'Raging hormones and powerful cars: the construction of men's sexuality in school sex education and popular adolescent films', in H. Giroux (ed.) *Postmodernism, Feminism and Cultural Politics*, Albany, New York: SUNY Press.

Whitty, G. (1985) *Sociology and School Knowledge, Curriculum Theory, Research and Politics*, London: Methuen.

Whyte, W.F. (1981) *Street Corner Society: the Social Structure of an Italian Slum*, Chicago: Chicago University Press.

Wilkinson, S. and Kitzinger, C. (eds) (1993) *Heterosexuality: a Feminism and Psychology Reader*, London: Sage.

Williams, R. (1965) *The Long Revolution*, Harmondsworth: Penguin.

Willis, P. (1974) *Symbolism and Practice: a Theory for the Social Meaning of Pop Music*, Centre for Contemporary Cultural Studies Stencilled Paper, No. 13, University of Birmingham.

Willis, P. (1977) *Learning to Labour, How Working Class Kids Get Working Class Jobs*, Farnborough: Saxon House.

Willis, P. (1978) *Profane Culture*, London: Routledge & Kegan Paul.

Willis, P. (1996) 'Ethno CS', paper presented at *Crossroads in Cultural Studies* conference, Tampere, Finland.

Willis, P. (2000) *The Ethnographic Imagination*, Cambridge: Polity.

Willmott, P. (1966) *Adolescent Boys of East London*, Harmondsworth: Penguin.

Winship, J. (1985) 'A girl needs to get streetwise: magazines for the 1980s', *Feminist Review* 21: 25–46.

Winship, J. (1987) *Inside Women's Magazines*, New York: Pandora.

Wolpe, A.M. (1988) *Within School Walls, the Role of Discipline, Sexuality and the Curriculum*, London: Routledge.

Wood, D.R. (1992) 'Teaching narratives: a source of faculty development and evaluation', *Harvard Educational Review* 62(4): 535–50.

Wood, J. (1984) 'Groping towards sexism: boys' sex talk', in A. McRobbie and M. Nava (eds) *Gender and Generation*, London: Macmillan.

Woods, P. (1985) 'Conversations with teachers: some aspects of life history methods', *British Educational Research Journal* 11(1): 13–26.

Magazines cited

More!, Issue 198, 25 October–7 November 1995, publisher EMAP Elan.
More!, Issue 206, 14–27 February 1996, publisher EMAP Elan.
More!, Issue 208, 13–26 March 1996, publisher EMAP Elan.
'He left me for my gay friend Ian', in *More!*, Issue 198, (details above).

Index

abjection 141–5, 162
abstinence 61–2
abuse, sexual 87–91
accountability 51
Acker, K. 99
adolescence 65–6
African-Caribbean masculinities
    156–7
agency 61–2, 208; body-reflexive
    practice 132, 141; discursive
    practices and 57–71, 202; sex
    education and student cultures
    65–71, 71
aggression 148–9; see also violence
'agony aunts' see problem pages,
    sex education lesson
Agony Aunts video 74–5
alcohol 80
Alderson, C. 100
Altman, M. 119
ambivalence 189–90
arranged marriage 157–8
Asians 157–9
Association of Teachers of African,
    Caribbean and Associated
    Literature (ATCAL) 26
assumed knowledge 122–5, 134
assumptions: cultural assumptions
    and sexuality 35–6; teachers'
    15–16
authoritarian approach 194
auto/biographical methods 11–14;
    Kehily's personal narratives

10–32, 200–1; teachers' work and
    culture 167–8, 172–99, 205

balkanisation 166
Ball, S.J. 15, 51
banding system 15, 215
banking concept of education 23
Barker, M. 104–5, 106, 112, 160
becoming a teacher 173–6
Benton, M. 27
Benton, P. 27
binary opposites 5, 34; teacher/
    pupil relations 170–1
biographies, sexual 176–85; see also
    auto/biographical methods
biological determinism 186–7
bio-power 24, 129
black masculinities 156–7
blame: self-blame and sexual abuse
    87–91; teachers and schools as
    objects of 51
body 18–19, 204, 210, 213;
    fetishisation of women's bodies
    142; institutions and
    embodiment of masculinities
    132–3; maternal body 85–6;
    theorising 129–32; young men,
    disgust, abjection and 141–5, 204
body-reflexive practice 132, 141
Bordo, S. 213
boundaries 97–8
Bourdieu, P. 130
bravado 124, 134–5

Brook Pregnancy Advisory Service 8
Brooks, A. 43
Bunty 48, 101
Butler, J. 43, 44, 56, 73

Cameron, D. 88
camp 109
Canaan, J. 117
Carbonell-Medina, D. 62
castration complex 38–9, 143
casual sex 78–80, 154–6, 212; *see also* reputation
'Cathy and Claire' page 112
censorship 119–20
Centre for Contemporary Cultural Studies 31
challenge, discourse of 136
child development 38–40, 104
childhood: innocence 47, 178–80; sexual latency 120–1; sexuality 47
Christianity: desire 59, 129; sex education from a Christian perspective 58–9, 61
Clandinin, D.J. 13
class, social 4, 130, 174–5
classroom management 132–3
close-reading technique 7
colloquial language 196–7
Comfort, A. 119
comics 125–6; *see also* teenage magazines
compulsory heterosexuality 34
concealment 85–6, 191–2
conformity 102
connected knowledge 121–5, 134
Connell, R.W. 54–5, 131–2, 133, 137, 141
Connelly, F.M. 13
consciousness 23; intensive, anti-sexist consciousness raising 96
conservative sex education 65, 169
constraint 5, 59
contemporary approaches to sexuality 41–3
contractual understanding 105–6, 126

control: in the classroom 14–25; self control 24
Cortazzi, M. 13
counselling 74, 86
Coward, R. 110–11
critical awareness 27
critical pedagogy 21, 22
cultural resources 191–2
culture: cultures of femininity 104–5, 114–17; gender learned through 34; student sexual cultures *see* student sexual cultures; teachers' 165–7
curriculum: hidden 29, 49, 101–2, 194–5; National Curriculum 207; official 57–60, 101

danger, pleasure and 85–7
Davies, B. 18
debunking of myths 90–1
deconstruction 56
defensive teaching 172
Department of Cultural Studies, University of Birmingham 12
desire 129–30; Christianity and 59, 129; and fear/revulsion 85; female sexuality and 42–3; teaching and relations of 168–9
determinism 186–7
development 38–40, 104
dialogic teaching 22
disbelief 112–13
disciplinarity 27–8
disciplinary technologies 24
discourses 17, 36–7, 40, 52–72, 202; and debates over sex education 97–8; official curriculum as discursive practice 57–60; pedagogy as discursive practice 60–5; student culture as discursive practice 65–71
discursive clusters 7
disgust 141–5
distance 194
diversity, sexual 185–93
Dollimore, J. 43
Donald, J. 23–4
Dyer, R. 56

economic change 4–5, 206
education: banking concept of 23; discursive field 37; disempowering environment for students 207; legislative change 2–3, 51, 165–6; and popular culture 101
Education (No. 2) Act 1986 58
Edwards, T. 43, 44–5
Ellsworth, E. 21, 22
emancipatory authority 22
emancipatory pedagogy 19–20, 21, 23, 30
embarrassment 116, 119–20
embodiment 129–32, 210, 213; of masculinities 132–3
emotional insecurity 78, 97
emotional learning 121–2
empathy 89
empowerment 21, 22, 27, 61
English teaching 25–8
engulfment, fear of 151–3
Enlightenment tradition 130
Epstein, D. 29, 172
Erben, M. 12
essentialism 33–4
ethnicity 156–62, 213
ethnography 6
exhibitionism 84–5
exposure, indecent 82–7

family 58–9, 181–2
Fanon, F. 18
fantasy 48
fear: of being gay 91–5, 144–5; male fear of female sexuality 151–3
Featherstone, M. 213
female friendship groups 107, 116–17, 121, 122, 123
female sexuality 42–3, 205; male fear of 151–3
femininity: cultures of 104–5, 114–17; and heterosexuality in student cultures 68–71; as performance 47–8; teenage magazines and 100–1, 104–5, 114–17

feminism 61; approaches to heterosexuality 54; approaches to sexuality 41–3; and sexual abuse 89–90
feminist sex education 169–70
Fine, M. 62, 97, 210
Firestone, S. 39
flasher 82–7
Foucault, M. 5, 24, 63–4, 111, 118; body and power 129–30; Christian perspective on sexuality 59; self 40; sexuality of children and schools 60, 132; sexuality and discourses 36–7, 52
Frazer, E. 88
Freire, P. 23
Freud, S. 38–9, 85, 120
Friedan, B. 39
friendship 99; male 80–2
friendship groups 107, 114, 208; female 107, 116–17, 121, 122, 123; male 135–6; see also student sexual cultures
Frosh, S. 162
Fuller, M. 101
Furlong, V. 101

gaze 18, 82–7
gender 73; contemporary approaches to sex and 42–3; difference and school-based reading practices 106–10; differentiation and reputation 79–80; inequalities and materiality of the body 131; and performance 44, 45; polarisation and homosexuality 94; sexuality, the domain of the school and 49–51; social constructionism and 34
gender displays 45, 100, 106, 125, 126, 203, 208
gender reform 208–11
Girlie Show, The 152, 153
Gordon, T. 49
gossip magazines 109
governing bodies 58
Grace, G. 165

graffiti 25–6
guardianship, Christian 60
Guillaumin, C. 130–1

Hammersley, M. 101–2
Hargreaves, A. 165, 166
Hargreaves, D. 165
Haug, F. 12
Haywood, C. 56, 124
health: promotion 177–8; public
   health 64–5, 176–8; sexual health
   64–5, 75–8
Hedonists 157
hegemonic masculinities 133
Henriques, J. 40–1
Hermes, J. 105, 106, 109, 121,
   122
heterosexuality 128, 162–3, 201,
   208; approaches to 54–7;
   homophobic performance and
   92–3; masculinities and
   consolidating 140–5, 204;
   masculinities and constituting
   133–40, 204; naturalisation in
   schools 57–60, 71; queer theory
   43–4; schools as sites of
   discursive practice 52–72, 202
hidden curriculum 29, 49, 101–2,
   194–5
history: narratives and creation of
   a history 90–1; socio-historical
   approaches to sexuality 35–8
HIV 75–8
Hoggart, R. 7
Hollway, W. 31, 55, 140
homophobia 44, 55, 57, 144–5,
   187–8, 189, 208; masculinities
   and 145–9; performance by
   young men 92–3; and the power
   of girls 91–5; teachers and
   challenging 192–3; teen
   magazines 109–10
homosexuality 36; fear of 91–5,
   144–5; queer theory 43–5, 56;
   teachers and sexual diversity
   185–93; teen magazines and
   109–10; young men and
   lesbianism 149–51
Hood-Williams, J. 125–6

hooks, b. 168, 169
humiliation, ritualistic 18
humour 29; and homophobia
   146–7; and problem pages
   112–13

ideal model 168
idealism 173–4; Kehily's 21–2, 23,
   31
identity 31–2; female friendship
   groups and feminine identities
   116–17; teachers and 16–18,
   167–8, 176
immigration 4
indecent exposure 82–7
industrial heritage 4
inequality 21; gender inequalities
   49
informal approaches 170–1
insatiability 152, 153
institutional anxieties 59–60
investment 40–1
Islam 159–60
isolation 187–8

Jackie 104–5, 107, 112
Jackson, S. 41, 54, 56, 143
Jenny Jones programme 148–9,
   216
Johnson, R. 29, 55, 56, 172
Jones, A. 65
Joy of Lesbian Sex, The 192
Julien, I. 157

Kehily, M.J. 2, 10–32, 45, 92,
   144–5, 200–1; auto/biographical
   methods 11–14; 'drift' into
   teaching 10–11; early teaching
   career 11; English teaching and
   radical pedagogy 26–8;
   experiences of schooling 11;
   fourth year class 14–19; girl in
   the toilet 28–9; graffiti 25–6;
   politicised approach to teaching
   8–9; and sex education 8–9,
   29–31; third year class 19–25
Kenway, J. 194, 195, 208
kinship based systems 42
kissing 142, 143, 144

Kitzinger, C. 56
Kristeva, J. 143–4

labour process 164–7
Labov, W. 30
Lacan, J. 39–40, 85–6, 94–5, 169
language 63–4, 196–7
late period, concerns over 75–80
Lather, P. 23
Lawn, M. 165
Lawrence, D.H., *The Rainbow*
    18
learning, sexual *see* sexual learning
Lees, S. 169–70
lesbianism 149–51; *see also*
    homosexuality
Levi-Strauss, C. 39
liberal sex education 169–70
liberation: emancipatory pedagogy
    19–20, 21, 23, 30; sexual 119
life history approaches: Kehily's
    personal narratives 10–32, 200–1;
    teachers' work and culture
    167–8, 172–99, 205
literary canon 26–7
Local Government Act 1988
    Section 28 186
'look' (gaze) 18, 82–7
love, romantic 75–8, 104
Luff, P. 103, 126, 216
Lupton, D. 96

Mac an Ghaill, M. 50, 56, 147,
    156–7, 166, 190
MacLure, M. 167–8
Make Love Last 61, 215
male friendship 80–2
male friendship groups 135–6
male sex drive discourse 88, 90, 140
marketisation 166
masculinities 50, 128–63, 204–5,
    208; assumed knowledge 124–5;
    consolidating heterosexuality
    140–5, 204; constituting
    heterosexuality 133–40, 204; and
    ethnicity 156–62; fear of
    engulfment 151–3; heterosexual
    activity and reputation 154–6;
    and heterosexuality 54–5,
133–45, 162–3; and
    homophobias 145–9; institutions
    and embodiment of 132–3; and
    strategies for sex education
    209–11; theorising the body
    129–32; young men and
    lesbianism 149–51
masturbation 137–8
materiality of the body 130–1
maternal body 85–6
McCourt, F., *'Tis* 18
McIntosh, M. 36
McRobbie, A. 4, 100, 117, 120;
    Jackie 104, 107, 112
Measor, L. 96
memory 31
memory-work 11–12; Kehily's
    personal narratives 10–32, 200–1;
    see also auto/biographical
    methods
Mercer, K. 157
methodology 5–7
Midlands region 4
Miller, J. 10, 168–9
Millett, K. 39
Mitchell, J. 39, 40
mixed relationships 159–61
moments 7; biographical 10–11
moral panic 103, 180–1
moralism 22; tensions with health
    imperatives in sex education 65;
    teachers 180–1; young men
    139–40, 154–6; young women
    116–17, 119–20
morality 211, 212; sexuality as
    individual morality 97–8
More! 103, 104, 126–7; too sexually
    explicit 115–16, 117–21;
    treatment of homosexuality
    109–10
multiculturalism 161
myths, debunking of 90–1

narratives: emergence of new forms
    90–1; personal *see* personal
    narratives
National Association of Teachers
    of English (NATE) 26
National Curriculum 207

Nayak, A. 45, 92, 144–5
Network 7 152, 153
new racism 160
New Right 51, 186
noticeboard for PSE information
    62

occupational culture, teachers'
    165–7
odour 142–3
Oedipal complex 38–9
Office for Standards in Education
    (Ofsted) 62
official curriculum 57–60, 101
oppression 21
oral sex 142, 143, 144, 145
organisational routines 24
ownership of classes 15

parental attitudes 193
patriarchy 39, 42, 54
Pattman, R. 210–11
Patton, C. 116
pedagogy: development of
    sexuality education 211–12;
    discursive practice 60–5;
    progressive 19–20, 21–3, 26–8,
    30, 62–3; radical 19–20, 21–5,
    27–8, 30
peer group *see* friendship groups,
    student sexual cultures
Penguin English Project 26–7
penis/phallus, possession of 38–9,
    94–5
penis envy 39
performance: femininity as 47–8;
    gender displays 45, 100, 106,
    125, 126, 203, 208; homophobic
    performances 45, 92–3; identity
    as gendered performance 44;
    male sex-talk 134–5
Perlstein, R. 27
personal narratives: Kehily's
    10–32, 200–1; teachers' 167–8,
    172–99, 205
Personal Narratives Group 12
Personal and Social Education
    (PSE) 1–2, 8; pedagogy as
    discursive practice 60–5; student

cultures and 65–71; teachers'
    approaches to students 193–7;
    see also sex education
personal vision 64
perversions, sexual 84
physical capital 133
play 131
pleasure, danger and 85–7
Plummer, K. 90–1
political economy of sex 42, 66
political plot 90–1
Politics of Sexuality Group,
    University of Birmingham 56
polymorphous perversity 38, 55
popular culture 91, 150, 203–4,
    208; education and 101; gender
    differences 81–2; soap operas
    103; suitability for use in sex
    education 209–10; teen
    magazines *see* teen magazines
pornography 138–40
poststructuralism 7
power 37, 50, 202; bio-power 24,
    129; empowerment 21, 22, 27,
    61; of girls and homophobia
    91–5; male 46, 88, 141;
    powerlessness of women and
    children 90
practitioner-produced resources
    213–14
pregnancy: changes in social
    attitudes 180, 182–3; fear of and
    problem pages 75–80; girl in the
    toilet 28–9; knowledge and
    teenage pregnancy 178–9; PSE
    teaching and 64, 176–8
Pretty Woman 143
problem pages: boys and 80–2, 96,
    123; sex education lesson based
    on 74–98, 203; sexual learning
    110–14, 114–15
production of gendered/sexualised
    identities 50
progressive pedagogy 19–20, 21–3,
    26–8, 30, 62–3
projection 76, 81–2
promiscuity, sexual 78–80, 154–6,
    212
prostitution 143

psychic splitting 24–5
psychoanalysis 213; approaches to
    sexuality 38–41; heterosexuality
    55–6; pleasure and danger 85–6
pupil-centred approaches 20, 22,
    62–3, 175
public health 64–5, 176–8

queer theory 43–5, 56

radical pedagogy 19–20, 21–5,
    27–8, 30
rape 139–40; discussing sexual
    abuse 87–91
Rasta Heads 156–7
reading effect 2
reading practices 105–6, 125–6;
    school-based and gender
    difference 106–10
reassurance 77
reception area noticeboard 62
reflexivity 48
regulation, sexual 154–6
relationships: student cultures and
    65–71; young men and fear of
    engulfment 151–3; young men
    and relationships with women
    140–5
repressive hypothesis 36
reputation 208, 212; classes and
    15–16; girls and 78–80, 117, 183;
    young men and 154–6
research: context 2–5; methodology
    5–7; suggestions for further
    212–14
restriction 5, 59
Rich, A. 34, 54
Ricki Lake programme 148–9,
    216
ritualistic humiliation 18
Robertson, J. 168, 169
Rofes, E. 108
romantic love 75–8, 104
Rose, J. 40, 41
routines, organisational 24
Rubin,G. 42

Saxby, H.M. 26
school nurse 172–3, 176–8, 197

schools 52–72, 202; bodies in
    school 132–3; context and
    radical pedagogy 22; discursive
    practices 37, 57–71; hidden
    curriculum 29, 49, 101–2, 194–5;
    legislative changes 2–3, 51,
    165–6; official curriculum 57–60,
    101; organisational routines
    23–4; pedagogic discourses and
    child sexuality 46–7; pedagogy
    60–5; schooling and domain of
    the sexual 53–4; sexuality, gender
    and 49–51; student cultures
    65–71
scopophilia 84–5
Scott, S. 121, 171, 194
Searle, C. 26
secrecy 191–2
Sears, J. 59
Sedgwick, E.K. 43, 44
Segal, L. 88, 96
Seidman, S. 44, 45
self 12–13, 40, 111; abjection
    143–5; reputation and 80
self-blame 87–91
self control 24
Sewell, T. 157
sex education 1–2, 13, 71–2, 205,
    208; boys' needs unmet 123;
    implications of research for
    208–12; Kehily and 8–9, 28–31;
    pedagogy in a Christian school
    60–5; practitioner-produced
    resources 213–14; school policy
    58; student cultures 65–71;
    teachers' approaches to students
    193–7, 198–9; teachers' sexual
    biographies and 176–85, 198;
    teaching 169–72; see also sexual
    learning
sex education lesson 73–98, 203;
    approach 74–5; boys, friendship
    and girlfriends 80–2; fear of
    homosexuality 91–5; flasher
    82–7; girls and reputation
    78–80; romantic love, pregnancy
    and HIV 75–8; sexual abuse
    87–91
sex manuals 119

sex-talk 133–7
'Sextalk' 118–19, 127
sexual abuse 87–91
sexual activity 179–80; choice and
    61; gender differences, reputation
    and 154–6; promiscuity 78–80,
    154–6, 212
sexual biographies 176–85
sexual diversity 185–93
sexual economy 42, 66
sexual health 64–5, 75–8
sexual learning 110–17; boys and
    134, 140–1; and cultures of
    femininity 114–17; piecing
    together 121–2; problem pages
    110–14
sexual liberation 119
sexual perversions 84
sexual promiscuity 78–80, 154–6,
    212
sexuality 33–51, 52–3, 201, 208;
    contemporary approaches 41–3;
    discourses of and sex education
    97–8; femininity as dangerous
    form 70–1; gender and domain
    of the school 49–51; problems of
    researching sexuality in schools
    5–6; psychoanalytic approaches
    38–41; queer theory 43–5;
    schooling and domain of the
    sexual 53–4; social
    constructionism 33–4; socio-
    historical approaches 35–8;
    Walkerdine's work 45–8
Shilling, C. 18–19, 133
shock 146–7
Sikes, P. 168
single mothers 180–1
'sissy' boys 107–8
Skeggs, B. 69, 150
'slushers' 154–6
soap operas 103
social change 180–1, 183, 206
social class 4, 130, 174–5
social constructionism 33–4,
    41–2
socio-historical approaches 35–8
spoiled identities 168

Stanley, L. 6, 12–13
state 37
Steedman, C. 17
student-centred approaches 20, 22,
    62–3, 175
student sexual cultures 1–2, 6, 54,
    205–7, 207–8; reception of sex
    education 65–71; see also
    masculinities, sex education
    lesson, teenage magazines
students: cooperation and
    classroom order 18; participation
    in lessons 96; and physicality of
    teachers 18–19; teacher-student
    relationships 16–17, 170–1,
    193–7, 198–9; teachers'
    approaches to 193–7, 198–9
subversive identities 168
Sugar 84, 103, 104, 114–15
surveillance 60
Symbolic order 39–40, 85, 94–5
Synnott, A. 142–3

tabloid press 125–6
teacher-pupil relationships 16–17,
    170–1, 193–7, 198–9
teachers 2, 13, 164–99, 205, 211;
    approaches to students 193–7;
    auto/biographical approaches
    167–8, 172–99, 205; becoming/
    being a teacher 173–6; and
    identity 16–18, 167–8, 176;
    Kehily's experience of schooling
    11; and the labour process
    164–7; life history approaches
    167–8, 172–99, 205; ownership of
    classes 15; ritualistic humiliation
    18; sexual biographies, teaching
    and learning 176–85, 198; and
    sexual diversity 185–93; teaching
    and relations of desire 168–9;
    teaching sex education 169–72
technical knowledge 66–7, 118–19
teenage magazines 76, 83–4, 95,
    99–127, 203–4, 209; burden of
    assumed knowledge 122–5; in
    context 103–6; More! see More!;
    piecing together sexual learning

121–2; problem pages *see* problem pages; school-based reading practices and gender difference 106–10; sexual learning and cultures of femininity 114–17
teenage pregnancy *see* pregnancy
text 7
therapeutic approach 194
Theweleit, K. 143–4, 152
Thomson, R. 121, 138–9, 171, 177, 178, 194
Thorne, B. 65–6
Tinkler, P. 104
Tong, R. 39
Touchstones 27
transference 169
triangulation 6
Troyna, B. 168
Trudell, B. 172
Tulloch, T. 96
Turner, B.S. 130

uncleanliness, feelings of 87–91
uncoupling of sex/gender 51
United States 61–2

Vance, C. 41–2, 42–3

victimisation 97–8
violence 97–8; homophobia and 148–9; *see also* rape, sexual abuse
vision, personal 64

Walkerdine, V. 18, 40, 41, 201; approach to sexuality 45–8; girls' comics 100–1, 107
Weeks, J. 35–6, 42, 44
Weiss, L. 62
Whitty, G. 16
Wilkinson, S. 56
Williams, R. 101
Willis, P. 4, 7
Willis, S. 194, 195, 208
Willmott, P. 137
Wolpe, A.M. 170
women's bodies, fetishisation of 142
Wood, J. 124, 134
Woods, P. 101–2
Word, The 152, 153
work 4–5
working class 4; teacher's working-class regional identity 174–5

'Yoof TV' 152–3